THE BATTLE OF
THE ST. LAWRENCE

NATHAN M. GREENFIELD

THE BATTLE OF THE ST. LAWRENCE

THE SECOND WORLD WAR IN CANADA

HARPER **PERENNIAL**

HARPER ● PERENNIAL

Published by HarperPerennial, an imprint of
HarperCollins Publishers Ltd

First hardcover edition: 2004
This trade paperback edition: 2005

HarperCollins books may be purchased for educational, business, or sales promotional use through
our Special Markets Department.

HarperCollins Publishers Ltd
2 Bloor Street East, 20th Floor
Toronto, Ontario, Canada
M4W 1A8

www.harpercollins.ca

Library and Archives Canada Cataloguing in
Publication

Greenfield, Nathan M., 1958-
The battle of the St. Lawrence : the Second World
War in Canada / Nathan Greenfield.

Includes index.
ISBN-13: 978-0-00-639450-1
ISBN-10: 0-00-639450-7

1. World War, 1939-1945 – Naval operations,
German. 2. World War, 1939-1945 – Saint Lawrence
River. 3. World War, 1939-1945 – Naval operations –
Submarine. 4. World War, 1939-1945 – Naval opera-
tions, Canadian. 5. Canada. Royal Canadian Navy –
History. 6. World War, 1939-1945 – Canada. I. Title.

D779.C2G73 2004   940.54'5943
C2005-901857-7

HC 9 8 7 6 5 4 3 2 1

Printed and bound in the United States

This book is dedicated to my children—
Pascale, whose excitement when I turned up something or
someone new almost equalled my own, and Nicolas, who
asked all the right questions when we toured the naval
base in Halifax, and to Micheline, my wife, who walked with
me as I travelled through the undiscovered
country of the past.

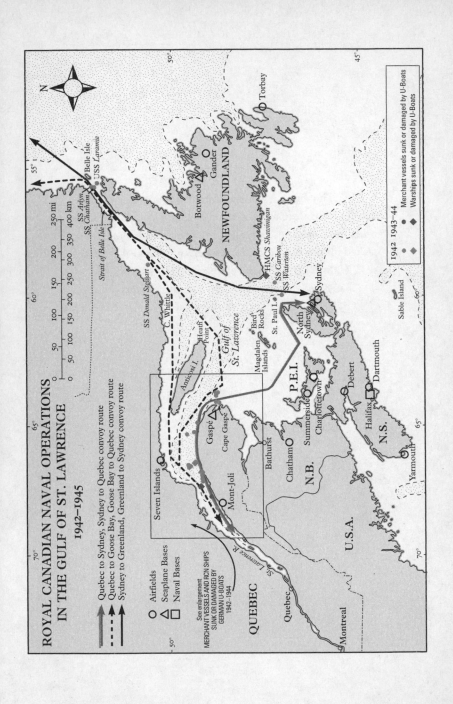

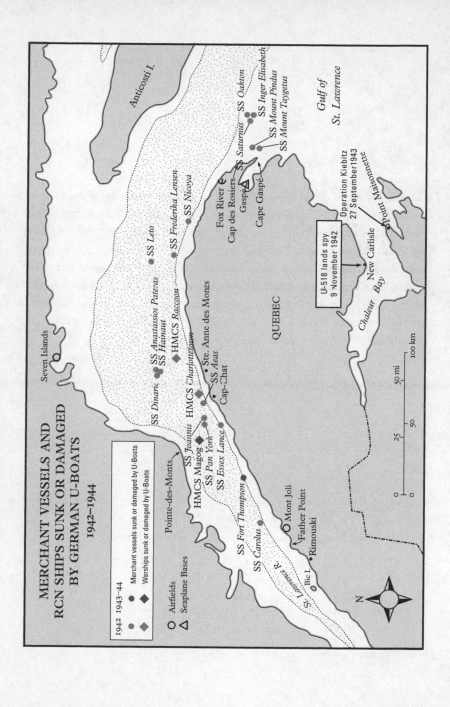

MERCHANT VESSELS AND
RCN SHIPS SUNK OR DAMAGED
BY GERMAN U-BOATS

1942–1944

1942 1943–44

● ◆   Merchant vessels sunk or damaged by U-Boats
◆ ◆   Warships sunk or damaged by U-Boats

1942 1943–44

○   Airfields
△   Seaplane Bases

Anticosti I.

Gulf of
St. Lawrence

SS Oakton
SS Saturnus
SS Inger Elisabeth
SS Mount Pindus
SS Mount Taygetus

Fox River
Cap des Rosiers
Gaspé
Cape Gaspé

Operation Kiebitz
27 September 1943

Point Maisonnette

SS Leto
SS Frederika Lensen
SS Nicoya

SS Anastassios Pateras
SS Hainaut
HMCS Raccoon

U-518 lands spy
9 November 1942

New Carlisle

Chaleur Bay

QUEBEC

Seven Islands

SS Dinaric

Ste. Anne des Monts

HMCS Charlottetown
SS Aeas
Cap-Chat

Pointe-des-Monts

SS Joannis
HMCS Magog
SS Pan York
SS Essex Lance

SS Fort Thompson

Mont Joli
Father Point
Rimouski

SS Carolus

St. Lawrence R.

Bic I.

N

0   25   50 mi
0   50   100 km

No Allied seaman could ever stomach the arrogant posturing of the U-boat men that we watched in movie newsreels: the brass bands, the vainglorious songs, the strutting admirals, the buxom maidens draping garlands of flowers about the necks of their returning warriors. Only a Nazi could transform the sinking of helpless merchant ships and the drowning of unarmed sailors into Wagnerian heroics. Certainly we had no such illusions, and when one U-boat survivor attempted an arrogant, arm-in-the-air Nazi salute upon being hauled aboard a Canadian corvette, he was unceremoniously bundled back over the side to rethink the situation.

—JAMES LAMB

CONTENTS

ACKNOWLEDGMENTS

When I undertook this project over two years ago, my knowledge of naval warfare consisted of hazy memories of having watched *Victory at Sea* with my father thirty years earlier. The crash course I undertook before and while writing *The Battle of the St. Lawrence* was taught by a small squadron of unpaid teachers. The first was Dr. Roger Sarty, then the director of the Canadian War Museum, who generously gave of his time and his unpublished research and who graciously offered to read the unpublished text. I owe much to Dr. Michael Hadley, who, while I was still getting my sea legs, e-mailed me permission to come up to the bridge. Dr. Marc Milner has also been an invaluable resource, and a fine stylistic critic of this text. Mr. André Kirouac, director of the Quebec Naval Museum, not only opened his files to me but has been there to help me find the smallest detail; *merci aussi, André, pour l'invitation à la colloque sur la bataille de St. Laurent.* Drs. Michael Whitby and Serge Bernier, and Charles Rhéaume of the Canadian Defence Department's Directorate of History also gave of their time both in answering my questions and in catching errors in the book's first draft.

I owe a special debt to Ted Read of Alexandria, Ontario, whose story of surviving the torpedoing of SS *Oakton* convinced me and Michael Benedict at *Maclean's* magazine—and subsequently my agent, David Johnston—that the Battle of the St. Lawrence was a gripping story. Protecting me from error—especially the landlubber's faux pas of writing "men on a ship" instead of "men in a ship"—has been Ian Tate of Port Hope, Ontario, who has also graciously allowed me to reprint many of the pictures he took at HMCS Fort Ramsay three score years ago. Geoffrey Smith of Oakville,

Ontario, has also been an invaluable resource. Joe Connolly, who during the war was an EAC pilot, taught me much about the intricacies of anti-submarine air patrols. I must not forget Max Reid of Ottawa, who explained to me much about life aboard ship and how naval guns were fired. Ron McGuire gave generously of his time and of his research on SS *Caribou*. Terry Manuel told me the horrifying story that ends this book.

My understanding of U-boat operations owes much to five men who served on U-boats. Werner Hirschmann, now of Toronto, was chief engineer on U-612 and U-190; ironically, the latter U-boat torpedoed Terry Manuel's HMCS *Esquimalt* off Halifax in the closing days of the war. Dr. Günther Spohn of Düsseldorf and Mr. Egon Martens of Beverstedt served aboard U-1228 and recall the torpedoing of HMCS *Shawinigan*. Before being captured in 1942 and sent to a POW camp in Bowmanville, Ontario, Volkmar Koenig served aboard U-99 under U-boat ace Otto Kretschmer. One former U-boat officer whom I interviewed has asked that I not record his name.

The men and women whose answers to my and other people's questions on the forums at uboat.net are too numerous to mention. Several, however, must be singled out: Rodney Martin, Roger (rogerhollywood), Douglas Struthers, hubertusw, Rainer Bruns and Rainer Kolbicz.

Both John MacSween of Glasgow, Scotland (another uboat.net connection), and Francis MacLaughlin of Kingston, Ontario, were more than graceful in explaining to me the physics of how a ship sinks. Both will recognize their labours, I trust, in my description of the death of SS *Nicoya*.

Both International Marine Research, a volunteer organization in Norfolk, England, and Tim Hughes, my researcher in England, worked miracles. So did Janice Summerby of the Canadian Department of Veterans Affairs. Claire Roy of Algonquin College's interlibrary loan service could find the proverbial needle in the haystack.

Richard Martin, my colleague in Algonquin's English department, performed yeoman's work proofreading this manuscript. And thank you to Mairi McKissock for preparing an excellent index.

Finally, thanks to Chris Bucci at HarperCollins, who has wielded his blue pencil skilfully and ensured that this narrative flows.

I, alone, of course, am responsible for any errors that follow.

AUTHOR'S NOTE

The four navies and different merchant fleets whose story this is had three different ways of reckoning time. The U-boats used German War Time, the prime meridian of which was Berlin rather than Greenwich, England. The Royal Navy, the Royal Canadian Navy and the United States Navy used Greenwich Mean Time. Thus, German war logs recorded events two hours ahead of whatever time the RN, RCN or USN recorded them, 1445 for the U-boats being 12:45z for the RN, RCN and USN (the "z" stands for "Zulu" and denotes GMT). Some merchant ships used GMT; others used local time, which was four hours earlier than GMT.

Since my main concern is to tell of the events that were unfolding in the St. Lawrence, I generally use local time, though to give the reader a taste of the military record I sometimes use both Zulu and German War Time, trusting that in context all will be clear.

A similar type of confusion reigns in the question of distances. Here the *Kriegsmarine* is most eclectic. Cruising distances were reckoned in nautical miles, and speed in knots; a knot is one nautical mile an hour, and a nautical mile is slightly longer than a mile measured on land. Distances between ships and when diving, however, were reckoned in metres; torpedo runs were, of course, also measured in metres. By contrast, the RCN, RN and USN, all of which used nautical miles and knots, measured distance between ships and from torpedoes in yards (and, less frequently, in cables, a cable being 4,256 feet). At the risk of a certain inconsistency but in the service of giving my reader a sense of the historical documents, I use all units of measure. As well, in order to give my reader a sense of the German navy, at times I use German phrases and titles, supplying translations where necessary.

I have distinguished between written material being quoted and interviews by using the present tense in the attribution for interviews—for example, "Read recalls"—and the past tense for written sources.

The distances given in the snapshots of the war are calculated from Gaspé, Quebec, and are rounded off to the nearest 500 miles.

PREFACE

The subtitle of this book—"The Second World War in Canada"—will, no doubt, surprise many.

Wasn't the Second World War "over there"? In the skies over England? At Dieppe? Across North Africa, Italy, Normandy, Belgium and Holland and in Germany? Weren't its greatest battles on the Russian steppes and across the Pacific? Canadians fell at Juno Beach, in Ortona, along the canals of Holland, in Hong Kong, and thousands died on the North Atlantic.[1] Over there? Yes—surely not "in Canada."

But between 1942 and 1944, more than 28 ships were torpedoed, 24 of these sunk, and more than 270 Canadians and scores of others did die—*in Canada*. They died in the Battle of the St. Lawrence, the only Second World War campaign fought inside North America.[2]

Many died within sight of land or of the lights that shone from the small towns and villages strung out along the rugged coast of the north shore of the St. Lawrence and Quebec's Gaspé Peninsula. One hundred and forty-five were officers and ratings aboard HMCS *Raccoon*, *Charlottetown*, *Magog* and *Shawinigan*, four of the dozens of Royal Canadian Navy warships that, after the torpedoing of SS *Nicoya* and *Leto* on the night of May 11, 1942, were tasked with escorting convoys in Canada's largest river and the gulf. One hundred and thirty-seven men, women and children—including forty-nine civilians (of whom eleven were under ten years old), forty-nine Canadian and British servicemen, eight American servicemen and thirty-one crew members, most of whom were from Port aux Basques—died when a torpedo fired from U-69 mortally wounded the Newfoundland–Nova Scotia ferry SS *Caribou* at 2 a.m. on October 14, 1942. Another hundred men—Finns, Belgians, Dutchmen, Greeks, Englishmen and American GIs and sailors—died, victims too of the torpedoes fired by the fifteen German U-boats that between 1942 and 1944 invaded Canada's home waters; one ship, SS *Carolus*, was torpedoed 10 kilometres downriver from Rimouski, Quebec, fully 600 kilometres from the Atlantic and some 250 kilometres from Quebec City.

Like all battles, myths have accreted to the Battle of the St. Lawrence. One holds that the government staged the sinkings to help sell Victory Bonds. Another, which surfaces from time to time on uboat.net, is that U-boats landed to buy groceries. Still another tells of German officers stopping for a beer and to listen to music at an *hôtel*. By far, however, the most persistent myth is that wartime censorship prevented word of the battle from reaching beyond the Gaspé.

The claim appears to have a good pedigree, stretching back to the hours after SS *Nicoya*'s sinking on the night of May 11, 1942. The news release that confirmed the sinking declared that "any possible further sinkings in this area will not be made public in order that information valuable to the enemy may be withheld from him." At first, the policy seemed to have teeth, at least in the House of Commons, where on May 13 the Speaker ruled against Gaspé MP Sasseville Roy's attempt to pry more information from Prime Minister Mackenzie King's government. The cutline on Jack McNaught's October 15, 1949, *Maclean's* magazine article, "The Battle of the St. Lawrence," is "A story that's never been told." Twenty-three years later, Peter Moon's "The Second World War Battle We Lost at Home," published in *Canadian Magazine*, was subtitled "The War Story Our Leaders Kept Quiet." James Essex subtitled his 1984 memoir, *Victory in the St. Lawrence*, "Canada's Unknown War." The claim was repeated in 1995 in Brian and Terence McKenna's NFB film *U-boats in the St. Lawrence*.

The famed "fog of war" conceals much, but in this case it hardly hid much about the Battle of the St. Lawrence from Canada's kitchen tables and radios.[3] The newspapers of May 13, 1942, jumbled *Nicoya* and *Leto*'s stories, but they clearly told Canadians that ships had been sunk in the St. Lawrence. Three days later, the *Ottawa Evening Citizen* reported that the sinkings had caused the war risk premium for ships using the St. Lawrence to double from 1.5 to 3 per cent.

On July 10, Roy asked in the House if the "minister is disposed to make a statement" about the torpedoing of "three more ships . . . last Sunday night." According to *L'Action Catholique*, "half the people in Quebec City" knew of the sinkings before Roy asked the question. The sinkings of USS *Laramie* and SS *Chatham*, *Arlyn* and *Donald Stewart* in late August and early September 1942 did not make the newspapers. The sinkings of HMCS *Raccoon* and SS *Aeas* on September 6 and SS *Oakton*, *Mount Taygetus* and *Mount Pindus* on September 7 did. A week later, headlines told of the loss of HMCS *Charlottetown*. Canadians read that "the torpedo tore into the engine room, trapping the men on watch before they could reach the upper deck. Clouds of black smoke rolled along the decks. Before they could launch the lifeboats the vessel went down by the stern, just as the survivors jumped clear and into the frigid water." They read of their sailors being killed within sight of land when their own depth charges exploded.

On September 13, the *Ottawa Evening Journal* told of the "daring mid day attack" that had sunk SS *Frederika Lensen* the previous July. Two days later, the *Journal*'s headline read "U-BOAT SINKS SHIP BELOW RIMOUSKI." *L'Action Catholique* asked, *"Ce qui se passe en Gaspésie?"* ("What is going on in Gaspé?"). The stories that followed the sinking of *Caribou* on October 14 spared readers little: "Bodies were found floating a short distance from where the ship was attacked," and a "number of caskets are being forwarded by train to Port aux Basques."

In early November 1942, Naval Minister Angus Macdonald spoke out against the rumour that U-boat crews were coming ashore to buy supplies; he gave the number of ships sunk in the "whole river and gulf area" as twenty. The *Halifax Herald* overstated things by saying, "R.C.A.F. 'Gets' Another U-boat," but, nevertheless, gave Canadians more than a few details about the air war being conducted against the Nazi invaders.

In March 1943, newspapers reported Quebec legislators Onésime Gagnon's and Roy's charges that the problems in the navy's command structure had prevented it from reacting to save a convoy that was attacked the previous September 15 and that as many as forty ships had been sunk in 1942. On March 17, 1943, papers reported Macdonald's speech, which not only defended the navy but also included the names of every ship sunk in 1942. After a tour of the Gaspé's naval and army bases, *La Presse*'s Roger Champeaux declared, "*Tout Gaspésien est devenu un soldat.*"

In mid-1944, thousands of Canadians received copies of *Canada's War at Sea*, a government-sanctioned book they had subscribed for a year earlier. Entitled "The Battle of the Gulf," chapter 4 tells a remarkably complete story of what was happening both on the St. Lawrence and in Parliament in 1942 and 1943. The torpedoing of HMCS *Magog* in October 1944 was not reported until April 18, 1945, less than a month before the end of the war. On December 7, 1944, under the headline "Canadian Corvette Sunk with All Crew—Five Drown, 85 Missing on Shawinigan," the *Ottawa Evening Journal* told of the corvette that had been torpedoed on the night of November 24.

Why then the myth that the Battle of the St. Lawrence is Canada's "unknown war"?

Professor Roger Sarty, whose pioneering work on the history of Eastern Air Command (EAC) is a model of both scholarship and clear writing, suggested one reason at a conference held in Rimouski, Quebec, in May 2002 to commemorate the sixtieth anniversary of the start of the battle. The generation of historians that immediately followed the war viewed the battle as a defeat—a view from which Sarty politely, but firmly, dissents—and thus sought to downplay it. In his *Far Distant Ships: An Official Account of Canadian Naval Operations in World War II*, Joseph Schull devotes a mere 14 (of 432) pages to the only naval campaign in Canadian waters; he characterized the battle as a "defeat," *tout court*.[4]

The second reason has less to do with wounded service pride than with the context in which history, especially military history, exists in Canada. No province or school board has ever included the Battle of the St. Lawrence in its curriculum. Accordingly, there is no mental envelope for the information contained in the cavalcade of commemorative articles or television shows that appear on solemn anniversaries or on such occasions as the launching of HMCS *Charlottetown III*.

The Battle of the St. Lawrence wasn't hidden from Canadians *during* the war. Rather, for three generations the nation's curriculum writers have been engaged in an ongoing act of forgetting. Forgetting that in the darkest days of the Second World War, hundreds of men, women and children were killed by Nazis who plied our inland waters. Forgetting that thousands of Canadians volunteered to defend our shores.

This book, then, is an act of historical recovery. Though this is not an academic history, I have tried to write as objectively as possible. However, while it is necessary to remain objective regarding tactical and strategic matters (such as the RN's failure to equip its ships with up-to-date radar), it is entirely inappropriate to say, as Martin Middlebrook does in his famous (and otherwise excellent) book *Convoy*, that "after more than thirty years, courage and patriotism can surely be admired whichever side a man fought on."

It is important and necessary to tell of U-boatmen's experience, of the sheer horror of being depth-charged. But to admire their "courage" is to imply that there is something in their actions that was morally courageous, for, as Gerald Linderman shows in his *Embattled Courage: The Experience of Combat in the American Civil War*, the word *courage* properly used means something much more moral than naked bravery.[5] "Only a Nazi," wrote James Lamb, who served aboard the corvette HMCS *Trail* during the 1942 portion of the battle, "could transform the sinking of helpless merchant ships and the drowning of unarmed sailors into Wagnerian heroics." Still less is it proper to "admire" U-boat captains Eberhard Hoffmann's, Ernst Vogelsang's or Paul Hartwig's "patriotism." They were not, as one of my correspondents who served aboard a U-boat tried to convince me, simply men who lived at a particular time in a particular set of circumstances and who did the job they were trained for without rancour or hate. Each and every one of the men who served aboard the U-boats that invaded Canada was a volunteer; each and every one had taken an oath of fidelity to Germany's *Führer*, Adolf Hitler. Each and every one served the Nazi state, Vogelsang with the swastika emblazoned on his conning tower. To forget this, to forget that their "Iron Coffins" fired torpedoes—Nazi steel shaped to kill—is to forget that had Germany won the war or at least fought the Allies to a draw, Hitler would have remained supreme in Europe and millions more would have been turned to dust in Auschwitz, Treblinka and Birkenau.

To admire their "patriotism" is to dishonour that of Ted Read, Ian Tate,

Geoffrey "Jock" Smith, Rear-Admiral Desmond "Debbie" Piers, Rear-Admiral R. J. Pickford, Max Korkum, John Chance, Herb Montgomery, Léon-Paul Fortin, Arthur Alvater, Bill "Mac" McRae, Lorraine Guilbault, Gaétan Lavoie, Roy Woodruff, Laurent Marchand, Gavin Clark, Frank Curry, Marilyn Whyte, Grace Bonner, Donald Murphy, Francis MacLaughlin, Ray MacAuley, Allan Heagy, Cyril Perkin, Ruth Fullerton, Donald Crowther, Fred Linnington, Richard (Dick) Powell, Leilo Pepper and Norman Crane, whose stories now stand for the thousands who lived—and the hundreds who didn't—through the Battle of the St. Lawrence.[6]

INTRODUCTION

His Majesty's Royal Canadian Navy and Nazi Germany's *U-Bootwaffe*—the two navies that from May 1942 through November 1944 were locked in a bitter conflict stretched over the almost quarter million square kilometres of the Gulf of St. Lawrence and as far inland as Rimouski, Quebec—were almost mirror images of each other.

Shortly after the 1922 election, which returned the Liberals under Mackenzie King to power, Parliament slashed the Naval Estimates from $2.5 million to $1.5 million, causing what Commodore James Polmer called "a scar that never healed." The loss of two-fifths of its budget forced the RCN to dispose of HMCS *Aurora*, a 3,500-ton cruiser, and two H-class submarines, and to cut hundreds from its active lists.

During the budget debate, Defence Minister George Graham argued that the cut in the Naval Estimates put Canada in line with both the spirit and the commitments undertaken by the United States, the United Kingdom and Japan at the 1921 Washington Disarmament Conference: "Every country in the world today is endeavouring to reduce its armament. . . . The great nations of the world agreed not only to take a holiday in naval construction, but to scrap many of their fighting ships." The conference fixed the ratio of capital ships between the three powers at 5:5:3.[1]

Like both J. S. Woodsworth, leader of the Independent Labour Party (a forerunner of the CCF, which later became the NDP), and T. A. Crerar, leader of the Progressive Conservative Party—who asked the minister, "Who has Canada to fear?"—Graham was influenced by what military historian

Correlli Barnett has called "moralizing internationalism." As did his counterparts in London, Graham put his faith in international covenants and the League of Nation's "machinery of talk instead of the traditional accoutrements of national power—armies, navies or air forces." Graham's desire to replace the permanent naval force with volunteers, who, he told the House, would provide "better service on our own behalf [and] a better service for the Empire at large," was in accord with what he was hearing from London. At the same time that Graham was reducing the RCN, British prime minister Ramsay MacDonald decided to delay completion of the Royal Navy base at Singapore as a "demonstration of sincerity" to the Japanese. Graham claimed that the volunteer force would be better for the Canadian economy because it would "not take a single man out of industrial employment." Graham's boss, Prime Minister King—who in 1918 wrote, in *Industry and Humanity*, that industrial production is key to economic development—no doubt agreed that it was unwise to take men out of industrial employment and place them in the military, which produced, apparently, nothing. By the end of 1922, His Majesty's Royal Canadian Navy had been reduced to a complement of 483 officers and ratings, and Canada's newly opened naval college had been closed.

Six years later, after King shuffled Graham out of and shuffled Colonel J. L. Ralston, a Nova Scotian, into the Ministry of National Defence, the Naval Estimates grew to $2.7 million, and a year later to $3.6 million. The bulk of the increased funds went to purchasing two older destroyers from England and to ordering two new destroyers, HMCS *Saguenay* and *Skeena*, the first warships built specifically for the RCN. To crew these ships, the navy's list grew to 896 officers and men.

In 1934, the year Hitler openly began to rearm and one year after Germany withdrew from the League of Nations, the Conservative government of R. B. Bennett responded to the crisis of the Depression by slashing government spending. Bennett's Naval Estimates proposed cutting the $2.4 million budget by $2 million. Chief of Staff Major-General Andrew McNaughton proposed paying off the Royal Canadian Navy and protecting Canada's coasts with aircraft alone. A ferocious bureaucratic battle, led by the navy's chief of staff, Commodore Walter Hose, kept the cuts to only $200,000. Years later Rear-Admiral Leonard Murray summed up the attitude toward the Canadian navy during these years: "They would be pleased if someone made up his mind to take the whole navy out into the middle of the ocean and sink it without a trace."

As international tensions built through the mid-1930s, the King government began increasing the Naval Estimates. In 1936 the Estimates more than doubled, to $4.4 million, as the navy bought two additional destroyers from England. Two years later, the Estimates jumped again to $6.6 million as the RCN purchased another two, giving the navy six relatively modern destroyers, three on each coast. Together, these ships could have made a credible defence of Halifax. In late May 1939, however, King's cabinet abruptly cut four anti-submarine vessels and two motor torpedo boats from the building program.

Thus, when war broke out in September 1939, the RCN found itself with a complement of 129 officers and 1,456 men, and with 13 ships—a woeful mismatch for the mission fate handed it. The primary mission of the Canadian navy had none of the glamour that fired the imaginations of generations of boys. Save for a few officers serving on RN ships during the hunt for *Bismarck*, there would be no latter-day Trafalgar, Copenhagen or Jutland for Canadians. Canada's war at sea—and its war at home—was the defence of the merchant ships that carried the men, machines, food and fuel needed to defeat Hitler.

Only a crash industrial program, scarcely imaginable just a few short years earlier during the Depression, gave Canada the hundreds of ships needed for convoy escort work. By the end of 1940, Canada's shipyards had turned out 11 corvettes and had converted 12 yachts into armed yachts. A year later, another 57 corvettes, 26 Bangor-class minesweepers and 13 Fairmile motor launches went into service. By the end of 1942, the Naval Estimates totalled $129,367,632 and the navy's rolls counted 179 warships; by the end of the war, Canada's fleet numbered 378 ships, the world's fourth largest, and the Dominion government was spending $427,098,883 on His Majesty's Royal Canadian Navy.

In 1944, journalist Leslie Roberts apostrophized the RCN as "a Navy of bank clerks, dirt farmers, fishermen, bond salesmen, mechanics and machinists, telegraphers and pre-war amateur radio enthusiasts." It had to be.

To crew the first group of ships that Canada put to sea, the navy called upon the 66 officers and 196 men enrolled in the Royal Canadian Naval Reserve (RCNR) and the 115 officers and 1,435 volunteers in the Royal Canadian Naval Volunteer Reserve (RCNVR). The men of the RCNR— men such as Captain John Willard Bonner, who died in the St. Lawrence when his corvette, HMCS *Charlottetown*, was torpedoed in September 1942, and Captain Alfred Skinner, whose corvette, HMCS *Arrowhead*, fought three actions in the St. Lawrence during 1942—had decades of experience at sea. As captains of merchant ships, Skinner's and Bonner's naval training consisted of a couple of weeks every year or so. The men of the RCNVR had even less training; they were, according to Roberts, "pre-war Sunday Sailors, members of yacht clubs and only partially trained." From 1939 through 1942, Canada's navy was manned by a maritime equivalent of the militia myth—a myth that holds, as Jack Granatstein has recently shown, that hastily drilled volunteers filled with pluck and a self-evidently just cause will produce great victories.

The navy didn't lack men to crew the ships that poured off Canada's slipways; it lacked time to train them. An old navy adage holds that "while it takes two years to build a ship, it takes five years to train a sailor." On March 1, 1943, the RCN counted 603 officers and 4,002 ratings. The RCNR's totals were 924 officers and 5,000 ratings. The bulk of the navy's volunteers, however, came through the RCNVR, which then carried 4,437 officers and 40,713 ratings; later in 1943 the RCNVR totalled almost 70,000 men.

After the fall of France in 1940 gave U-boats relatively unfettered access to the North Atlantic, the RCN rushed thousands of RCNVR men through two-week-long training courses. Léon-Paul Fortin, who survived the torpedoing of *Charlottetown* off Sainte-Anne-des-Monts on September 11, 1942, had never been to sea before December 13, 1941, the day *Charlottetown* was commissioned. The rest of the crew was so green that they were seasick within hours of leaving the jetty in Quebec City. Weapons specialists such as Radar Operator Allan Heagy, also of *Charlottetown*, had scarcely more sea training.

Out on the North Atlantic, RCN ships—equipped at first with 123 asdic (sonar) and 286 radar, both of which were a technological generation behind the RN's 127 asdic and 271 radar, which could pick up a periscope— were almost overmatched by the "grey wolves" that prowled the sea. In May 1941, the RN complained that the Canadians "showed a complete lack of understanding of what was expected of divisions within individual ships (the Asdic operators, depth charge crew, gunners, and so on) and of ships operating as a group." Just six months later, after the bulk of the US Atlantic Fleet was sent to the Pacific following Pearl Harbor, the RCN supplied 48 per cent of the escort ships on the "Newfie–Derry" run; the RN supplied 50 per cent and the USN 2 per cent.

Before 1942 was out, the strain of expansion and the slow upgrading of radar and asdic (years after RN corvette captains were furnished with gyro-compasses, which continued to function during depth-charge attacks, Canadian corvette captains relied on inaccurate magnetic compasses mounted on the binnacle) came close to breaking the Canadian navy. Sixty of the eighty ships lost in convoying were lost while under RCN escort, eighteen of them in the Gulf of St. Lawrence and the St. Lawrence River.

Responding to the fact that between February and March 1917, 148 U-boats destroyed 1.9 million tons of shipping, which nearly forced England out of the Great War, Article 191 of the Treaty of Versailles, signed on June 28, 1919, declared, "The construction and acquisition of any kind of submarine, even for trade purposes, is forbidden to Germany."[2] Within two years, a secret U-department had been organized within the permitted Torpedo and Mines Inspectorate based in Kiel. Together with inspectorate officials, engineers from the firm Blohm & Voss were soon in Kobe, Japan, helping Germany's former enemy (and future ally) build its first submarine fleet. That same year, Krupp sent engineers to Argentina to supervise the construction of ten submarines.

In 1922, the year Canada slashed two-fifths from the RCN's estimates, the three German shipyards led by German steel-producing giant Krupp formed a dummy company in Rotterdam, Ingenieurskantoor voor Scheepsbouw (IvS), staffed by former U-boat captains and engineers. IvS built submarines for four countries—submarines that served in effect as prototypes of the U-boats Germany would use against the Allies. Turkey's 1923 order was filled in 1927; the boat's sea trials were carried out by a former U-boat commander and chief engineer who made a report to a secret division of the German Naval High Command.

In 1926, a year during which the Naval Service of Canada failed to spend $60,000 of its $1.4-million budget, IvS received orders from Spain, Finland and the Soviet Union, this last sale preceded by three secret missions to Moscow. A large part of an 800-million-gold-mark loan granted to the Weimar Republic by the International Control Commission in 1926 was dispersed to Krupp and other industrial firms involved in secret rearmament, including the electronics giant Siemens.

In 1930, two years before Hitler's rise to power and seven years before the formal abrogation of the Treaty of Versailles, Rear-Admiral Walter Gladisch was already signing himself *Führer der Uboote* (FdU). From July to September 1930, some of his officers, disguised as civilian tourists, carried out the sea trials for one of the 500-ton submarines that IvS had built for Finland. In 1935, the British Admiralty, convinced, as the Defence of Trade Committee put it a year later, that "the problem of dealing with the submarine is more than simplified by the invention of ASDIC [sonar]," raised no objection to the London Naval Treaty, which removed the prohibition on building submarines that Versailles had placed on Germany. The main thrust of the London Naval Treaty was to try to limit Germany's surface ship fleet and thereby prevent the start of the type of naval arms race that preceded World War I.[3]

The *U-Bootwaffe* quickly took shape after February 1, 1936, the day Hitler ordered the construction of the first boats. In March, the 1st Flotilla was organized in Kiel. (After the fall of France it moved to Brest.) Several months later, Hitler appointed Karl Dönitz, a former U-boat captain and World War I Iron Cross winner, to the position of FdU. Despite Hitler's and *Grossadmiral* Erich Raeder's commitment to large capital ships such as the battleship *Bismarck* (only 10 per cent of Germany's steel production was dedicated to the building of U-boats), Dönitz argued that the *U-Bootwaffe* was the *Kriegsmarine*'s most potent arm in the coming *guerre de course*, the war against England's trade. In October 1936, the 2nd Flotilla, based first in Wilhelmshaven and later in Lorient, was organized. Within a year, Dönitz, who had told Hitler, "give me three hundred submarines and I'll win the war for you," was organizing group exercises that presaged the wolf-packs that savaged the ships on the North Atlantic run.

The conditions endured by Dönitz's men were not all that different from those cursed by the thousands of Canadians who served in corvettes. Like the "patrol vessel, whaler type" (as the ships were called before Churchill dubbed them "corvettes"), U-boats were cramped, wet ships. Designed for a crew of forty-five, corvettes routinely carried eighty or more, the number growing through the war as they were fitted with more specialized anti-submarine gear. Because of the corvette's low fo'c'sle, water poured into the ship's hatchways and down ventilators until it came to rest in the crew's mess.[4] Uniforms were almost always damp, and men slept in damp hammocks abutting each other, strung up above the water sloshing on the deck beneath them, upon which floated bits of food, personal belongings and the detritus of daily life.

The forty-four men in a Type VIIC U-boat, the workhorse of Dönitz's fleet, lived in a steel-encased cigar-shaped bubble not more than a few metres in diameter. On paper their underwater trench measured 150 square metres. In reality, it was much smaller, for within that space were crammed their diesel engines (which took up 33 metres), electric motors, two battery rooms, tanks for drinking water, thousands of metres of piping, and their ship's stores. In addition, when the U-boats left port, four extra torpedoes were stored in the mess decks; the men would sleep on hammocks strung above them or on the hard deck plating. (Another ten torpedoes, which could only be accessed while on the surface, were stored between the outer hull and the pressure hull.) Almost every other spare place, including one of the two toilets, was stuffed with food and other provisions. The air was not only damp, it was fetid; U-boat men could go six weeks without bathing. Diesel and other oil smells and the foul odour of mouldy food filled the boat's air.

Unlike Canadian sailors and airmen, who had to learn their trade at sea in the real time of battling U-boats scant miles off Canada's home shores, Dönitz's men were superbly trained.[5] At twenty-eight, *Korvettenkapitän* Paul Hartwig, the ace of the Battle of the St. Lawrence who sank nine ships, was decades younger than the men who captained *Charlottetown* or *Arrowhead*. Unlike them, however, he had had seven years of naval training, including service on the battleship *Deutschland*. Engineering cadets had over two years of training. "Even late in the war," recalls Werner Hirschmann, chief engineering officer on U-190, which sank HMCS *Esquimalt* in April 1945 before surrendering to the RCN on May 12, 1945, "every one of us on board was an expert in his own division." The training regimen was a vital part of the creation of the mythos of the *U-Bootwaffe* as the elite German military force.

The map Dönitz had prepared for the January 1939 war games identified the North American supply route to England as *Kanada-Transporte*. The title, which harkened back to the First World War (for more than three years the convoys that sustained England left from Halifax, Sydney and Gaspé) was also prescient. For not only did the convoys that sustained England for two years after 1939 leave again from Halifax and Sydney, but Canadian ships provided as much as 48 per cent of the escorts.

About 200 miles south of Burgeo, Newfoundland, *Kanada-Transporte* divides. One spur cuts southeast, running just off the coast of Nova Scotia toward Boston. The northern spur heads northwest, through the Cabot Strait, almost touching Cape Ray, the most western point of Newfoundland. The line continues through the Gulf of St. Lawrence, running between Anticosti Island and the Gaspé Peninsula. *Kanada-Transporte*, which correctly predicted the main shipping lane used by the St. Lawrence convoys, ends just shy of the mouth of the St. Lawrence River.

In 1939, a line on a war game map. Five years later, that same line described at least part of the course taken by each of the fifteen U-boats that invaded the St. Lawrence. It ran over the watery graves of hundreds of men, women and children and the shattered hulls of SS *Oakton, Inger Elizabeth, Mount Taygetus, Mount Pindus, Waterton, Nicoya* and *Caribou* and HMCS *Shawinigan*, eight of the twenty-nine ships destroyed in the only successful invasion of North America between 1812 and September 11, 2001.[6]

CHAPTER ONE
WAR IN PEACEFUL SEAS

MAY 11, 12 AND 13, 1942

Is there no silent watch to keep?
An age is dying, and the bell
Rings midnight on a vast deep.

—ALFRED NOYES

At 11:52 p.m. on May 11, 1942, Captain Edward H. Brice knew that his ship, SS *Nicoya*, was doomed.

He'd thought it a year earlier, in the early hours of May 20, 1941. Then, two thousand miles to the east, in the middle of the air gap (the area beyond the reach of protective aircraft where Hitler's U-boats carved ships from the convoys that sustained England), *Westgruppe*, a ten-boat wolfpack, pounced on the twenty-nine ships of convoy HX-126. Two days later, HX-126's commodore counted twenty-two ships.

"The attack began just after midnight on May 20th," recalls Bill "Mac" McRae, who, along with three other recently trained RCAF pilots, was on his way to Fighter Command in England. Lashed to *Nicoya*'s hatches was an equally important cargo: two crated Hawker Hurricanes built in Fort William, Ontario. "Bill Wallace and I were in our bunks in what before the war was a first-class cabin below the main deck. Suddenly, the steady throb of the engines ceased. We heard a dull thud and felt the ship heel sharply to the left. Immediately, a steward came running to our cabin and told us to get dressed and get up to the boat deck with our lifebelts on."

It took the twenty-one-year-old McRae and Wallace less than three minutes to get dressed and run up to the deck. When they got there, SS *Norman Monarch*, torpedoed some 180 seconds earlier, was already gone. Later, Brice told McRae he'd ordered the Hard to Starboard that McRae felt in order to avoid the other ship, which had been stopped dead in the water before plunging to the bottom.

Through the long night, *Nicoya*'s crew kept watch and its gunner stood at the ready (*Nicoya* was a defensively equipped merchant ship, or DEMS). McRae, Wallace, Jack Milmine and Wally McLeod—listed on the ship's manifest as "passengers"—alternated between standing nervously on deck and trying to catch a few moments' sleep on the wardroom's steel deck.

Late the next morning, the attacks began again.

"In quick succession, three more ships were hit, and sank before our eyes," victims, McRae learned years later, of U-556. "One, a tanker off to our starboard, burned fiercely. We could see the inky black smoke that billowed off her for hours."

*   *   *

Kapitänleutnant Herbert Wohlfarth, nicknamed "Sir Parsifal," one of Admiral Karl Dönitz's most enthusiastic volunteers, saw the horrific scene differently: "Both torpedoes hit. . . . The tanker was struck amidships and immediately bursts into bright flames. . . . The oil from the two tankers has spread over the water. The entire sea is on fire. In its middle, looming gigantically, the burning tanker. It is dreadfully beautiful."[1]

"Just after we saw the third ship go down," recalls McRae, "off our port quarter, not fifty yards away, a submarine broke surface. The gunner tried to depress the 3-inch gun, but before he even tried to get off a shot, Captain Brice, who was up on the bridge, yelled down, 'Don't shoot!' through a megaphone. Later I heard a rumour that our convoy had a British submarine escorting us."

Moments after the submarine disappeared, a loud thud reverberated through the ship.

Thinking that his ship had been torpedoed, and hoping to prevent it from blowing up when the cold water of the North Atlantic washed over its hot boilers and pipes, Brice rang Full Stop and ordered the mate to blow the whistle and let off the steam that *Nicoya*'s boilers had produced from Canadian coal. The ship was dead in the water. Brice ordered that the lifeboats be swung out on their davits and that the seacocks be put in place.

Standing by his assigned lifeboat, McRae watched the wreckage of war around him. "Off to our port, we could see the burning tanker and the gaps left by the ships that had already been sunk. Among the broken bits of wood, oil and other wreckage were the fuselages of two Lockheed Hudsons that must have been cut loose by men desperate for anything that could serve as a raft."

Brice did not, however, order Abandon Ship. Instead, he told his chief engineer to go below and report on the damage. The chief engineer came back a few minutes later and reported that there had been none. Brice ordered the engine room to raise steam. "We'd all felt the thud—we'd definitely hit something or been hit," recalls McRae. "Later, Captain Brice said that maybe it was a dud torpedo or that we'd run over the submarine that we'd seen."

The first two letters of convoy HX-126 designated it a fast convoy that left from Halifax; slower convoys (the SC series) were capable of making up to 7 knots and left from Sydney, Nova Scotia. According to Admiralty regulations, HX-126 should have been able to make 14 knots, but in reality, some of its ships could make only 7 knots, which became the whole convoy's speed.

Built for the "banana run" from Jamaica and the islands to Liverpool and the Mersey, Brice's *Nicoya* could do better than 14 knots. Still, it took over an hour to get enough steam to get underway again. "All the time," McRae recalls, "we stood at our lifeboat stations and stared out at the wreckage and the still-burning tanker, expecting at any moment that we too would be torpedoed."

Shortly after *Nicoya* had caught up with the other survivors of *Westgruppe*'s attack, what to the Port Arthur (now Thunder Bay), Ontario, born and bred McRae looked like an armada passed HX-126. An Aldis lamp signal told them that "the mighty *Hood*," the pride of the British navy, had been sunk, and that these thirteen ships, including the battleship *King George V* and the aircraft carrier *Victorious*, were in hot pursuit of its slayer, the great battleship *Bismarck*.

Years later, McRae learned that had *Bismarck*, with its consort, *Prinz Eugen*, broken out into the Atlantic, *Nicoya* and the other ships in HX-126 would have soon been within its sights. He also learned that U-556 had sped away from its attack on HX-126 to protect the wounded *Bismarck* and found itself in perfect position to torpedo HMS *Ark Royal* and *Renown*, two of the warships that helped sink the battleship, but it could not. For Wohlfarth had expended his last torpedoes sinking three ships within hailing distance of *Nicoya*.

MAY 11, 1941

- Three thousand five hundred miles^2 east, workers at Flender-Werke in Lübeck lay the keel for U-313; at Bremer Vulcan in Bremen, U-266 is launched.
- Six hundred and fifty miles west in Ottawa, the Canadian government announces that— following victory of the "yes" side in the April 27 plebiscite, in which Prime Minister Mackenzie King's Liberal government asked to be released from the "no conscription" pledge it had made in the previous election—conscription will begin. The government pledges that conscripts will not be sent overseas.
- Five thousand miles east, German aircraft flying from the occupied island of Crete sink three British destroyers: HMS *Lively*, *Kipling* and *Jackal*.

- Nine thousand miles away in the South Pacific, the destroyer USS *Henley* arrives at the last known position of the US Navy tanker USS *Neosho*, which had been badly damaged during the Battle of the Coral Sea. Two days later, *Henley* will pick up more than 100 men from *Neosho*'s lifeboats.
- Four thousand miles east in Poland, deportations of more than 10,000 Jews from the ghetto in Łódź, Poland, to the Chelmno Concentration Camp continue.
- Eight hundred miles south in New York, American Zionists demand that the Jews be given sovereignty over Palestine; the British refuse.
- Eight hundred miles south in New York, SS *Queen Mary* leaves New York harbour bound for England with 10,000 American troops aboard.

At 11:52 p.m., two ships—U-553 and SS *Nicoya*—sailing in what German navigational maps designated grid square BB 1485 (some eight miles off the coast of the northern part of the Gaspé, just about where the peninsula begins to curve southward), were 400 metres, and almost a world, apart.

The distinctive colour scheme—silver-grey hull, red-topped buff ventilators and buff yellow funnels crowned by black top hats—that had for two decades marked the *Nicoya* as an Elders & Fyffes ship had long since given way to the dull grey of war. The crates on the deck were filled not with the exotic fruits of the Caribbean but with aircraft destined to fight Hermann Göring's *Luftwaffe*.

Still, as Brice and his first mate, Frederick Inch, looked ahead over the St. Lawrence and toward the rugged coastline of Quebec's Gaspé Peninsula on their right, they could just about push the war from their minds. Here, eight miles from Canada's shore, in the waters that flowed from Lake Superior, over the cataract at Niagara, past Montreal and down hundreds of miles through the world's widest river, *Nicoya* felt safe.

True, there had been warnings. In July 1939, Prime Minister Mackenzie King told the House of Commons that "within a few months submarines may well be found operating in the gulf, and even in the St. Lawrence river." On September 10, 1939, the day Canada declared war on Nazi Germany, King drew the House's attention to the reality that the "safety of Canada depends on the adequate safeguarding of our coastal regions and the great avenues of approach to the heart of this country. Foremost among these is the St. Lawrence river and gulf." No doubt, while resting at the Manning Pool on Montreal's Viger Street, some of *Nicoya*'s crew would have run across month-old newspapers that carried stories quoting Vice-Admiral Percy Nelles, chief of naval staff, and Rear-Admiral G. C. Jones, commander-in-chief of the Atlantic, warning that the start of the 1942 shipping season might very well bring U-boats into Canada's waters. Brice might even have known of the opera buffa of October 14, 1939, when His Majesty's Royal Canadian Navy consulted a "submarine diviner" before sending two harbour vessels, including the aptly named *Druid*, armed with a borrowed army cannon surrounded by sandbags, to investigate a reported U-boat sighting off Île d'Orléans. But everything Brice and Inch saw on the river and the fact that they were sailing independently (at least until they joined a convoy at Sydney) told them they were sailing in peaceful seas.

There were precautions aplenty, but these too bespoke safety. The Fusiliers du St-Laurent, wearing World War I–era uniforms, could be seen guarding the railroad bridge at Quebec while others manned the 7.5-inch guns that pointed down toward the river from Fort de la Martinière in Lauzon, opposite the heights of Quebec City. Unseen were the two 18-lb. mobile guns secreted on Île d'Orléans, the island just east of Quebec City at the centre of which was the degaussing station. There, during the 1942 shipping season, outbound ships stopped to have their hull's magnetic charge neutralized. Likely neither Brice nor his crew knew that the waters off Bic Island, ten miles west of Rimouski, Quebec, had seen Canada's first successful action at sea: the seizure of the 3,921-ton Italian merchantman *Capo Noli* by the minesweeper HMCS *Bras d'Or*.[3]

There was air cover, apparently improved from 1941 when *Nicoya* took McRae to England. When the war began in 1939, Eastern Air Command (EAC) had one lone squadron at an improvised base on the Sydney River (near Sydney, Nova Scotia, on the far end of the Gulf of St. Lawrence) to provide coverage of the almost ¼-million-square-kilometre area of the river and gulf in addition to the seaward approaches to Halifax. As historian Alec Douglas has shown in *The Creation of a National Airforce*, a year later (in 1940), this first squadron, now based at a permanent facility at Kelly Beach, Nova Scotia, was joined by a small squadron of Supermarine Stranraers, biplane seaplanes flying from Dartmouth, across the bay from Halifax. In 1941, more planes were available, from Kelly Beach, Sydney, Botwood and Gander and from American air bases in Newfoundland. By 1942, EAC had almost one hundred planes available, though most were assigned to North Atlantic convoy protection. Unarmed training squadrons based in Mont Joli, ten miles west of Rimouski, and at Charlottetown and Summerside, Prince Edward Island, did double duty as an anti-submarine deterrent force as they flew training patrols over the river and gulf.

Out toward the end of the Gaspé itself was the newly built naval base HMCS Fort Ramsay, equipped with a seaplane slip. And just outside the town of Gaspé, a chain of army forts: Prevel, Haldimand and Peninsula, positioned to guard Gaspé Bay. Plans called for Fort Ramsay to have a small force of two armed yachts and two minesweepers, designated as a "hunter group," that would spring into action once the location of a submarine was clear.[4]

*   *   *

Everywhere Brice and Inch looked there were the signs of safety.

Navigational lights and radio beacons were "operating as in peacetime," wrote *Kapitänleutnant* Karl Thurmann, commander of U-553, in his war diary (KTB) on May 8, 1942, three days before he fired the first salvo in the Battle of the St. Lawrence. *Nicoya*'s own lights shone.

Tomorrow, after passing Cape Gaspé, the crew would once again take up war positions. Watches would be posted. The guns that had been welded to the *Nicoya*'s deck would be manned.

But for one more night, the crew that would soon once again face Dönitz's wolves could sleep easy. *Nicoya* was sailing through peaceful seas, last roiled by war almost two hundred years earlier. In the Battle of the Restigouche in Baie des Chaleurs on July 8, 1760, a British squadron led by HMS *Fame* defeated the French fleet, led by Admiral François Chenard de La Giraudais's 500-ton frigate *Machault*, which had been sent to reconquer Quebec. La Giraudais's loss ended the Seven Years War and ended forever France's claim to Canada.

* * *

The four men crammed onto the top of U-553's conning tower knew differently. Now they were the hunters. The sounds of the hunt were the low throb of the 3,200-hp diesel engines that powered their Type VIIC *Unterseeboot*, the glide of water passing their 67.1-metre outer hull and the words of their captain—an Iron Cross First Class–winner—as he read off the co-ordinates and other target information from his attack binoculars to his *Oberbootsmann*. Generally referred to as *Nummer Eins* ("Number One"), Thurmann's first officer repeated the numbers as he fed them into the torpedo attack calculator, which computed the settings and then transmitted them by two wires directly into the guidance system of the "eel" in Tube I.

Two days earlier, after having entered the St. Lawrence to repair a hydroplane damaged in what Thurmann called a "chance" bombing (on May 7) some twenty miles southwest of Cape Breton's Scaterie Island, the sound of war was the alarm bell signalling an emergency dive after a lookout spotted a plane at 5:16 p.m. Thurmann's war diary entry—"Emergency dive because of 4-engine land-based aircraft on bearing 300, elevation 700 m., range = 5000 m. Aircraft flying parallel course. 5 bombs landed when at depth 20 m., at moderate range, normal damage"—hardly captures the horror of being caught on the surface by a bomber, or the organized chaos of an emergency dive.

The first glint of the setting sun reflecting off the silver skin of the US Army Air Force B-17 Flying Fortress set in motion a well-choreographed ballet of men, valves, steel and water that took the U-boat from the surface, where its conning tower was some 4.5 metres above water, to relative safety, more than 20 metres under. Immediately following the alarm, the four men on the conning tower scrambled down the hatch, more jumping than climbing down the steel ladders. The last down, the senior watch officer, closed the hatch. As soon as he had, and while still turning the wheel that locked it in place, he yelled *"Fluten!"*—"Flood the tanks!"

The first valves that were turned after the chief engineer ordered, "Vent ballast tanks 2, 3, 4 and 5," opened the air vents at the top of the boat's forward ballast tanks, which allowed water rushing into the bottom of the tanks to push out the air that kept the U-boat afloat. Simultaneously, the ship's hydroplane operators turned the wheels in front of them to pitch the heavy diving planes downward. In the engine room, artificers were at once shutting down U-553's diesel engines and engaging her silent electric motors in a tightly co-ordinated sequence designed to ensure that the boat's propellers did not miss a beat. Every bite the propeller blades took into the water drove the boat farther toward safety. Only after the boat had achieved a descent angle of between 20° and 25° did the chief engineer call for the aft ballast tank to be filled; this sequence ensured that the boat's stern did not pop out of the water.

Had the dive been occasioned by the sighting of a ship, Thurmann's engineering officer would probably have ordered it halted when they reached 13.5 metres (their depth being indicated by a mercury column similar to a barometer), which was periscope depth. Because they were diving to escape a plane, however, the engineering officer waited several more seconds, till they reached 20 metres, before ordering the dive plane operators to bring the hydroplanes back to their neutral position—and before ordering the complex pumping of water between the ship's fore and aft, starboard and port trim tanks that would keep the 1,070-ton ship on an even keel. As little as 36.3 litres (8 gallons) in the wrong tank could upset the boat's trim and buoyancy.

A little over three hours later, Thurmann radioed U-boat headquarters in Lorient telling *Führer der Unterseeboote* Karl Dönitz that his "forward hydroplane motor [was] again unserviceable," that even though he'd obviously been spotted, "navigational lights ashore are still operating," and that he had gone "into the river!" Ten hours later, he'd travelled 94.5 nautical miles farther into Canadian waters. Seventeen hours after that, he stood 400 metres off *Nicoya*'s port side, ten miles from Fame Point, ten miles west of the tip of the Gaspésie.

At nine minutes to midnight on May 12, 1942, the equation that described *Nicoya*'s ability to float was as old as Archimedes' famous naked run through Syracuse.[5] *Nicoya* floated because though the ship, its stores and cargo, and its men weighed some 10,670 tons (of which 4,400 tons was the ship's own weight), her 400 × 51 foot hull displaced its own weight in water. It did this because the tons of steel, glass, planes, frozen meat and men, all heavier than water, were part of an equation that also included the thousands of cubic metres of air trapped within the hull. In effect, the hull was a gigantic bubble. Even though the hull pushed down into the water as much as 26.9 feet, as long as it remained intact the hydrostatic force of the water pushed upward on it, creating what naval architects call "buoyancy."

That equation changed a minute later when, at the end of a 400-metre run, the torpedo fired from U-553's Tube I detonated. The torpedo hit *Nicoya* with the force of 57.6 metric tons about 100 feet from the stern, just behind the engine room on the port side.

Within milliseconds of the torpedo's pistol's igniting 268 kilograms of *Schiesswolle 36*—a high-explosive mixture of TNT, hexanitrodiphenylamine and aluminum flakes—a white-hot (3,000°C) gas bubble with a pressure of some 50,000 atmospheres (750,000 pounds per square inch) formed. If such a shock bubble forms close to a ship's keel, it is strong enough to lift even the largest ship. The bubble then acts like a pivot around which the keel bends and, finally, breaks. Set at three metres, however, Thurmann's torpedo hit too far above *Nicoya*'s keel to lift her and break her back. Instead, it blasted through *Nicoya*'s .46-inch steel plating, tearing, Brice reported, a "huge hole" in the ship's port side.

Though now aboard a doomed ship, Brice's crew were luckier than most torpedo victims. The blast that ripped through the hull entered a refrigerated hold. Tons of chilled meat absorbed some of the force. The dense cold cooled the rampaging stream of superheated gas, preventing the formation of the flash, an instantaneous burning that streams through passageways, ventilation shafts and whatever pathway the force of the explosion itself has bludgeoned. Had the torpedo hit a hold with vast empty spaces, the white-hot bubble would have expanded within the hold, its heat and force shredding even the thick steel bulkheads, turning them into pieces of shrapnel moving at hundreds of miles an hour. It's likely that had the flash erupted in an empty hold, *Nicoya* would have vanished in mere seconds.[6]

Before Brice and his crew felt their ship tremble, a secondary effect of the bubble tore through *Nicoya*. The detonation wave, now behaving like water flowing through the ground, followed the path of least resistance. Because the hold's bottom plating ranged between .72 inches and 1 inch in thickness, the torrent could not break out through the ship's bottom. Nor could it rupture the hold's fore and aft bulkheads, which were stiffened by frames spaced every 30 inches. The path of least resistance, therefore, lay upward. The explosion surged through the steel and wooden decking that covered the hold, blowing apart a crate and the plane within it. Then the explosive wave exhausted itself—at just about the time Captain Brice's bridge crew became aware of it—by blowing apart the aft port lifeboat.

Reaction aboard the *Nicoya* was instantaneous. The engineer stopped the engines even before the ship's telegraph rang Full Stop. Men and the one woman aboard, who before going to sleep had looked out upon the peaceful waters that lapped the shores of the Gaspé, jumped up. Some dressed before running out of their cabins or messes. Steward Russell Simpson didn't; he ran from his cabin barefoot and in his pyjamas.

Two of Brice's passengers had experienced this nightmare of broken glass, twisted metal and ruptured steam lines spewing forth scalding white smoke just a month earlier. One, Roman Ferreira, had survived the sinking of SS *Montevideo* that March; during the First World War, he had survived being torpedoed, and two weeks in an open boat. He didn't survive a fourth torpedoing 362 days after the *Nicoya*'s sinking. Either Ferreira or the other passenger (unnamed by the press) who had also survived a sinking just weeks earlier told a reporter that in addition to losing his new kit, he lost the marshmallows he was bringing home to his wife, "who had quite a liking for them."

Before running from the bridge, the wireless telegraphist likely given the watch, Second Wireless Officer Lewis Burby, paused for a moment to shove the secret code books that had been given to Brice in Montreal into the weighted bag. The bag was later thrown over the side.

Mrs. Michael Silverstone, on her way to England to join her husband, an RAF officer who had returned home earlier from a posting in Montreal, ran from her cabin, carrying her eighteen-month-old son, Nathan. Once on deck, they joined Captain Brice and seventy-four other souls in a grotesque ballet. Shrouded by steam, they picked their way over broken glass and twisted metal and over or around wrecked wooden hatches. All this and more is contained in Brice's words: "There was so much noise from escaping steam, it was impossible to give orders or hear anything, and it was difficult to see through the steam"—the laconic expression favoured by the writers of operations reports.

In the first minute after the explosion, hundreds of tons of water poured through the hole blasted by the torpedo. The water's first effect might be called beneficial. It cooled the hold and doused any fires that may have burned in its bottom.

Soon, maybe two minutes after the torpedoing, the water passed the critical mark. Fully loaded as it was, *Nicoya* had a reserve buoyancy of some 2,200 tons. As Hold No. 3 filled with water that quickly began to flow farther aft through the bilge and crankshaft spaces, *Nicoya*'s reserve buoyancy vanished.

Brice didn't need to work out the equation that says that a ship will sink when it has taken on so much water that its total weight (ship + water) exceeds its hull's ability to displace water. Every moment *Nicoya* pushed lower into the water told him that soon there'd be no more buoyancy to be found.

Nor was he fooled by the fact that his ship was still on an even keel. The fact that even with a gaping wound *Nicoya*'s hull was still able to distribute the added load across her length and breadth was a tribute to her designers as much as it was a twist of fate. Had the torpedo hit the forward hold, now, some two minutes after being hit, *Nicoya* would be going down by the bow. Again, Brice's words—"she was obviously sinking rapidly"—hide more than they reveal, but since Brice doesn't mention a list, it's safe to assume that *Nicoya* was settling quickly into the dark waters of the St. Lawrence.

Within minutes of Brice's ordering Abandon Ship, forty-one of the passengers and crew were safely aboard the one remaining portside boat and the aft starboard boat. Moments later, Brice and thirty-five men still aboard the fast-sinking ship watched in horror as the forward starboard boat they were preparing to board "was lowered too quickly and became waterlogged immediately [after] she hit water," Brice reported.

Even if there had been room in the two just-launched boats, neither would have returned to pick up Brice and the other men. Once shipped, lifeboats follow their own imperative: move as quickly as possible away from the stricken ship. This seemingly heartless manoeuvre is necessary to ensure that the lifeboat and the survivors in it are not pulled down by the suction caused by the sinking ship. As soon as his boat was free of its lines, Inch started his boat's Austin outboard engine and moved away from the wrecked *Nicoya*. Moments later, the men in the other boat used their oars to do the same. Twelve hours later, Inch's boat would be the first to reach shore and thus bring Canada the word that war had come to our inland shores.

Perhaps because *Nicoya* was settling on an even keel, Thurmann thought it had not been mortally wounded. Had she been torpedoed in the open sea, he would likely have surfaced and used his deck gun to hole her hull again and ensure that she sank while saving one of his few torpedoes for another ship. Eight miles from Canada's shore, such a gambit was too risky. Still, he could not take the risk that *Nicoya* might be beached ashore, where it could be salvaged. As historian Peter Padfield has shown, Dönitz's *guerre de course* demanded not that ships be badly damaged but that they be sunk: "The enemy's shipping constitutes one single, great entity. It is therefore immaterial where a ship is sunk. Once it has been destroyed, it has to be replaced by a new ship. In the long run the result of the war will depend on the result of the race between shipping and new constructions." This time, Thurmann's war diary doesn't record the co-ordinates or running time, saying only, "0611 *Coup de grâce* from Tube II, hit amidships."

In the moments before Thurmann's second torpedo hit, Captain Brice led the remaining men in launching the ship's Carley floats. Built out of balsa wood and shaped like a large square doughnut with netting in the middle, Carley floats were standard equipment on both merchant ships and warships. *Nicoya* carried four, each attached to a skid secured to the ship's rigging. On some ships, Carley floats launched themselves, their own buoyancy being enough to detach them from their skids. On others, such as *Nicoya*, Carley floats were launched by pulling a pin.

Just as Brice had ordered his men to dive into the water and make for the just-launched floats, Thurmann's second torpedo slammed into the stricken ship, setting off what one resident told the Canadian Press was a "terrific explosion that rocked the houses [several miles away from *Nicoya*] as though there was an earthquake." Scant seconds before Thurmann's *coup de grâce* hit their dying ship, thirty men reached one of *Nicoya*'s rafts. The disaster continued. *Nicoya* "plung[ed] to her grave," pulling the raft and the men on it under the St. Lawrence waters.

"The raft had been thrown over and we jumped in and swam to it," Burby told British United Press. "About thirty of us scrambled on. But no one had cut the rope attaching the raft to the ship, and as she plunged we were dragged right under the water."

As desperate men hacked at the rope with whatever they could find, the other end was securely attached to a now deadweight of some 10,000 tons. The raft was pulled under and then the rope parted. The raft sprang back to the surface with six fewer men than it had supported just moments earlier— the first men to die from enemy fire in Canada since the Riel Rebellion in 1885.

William John George, a sixteen-year-old ordinary seaman, was dead. So too were James Stanley Newcomb, a thirty-five-year-old third engineer, likely the man who ordered the *Nicoya*'s engines stopped. H.V.

Woodthrope, a twenty-year-old carpenter; and two other thirty-five-year-olds, Frank L. Smith and Douglas Phillips, too had drowned. Henry Mills, an anti-aircraft gunner, would also never be seen again. Brice didn't know the names yet—that would have to wait another two days—but within minutes, one count and then another had been taken, and he knew that six of his crew had vanished.

As U-553 cruised away on a northwesterly course that would take it farther into the river, *Nicoya*'s crew struggled to survive. Knowing that the raft would slow down whichever boat took it in tow, Brice ordered Inch to proceed independently to shore. Inch's orders were as simple as they were obvious: "send out assistance" and report *Nicoya*'s loss to Captain Armit, commander of Fort Ramsay, the newly opened RCN base at Gaspé. Through the rest of the night and well into the next day, Inch, the wind whipping his thick mane of hair, needed every ounce of his extensive knowledge of the sea to pilot his little boat, upon which forty-one souls depended, through the strong currents of the St. Lawrence.

The bitterly cold night was dangerous to the men in the remaining boat, but they were relatively dry. Brice knew that he and the men who swam to the raft were in mortal danger.[7]

Just moments after seeing his ship destroyed and learning of the death of six of his crew, Brice had to make the most difficult of command decisions. Leaving men, including himself, on the raft, where they would be partially submerged or constantly soaked by the choppy sea, was a death sentence. Ordering that a rotation be established with the men in the chief engineer's boat (which had taken the raft in tow) could be a death sentence to some already in the boat. Brice's report betrays no hint of the strain he faced, saying only, "It was bitterly cold during the night, so we pulled on the oars in order to keep warm, transferring the men from the raft to the lifeboat frequently during the night."

MAY 12, 1942

- Three thousand five hundred miles east in Hamburg, workers at Deutsche Werft AG lay down the keel for U-540; in Danzig, F. Schichau lays down U-742's keel. U-629, U-630 and U-710 are launched.

- Five thousand miles east in the centre of the Donets Basin in southern Russia, 854 tanks under the command of Soviet marshal Semyon Konstantinovich Timoshenko attack the German lines behind the city of Kharkov. Seven days later, the German general Paul L. E. von Kleist will report the destruction of more than 600 Soviet tanks and the capture of 241,000 men.

- Two thousand miles east, in the middle of the air gap, two U-boats carve five ships from ONS-92, escorted by the corvettes HMCS *Algoma*, *Arvida*, *Bittersweet* and *Shediac*.

- Three thousand miles south, off the coast of French Guiana, on his first patrol as commander of U-69, Ulrich Gräf sinks the Norwegian merchant ship SS *Lise*. On October 9, Gräf will see the lights of Rimouski when he sinks the SS *Carolus*. Five days later, he will kill 137 men, women and children when he torpedoes the Newfoundland–Nova Scotia ferry SS *Caribou*.

Sixteen miles southwest of the waters in which Brice and his men were struggling to survive, the St. Lawrence rolls on to the Gaspé Peninsula, the southern shore of the St. Lawrence River. Four miles from the centre of the town of Gaspé, a mixed crew of sailors and two local civilian women, all specially trained in wireless, codes and ciphers, were on duty with their sub-lieutenant in the Signals Office on the second floor of a clapboard building in Fort Ramsay. Through the long hours of their watch, which began a scant five minutes after Thurmann fired his first torpedo, the wireless receivers brought not a word of the sinking of *Nicoya*. Nor did the telegraphists hear of Thurmann's second victim, SS *Leto*, a Dutch freighter torpedoed seventeen miles north of Cap-de-la-Madeleine at 2:38 a.m. on May 12, two hours later.

"I wasn't on duty that night, or even the next watch, when word of those sinkings reached the base," recalls Ian Tate, then a twenty-one-year-old sub-lieutenant just arrived from Halifax. "That watch, the one that came on duty at midnight on the eleventh, was the last of its kind, the last before the war moved into the St. Lawrence.

"We all knew why we were there, even though, to be frank, the whole thing had a certain unreality to it. We knew, and, looking back on it, surely our C/O, Commander Armit, knew that there was a real threat, but it was still so hard to believe. True, for two years we'd been hearing of sinkings: 'the mighty *Hood*,' HMS *Repulse*, Pearl Harbor, HMCS *Spikenard* (one of our corvettes sunk in the mid-Atlantic earlier that year in February). And, of course, we knew of the slaughter of the 'Second Happy Time' off the American coast and up to the approaches to Halifax.

"But the news was always 'over there.'

"Here we were, in a naval base commissioned just twelve days previously, that wasn't even finished. The wardroom wasn't up and running yet, and neither were the barracks. The half dozen officers weren't even able to sleep on the base, staying instead at Baker's Hotel in the town of Gaspé.

"I was one of the four pretty green officers in charge of a mixed watch system, varying from eight to twelve hours. I'd had all of one month's training. Two months earlier, I'd been at University of Toronto studying arts so that I could go to law school."

At 2:30 a.m., at the end of a 1,200-metre run, the torpedo fired from U-553's Tube III struck the SS *Leto*'s starboard side some 60 metres from her bow, 3 metres below the waterline. For a moment a "big stream of water and coal" towered over the Dutch ship. Before it collapsed, forty-three men were running for their lives through a ruined ship.

The *Leto*'s first chief engineer, C. Spaan, ran to the engine room but never made it. Finding his way blocked by steam and feeling that the engines had stopped, Spaan knew that the engine room had been blown apart. Through the torn bulkheads he could hear "two screams and that was it," as the six men of the third watch who weren't incinerated by the $3,000°C$ bubble or obliterated by the 50,000 atmospheres of pressure were scalded to death by the ship's own steam. The explosion trapped a seventeen-year-old trimmer in the coal hold at the bottom of the ship.

As Spaan ran toward the engine room, his captain, Egbert Henrik Van Der Veen, paused only long enough to don his life jacket before running to the bridge. Once there, he sent his second navigation officer to the quarterdeck to supervise preparations for launching *Leto*'s boats. Then, together with J. Breet, his first navigation officer, Van Der Veen scanned the night for the submarine, ready to issue orders to twenty-year-old George Brown and twenty-one-year-old Leonard Clepson, two British DEMS gunners who had been able to make it to their guns.

Asleep in their bunks deep in the ship when the torpedo hit, London-born twenty-five-year-old Bill Middladitch and James Hullican, twenty-four, of Welsey, never got to their guns. "We couldn't realize what had happened at first," Hullican told the *Ottawa Evening Citizen*'s reporter a day later. "But when we leaped out of [our] bunks and stepped in knee deep water we knew we must have been hit."

By the time they got to the deck, *Leto* had started to list and Van Der Veen had ordered Abandon Ship. Before leaving the bridge, he threw the secret code books into the water he'd soon be swimming in.

Unlike *Nicoya*, which settled on an even keel, *Leto* quickly took on a list to starboard as thousands of tons of water poured into her ruptured hull. Just moments after reaching the boat deck to help launch the lifeboats, maybe two minutes after the ship had been hit, Van Der Veen heard "water entering the between-decks" (an area several decks above the waterline) when he ran past the starboard bunker window.

Leto carried five lifeboats, more than enough for her forty-three men and two passengers (including O. Nuzink and M. A. A. Overzier, both from Rotterdam, who were returning to England after having been torpedoed seven weeks earlier in the North Atlantic)—had they all been launched.

One boat on the starboard side had been destroyed by the explosion. Because of the list, the main port boats lay heavily against *Leto*'s side. Johannes Boerklaar told the *Montreal Gazette* that in the few anxious moments before the ship began to heel over, "some of the men tried to swing [the boats] out in twos and threes, but it was useless."

While the men near Boerklaar tried to swing the boats out, Van Der Veen ran back up to the bridge, where still another lifeboat was lashed to the stricken *Leto*. He freed it, but his efforts were in vain. It slid down its stays too quickly and foundered when it hit the water.

By now, the first boat to be launched (a jolly boat designed for twelve men but carrying twenty-two, including gunners Hullican and Middladitch) had got safely away from the fast-sinking *Leto*. The portside boat that Van Der Veen ran for was in the water too. As he got to it, the *Leto*'s 4,712 tons began to heel over.

In the moments before *Leto* capsized, members of the crew heard the first navigation officer shouting that he had a passenger with him who couldn't swim. He asked the donkeyman, an oiler and a fuel man if they could take care of the passenger while he and the first navigation officer, who also didn't have a lifebelt, swam for it as the ship plunged.

The suction of the sinking ship drew several men into a maelstrom of twisted wreckage and water made oily by coal dust.

Seconds ticked by.

Then air bubbles, some filled with coal dust, burst to the surface. Next, wooden hatchways that had broken apart and been pulled into the vortex bounded up from the depths.

Had there been only twelve men in the jolly boat, they would have braced themselves for the outwash waves created by the plunging ship. The twenty-two men knew the horrible truth: nothing could keep the outwash waves from pouring over the boat's low freeboard, the first of many waves that would all but swamp the boat during the long cold night. "We were bailing the water as fast as we could, but we would just dip out one bucketful when two or three more would come surging in," recalled twenty-one-year-old crewman Tommy Maxwell.

Leto never got off a message; Gaspé knew nothing.

More seconds ticked by and then, among the detritus coughed up by *Leto*, were two living men: Captain Van Der Veen and George Brown. Van Der Veen's story was told only in the classified operations report: "Shortly after I got there [to the portside lifeboat], the ship capsized and sank, dragging the portside lifeboat, including the people in it, with it. When I reached the water's surface, I noticed that my watch stopped at 2:47 a.m." Brown's story, however, was read by millions. "That was the only time I was afraid," Brown told the Canadian Press. "I had no lifebelt and I was sucked down far under the water as our ship went down. I really did some praying then."

Later Brown was able to save his gunnery mate, Clepson. Clepson, who told interviewers of the painful irony of being able to "see the lights of shore about six miles away," didn't remember how he got off the dying ship. "I passed out cold," sprawled out on a bobbing packing case. After coming to, he saw Brown on a larger case and joined him there. As the night wore on, hypothermia began to affect Clepson. "I was wearing lighter clothes than Len, but the cold water didn't affect me as much as it did him," recalled Brown. Toward dawn, the cold almost claimed Clepson. "Shall we go over?" he asked Brown. "And, just as he got the words out I said, 'There's a ship in sight.' He never said another word until we were rescued."

Wilhelm Koning, who had survived another sinking just weeks earlier and was travelling back to England on the *Leto*, was picked up by another Dutch steamer, SS *Titus*, but died "because of the cold water and exhaustion."

Neither *Titus* nor SS *Dutch Mass*, which was travelling with *Titus* and which also picked up survivors, radioed to Gaspé to alert Commander Armit. Both ships proceeded upriver. At 7:30 the next morning, the survivors and Koning's body were transferred to the pilot's boat and then landed at Pointe-au-Père (five miles east of Rimouski, Quebec) directly outside the window of then eleven-year-old Gaétan Lavoie, the Pointe-au-Père lighthouse keeper's son.

"There were about twenty of them. I'd never seen anything like it before. There, at 7:30 in the morning, were twenty men covered in oil walking past my window from the wharf into the town. I didn't know where they were going, but later learned they went to the hotel, where they were given dry clothes and food," recalls Lavoie.

"I asked my father, the lighthouse keeper, what had happened. He told me he didn't know. I thought he knew but didn't want to frighten us.

"When I arrived at school, we learned something about them. We heard that they'd said they'd been sunk by a submarine. That's what some of the kids who had parents who took them in and gave them clothes said."

Young Gaétan almost certainly guessed right about his father. By the time *Leto*'s survivors and dead were coming ashore, Canadian authorities already knew that there had been at least one sinking in the St. Lawrence. Since 1939, Charles-August Lavoie and his fellow lighthouse keepers had listened for codes, broadcast on CBC and Radio-Canada, that told them when to dim their beacons because of enemy action.

Action Stations was rung at Fort Ramsay shortly after noon on May 12 after a phone call brought the first report of torpedoing survivors coming ashore. The boat that landed at L'Anse-à-Valleau, fifteen kilometres from Fox River (Rivière-au-Renard), carried the thirty-nine men as well as Mrs. Silverstone and her son, whom Brice had entrusted to First Mate Inch.

"The true impact of what had happened, that the war had now come home to Canada's inland shores, did not dawn on us," recalls Tate. "I don't remember where on the base I was when I first heard the news, but I know that within a few minutes I'd grabbed my camera and joined a rescue party of eight men, including Commander Armit and an army medical officer.

"It took us about an hour and a quarter to get there. We took the base station wagon as far as we could, but there was still a great deal of snow on the ground and it drifted across the only road on the coastline. Some ways away, we had to abandon the station wagon and walk, carrying the supplies through the village to the beach.

"By the time we arrived at the beach, the number of survivors had grown by more than a score. We arrived just in time to see another of the *Nicoya*'s boats land, towed by a motor fishing boat that was filled with survivors we later learned had been on the raft when the boat came out to get them."

Although Minister of Naval Services Angus Macdonald would soon be assuring the nation that the navy had put in place "long-prepared plans for the protection of Canada's territorial waters" and that the 1942 memorandum entitled "Defence of Shipping—Gulf of St. Lawrence" called for the immediate dispatch of "adequate hunting and striking forces," Canada's immediate military action was negligible.

Searching did not begin until dawn on the thirteenth. Even then, the existing plans could not be fully put into effect because the slipways, fuel dumps, seaplane tendering and even barracks necessary to base a detachment of Cansos (a flying boat) at HMCS Fort Ramsay were not yet complete.

HMCS *Medicine Hat*, a Bangor minesweeper tasked with being the lead ship to patrol the waters around Gaspé once a submarine alert was sounded, was in Sydney, Nova Scotia, over 250 miles away. It did not arrive in the area where *Nicoya* and *Leto* were torpedoed until the afternoon of the thirteenth. *Medicine Hat* "searched the area of the sinkings, Fame to Fox Points, with no results," reported the U-boat tracking report for May 1942.

The RCN's immediate local response was the launching of HMCS *Venning*, an 18-metre converted fishing trawler that first had to be taken off its winter chocks. Ordered into the water by twenty-five-year-old First Lieutenant Paul Bélanger, *Venning* had to manoeuvre around ice floes before getting out of Gaspé's harbour.

James Essex's memory of Engineer Clark trying to "squeeze every last ounce of energy from the wheezing engines" may sound like something out of a *Boy's Own Magazine* story. The hard reality was, however, that though Gaspé had been designated a strike force, it was totally unprepared for anti-submarine warfare. Not only did *Venning* lack sonar and radar, it carried no depth charges and no machine gun. "If they did see a sub," recalled Essex in his memoir, *Victory in the St. Lawrence*, "they did not even have a radio" to report it to Fort Ramsay.

MAY 13, 1942

- Three thousand five hundred miles east in Berlin, in a section of his diary in which he praises the *Protocol of the Elders of Zion* (a late-nineteenth-century Russian creation that "outlines" how Jewish interests will take over the world), Joseph Göbbels writes, "There is therefore no other recourse left for modern nations except to exterminate the Jew."

- One thousand five hundred miles to the east, in the middle of the air gap, in the second day of a two-day battle, ONS-92, a slow convoy bound from the UK to North America and protected by six escorts, including the corvettes HMCS *Algoma*, *Arvida*, *Bittersweet* and *Shediac*, loses two more ships.
- Two thousand miles south, Ulrich Gräf's U-69 sinks the US freighter SS *Norlandic*.

With the exceptions of the readers of the *Ottawa Evening Journal*, the *Vancouver Province* and the inside pages of Quebec's *Le Soleil* newspapers of May 11, most Canadians learned of the St. Lawrence sinkings from the headlines on May 12—just about the time Gaétan Lavoie was watching the survivors of *Leto* come ashore in Pointe-au-Père. The news stories went considerably further than simply reporting that sinkings had occurred off "a St. Lawrence Port" (a phrase that quickly took its place beside the ubiquitous "East Coast Port") and repeating the statement issued by Naval Services Minister Macdonald:

> The minister for naval services announces that the first enemy attack upon shipping in the St. Lawrence river took place on May 11 when a freighter was sunk. Forty-one survivors have been landed from the vessel.
>
> The situation regarding shipping in the river is being closely watched and long-prepared plans for its special protection under these circumstances are in operation.
>
> Any possible further sinkings in this area will not be made public in order that information of value to the enemy may be withheld from him. It is felt, however, that the Canadian public should be informed of the presence of enemy U-boats in Canadian territorial waters and they are assured that every step is being taken to grapple with the situation.

While subsequent days would see confusion as survivor stories became jumbled and with the publication and then retraction of the baleful rumour that "a woman and her baby [had been left] ominously alone in an oarless lifeboat," the articles that appeared on the thirteenth and on the days that followed were substantially accurate.

As he had for thousands of nights, before going to bed on the twelfth, Canada's tenth prime minister, William Lyon Mackenzie King, sat alone writing in his diary, accompanied only by his dog. King sat in a room on the second floor of Laurier House, a three-storey brick Victorian building that his predecessor, Sir Wilfrid Laurier, had given the Liberal Party. Amidst pictures of his mother and father, King recorded the first mention of the

Battle of the St. Lawrence in Parliament. Toward the end of a Liberal caucus meeting, in which the prime minister reminded his members of the need for both cabinet and caucus unity in dealing with the contradictory vote in the April 7 plebiscite that freed King from his 1940 campaign promise not to bring in conscription, he made a most uncharacteristic detour into technical military matters:[8]

> I then went on to say that I had pretty good evidence of what I had said about space and time being eliminated. Matters were moving very rapidly and distance being overcome. I drew from my pocket a brown envelope with red seals and said that they would be surprised to learn that therein was word that an enemy submarine had torpedoed a ship in the waters of the St. Lawrence west of Gaspé and that this morning the survivors were being landed on the shores of the river in the province of Quebec. I said that I hoped they would not imagine that this was an isolated happening, and that they might expect to find it followed by further raids and the probable approach of the enemy into our country both on the waters and overhead, with the probable destruction of Canadian lives, homes, etc.

Vague as ever, King's words did more than tell his MPs that new technologies were altering the time and space of war. His words were preparing them—and through them, ultimately, the nation—for something entirely new: battle deaths in Canada.

*   *   *

The stories pieced together by reporters grabbed the attention not only of the Canadian public but also of the German and Canadian governments. Even before Thurmann radioed his report to Admiral Dönitz at U-boat Command (*Befehlshaber der Unterseeboote*, or BdU), Germany knew of the sinkings from Canadian sources, published on the twelfth. At 9:15 a.m. on May 12, hours before young Gaétan saw *Leto*'s survivors arrive on land, Berlin radio broadcast the (somewhat fictionalized) report, which indicates, incidentally, that Radio Berlin's wordsmiths did not fully understand the geopolitical division of North America:

German U-boats are now operating in the St. Lawrence River, the nearest approach to land. A German U-boat sank an American 6,000-ton freighter yesterday, carrying a cargo of jute from India for Montreal. The ship had made the long voyage from India safely, only to be sunk in the St. Lawrence. This is the first time that U-boats have operated so far from the sea. The news broke like a bombshell in Canada and the United States. The United States Navy Department announced that no further report will be given of any future sinkings that may occur in this region.[9]

Concerned about the extent of detail published in the aftermath of the sinkings—including the naming of survivors and such information as "we never used watches in the St. Lawrence river and we were only due to start them the morning after we were sunk"—the director of censorship of the Canadian naval staff prepared guidelines that told news editors what types of information should not be published. The legal foundation for Memorandum No. 1, prepared by Walter Scott Thompson and entitled "Sinkings in the St. Lawrence, May 11, 1942: Notes on Publication of News Stories," was an Order in Council passed on September 1, 1939, nine days before King George VI signed Canada's Declaration of War: "No person shall print, circulate or distribute a book, newspaper, periodical, pamphlet, picture or documentary of any kind containing any material, report or statement, false or otherwise, intended or likely to cause disaffection to His Majesty, or to interfere with the success of His Majesty's forces . . . or which might be prejudicial to the safety of the state or the efficient prosecution of the war."

Sent to news editors on May 21, Memorandum No. 1 recognized the impossibility of imposing a complete news blackout when the battle front extended hundreds of miles into the country. The director of censorship's goal was, rather, to convince the nation's news editors to censor their own news and thus, as Macdonald told the House several months later, to establish two types of information: local rumour and official news, only the latter to be broadcast and hence accessible to the enemy.

The notes explained what type of information was useful to the enemy. In addition to such obvious points as the exact location of an attack (which revealed the strength of Canada's defences) or the type of ship (which revealed information about supplies of food or oil), the notes explained that such seemingly innocuous information as the nationality of the ship or the names of survivors was useful to the Germans: "If any crew members are nationals of German occupied territories, their [the crew's] morale can be attacked through persecution of relatives, or friends." The notes are equally clear on what German naval authorities could glean from such statements as "there were other ships within hunting distance" (that river traffic was unescorted), or even from statements about the weather.

Since high-frequency directional finding (HF/DF, or "huff-duff"), a system of listening posts in Greenland, the United Kingdom, eastern Canada and the United States that allowed the navy to locate a U-boat by triangulating on its radio broadcasts, was top secret, it's hard to know what crusty news editors would have made of the statement: "It is in our interest to encourage U-boats to use their radio. It is detrimental to our interest to spare them this necessity." No doubt, news editors winced at the navy's purple prose:

The morale in U-boats is a highly variable morale. Success will send it rocketing; failure will plunge it to the depths. Apparent success, without full knowledge of its extent, is irritating and tantalizing.

It is safe to assume that a comprehensive report on this exploit will now be made for the use of U-boat commanders, and that it will give the fullest particulars [i.e., details taken from Canadian news reports] regarding the whole matter. It will tell more of this operation than could have been told by the commander of the attacking U-boat.

This will increase the respect of U-boat commanders and crews for the German Naval Intelligence Department, and will, in every way, assist in building U-boat morale.

But, on the whole, they took the navy's admonition to heart while not flinching from reporting the horror of the war.

*   *   *

At 3 p.m. on May 13, as *Medicine Hat* and EAC's planes searched for *Nicoya* and *Leto*'s killer, two centuries-old rituals were about to begin: one in Ottawa, the other in the corner of a cemetery in Pointe-au-Père.

One hundred and fifty feet to the west of the hushed Hall of Honour, which to this day holds the leather-bound folio-sized Book of Remembrance that lists the names of Canada's dead from the Great War, is the entrance to the House of Commons. On May 13, as he did every day when the House was in session, at precisely 3:00 p.m., the black-robed Speaker rose, looked toward his left to the leader of His Majesty's Loyal Opposition and asked if there were any questions for the government sitting three swords' lengths away. A moment later, Thomas L. Church, the Progressive Conservative member for Toronto-Broadview, rose, answered "Yes" and, after looking across the green carpet at the cabinet, turned toward the Speaker and told the House of Commons that his question was for the minister of naval services.

Sixty years later, and even taking into account that over the year and a half Canada had been at war parliamentarians had learned that operational matters would not be discussed in open session, the exchange that followed has a certain unreality about it. Instead of asking whether the attacks inside Canada would affect the government's plans to send, if necessary, conscripts to Europe, or even whether the "long-prepared plans" Macdonald had referred to in his statement of the twelfth now required revision, Church asked, "Is the Government aware that for nearly the past two years German U-boats have been sheltering in the deep creeks, inlets and harbours of these islands, St. Pierre and Miquelon, where they flash signals at night from shores to sink Atlantic shipping?"

Macdonald's reply—"Does my honourable friend state that to be the case?"—violated the parliamentary tradition that forbids that a minister who is being asked a question reply with a question. Momentarily interrupted by Conservative house leader Richard Hanson's heckle, "He is asking you," Macdonald continued. "There has to be something more in this House than mere innuendo and suggestion."

Church's supplemental question—"Where was your navy when all this was going on in the St. Lawrence?"—ratcheted up the tenor of the debate to the level that it would remain over the next several months as more ships were sunk. Macdonald's reply evaded the supplementary question and sought instead to forewarn the House that the sinkings of *Nicoya* and *Leto* were not isolated instances because, as King had told the caucus a day earlier, technological changes had altered the time and distance of war:

> I will answer my honourable friend with the fact that I do not know, and he does not know, and no respectable, reputable authority knows that there is a German U-base on this side of the Atlantic.
>
> I have stated several times in this House that we knew definitely that German U-boats could leave European bases, come over to this side, operate for some days off the American coasts and get back to their bases in France or Germany or along the conquered coasts without the necessity of refuelling. There are no very deep inlets in the harbours of St. Pierre-Miquelon.

By the end of Question Period, Thurmann had cruised to grid square BA 3673, about fifteen miles off the small village of Tourelle, Quebec, some fifty miles upriver from where he sank *Leto* and some seventy-five miles from where *Medicine Hat* was looking for him. Thurmann left the St. Lawrence on May 22 without sinking another ship.[10]

Two of *Leto*'s dead were buried, the first in unhallowed ground.

Wearing oversized pants, old woollen sweaters and dark peacoats worn from long use, the men who stood in the far corner of the cemetery adjacent to the white clapboard church looked at the plain wooden casket the priest had refused to allow into his church. Their hands and faces still stained from the ooze created when coal dust and oil mixed with salt water, they stood; some choked back tears, some didn't. Through their minds ran images—of the explosion, the water, the grasping hands that pulled them onto floating bits of decks. Some still heard sounds far more striking than the gentle rustle of the breeze that came in off the waters of the St. Lawrence—the cracking of the ship, the screams of men trapped in the furnace that had been the engine room.

They looked at the church and wondered what it was like inside. They heard again their captain, now just a survivor of a torpedoing like them, tell them the priest would not allow a non-Catholic—a parishioner of the Dutch Reformed Church, a Protestant schismatic who looked not to Rome but to his own reading of the Bible to find the risen Christ—to cross the threshold of the church. They stood now not even on hallowed ground, for that too was denied to Wilhelm Koning.

In the far corner of the yard, far from the cross and distant from where other men, women and children slept, they stood and looked into the open casket, at Koning's body. They must have commented on Arsène Michaud's undertaker's art, for the body was no longer "blackened as if burned." Soon the words ended. The body was lowered, not as deep as the men who lay at rest in the shattered *Leto*, but deep enough to rest forever in the Gaspé.

Several days later, a body washed ashore near Grande-Vallée. To preserve it, local fisherman put it in an ice house and then transported it to Fort Ramsay in Gaspé, where Captain Van Der Veen identified it as donkeyman Frederick van Hoogdalem. Several days later, Captain Van Der Veen and several of his crew returned to Grande-Vallée where, since no one knew whether Hoogdalem was Catholic or not, the local priest agreed to bury him in hallowed ground.

Since 1943, every May 12 an emissary of the Dutch embassy has come to these little villages and placed flowers on the graves.

CHAPTER TWO

FOUR SINKINGS IN JULY

JULY 6 AND 20, 1942
SS *Anastassios Pateras, Hainaut, Dinaric* and *Frederika Lensen*

And found'ring like a man in fire or lime . . .
Dim, through the misty panes and thick green light,
As under a green sea, I saw him drowning.

—WILFRED OWEN

On August 10, 1940, as hundreds of *Luftwaffe* pilots struck England and hundreds more readied themselves for *Adlertag,* the 1,500-sortie-a-day attack against England's airfields, radar stations and aircraft factories, engineers at Bremen's Vulkar-Vegesacker Werft laid the keel for the yard's seventh Type VIIC U-boat. Over the next ten months, as *Adlertag* rose to its crescendo with the bombing of London and the obliteration of Coventry, as the Third Reich suffered its first defeat when Hermann Göring's planes were driven from England's skies, as Bomber Command made its first tentative raid on Bremen and as the *Wehrmacht* moved troops east for Operation Barbarossa, shipwrights spent 254,000 hours fashioning 268 metric tons of steel, 4 tons of wood and 4 tons of paint into U-132, a weapons platform that sank or damaged ten ships for a total of 45,629 tons of shipping, almost half of it in the St. Lawrence.

Der Tag. The Day.

Sailors in the *Kriegsmarine* lived for *der Tag,* the day when their capital ships of 26,000, 31,000 and 42,000 tons would once again sally forth and battle "perfidious Albion" for control of the seas. The British, including Canadians who served with the Royal Navy, dreamed of another Drake, another Nelson—for another Battle of Jutland, the First World War battle during which the RN drove the kaiser's much-vaunted Grand Fleet from the seas. For the men of the *Kriegsmarine, der Tag* would erase this stain and wipe out the ignominy of the surrender and self-scuttling at Scapa Flow in 1919. *Der Tag* never came.

The Second World War in the Atlantic saw epic engagements—in 1939, between the merchant cruiser HMS *Rawalpindi* and the battlecruiser *Scharnhorst*, and a year later between the merchant cruiser *Jervis Bay*, and the German pocket battleship *Admiral Scheer*. On May 24, 1941, *Bismarck* sank "the mighty *Hood*." Three days later, an armada sank *Bismarck*. The spectre of 16-inch guns hurling two-ton shells 20,000 yards at the merchant ships carrying food, fuel and the weapons of war to Britain continued to haunt the Admiralty even after *Bismarck*. The 40,000-ton battle cruisers *Scharnhorst* and *Gneisenau* were in the Channel port of Brest, France, as was *Bismarck*'s consort, the 20,000-ton *Prinz Eugen*. Trondheim on the Norwegian Sea sheltered *Bismarck*'s sister ship, the not-yet-finished *Tirpitz*. Dubbed a "fleet in being," these four ships tied down scores of the Royal Navy's battleships and destroyers.

But the Battle of the Atlantic was ultimately fought by smaller ships. Some, such as the corvette, the most numerous of Allied ships, weren't even in existence when the war broke over Europe in September 1939. The six-year total of some 700 U-boats sinking 2,259 ships hides more than it reveals. After the establishment of U-boat bases in occupied France gave Dönitz's men relatively untroubled access to the North Atlantic, losses rose from 375 ships representing 1.8 million tons of shipping in 1940 to 496 ships representing 2.4 million tons in 1941. In 1942, imports to the UK fell to one-third of the peacetime levels of 1938 (the last year of the Depression) as 5.4 million tons of shipping were sent to the bottom of the North Atlantic. Another 2.4 million tons were sunk elsewhere. In January 1943, the RN's stock of fuel oil dropped to two months' worth. Month after month, great convoys consisting of scores of ships covering 20 or 30 square miles put to sea from Sydney, Halifax and, later, New York. Until May 1943, when the air gap in the middle of the Atlantic was closed, month after month convoys repeated SC-42's fate: in a ten-day battle that unrolled over 1,200 miles of ocean, twenty-one U-boats sunk eighteen merchant ships totalling over 100,000 tons of food, fuel and war material.

*   *   *

It wasn't supposed to be this way. The British Admiralty was so sanguine about the prospects of asdic, invented in the last days of the First World War, that it raised no objection to the 1935 London Naval Agreement that legitimized Germany's violation of the Treaty of Versailles, which had forbidden Germany from building and possessing submarines. The 1936 report of the Royal Navy's Defence of Trade Committee reported that "the problem of dealing with the submarine," which before the introduction of convoys in 1917 had come close to forcing England out of the First World War, "is more than simplified by the invention of ASDIC. This instrument takes the place of the 'eye' and removes from the submarine the cloak of invisibility which was its principal source of strength in the late war. . . . It is considered that war experience will show that with adequate defences, the operations of submarines against merchant vessels in convoy can be made unprofitable."

Just weeks before the outbreak of the war, Canada's chief of naval staff, Admiral Percy Nelles, echoed the committee: "If unrestricted submarine warfare is again resorted to, the means of combating Submarines are considered to have so advanced that by employing a system of convoy and utilizing Air Forces, losses of submarines would be very heavy."

History would, ultimately, prove both the committee and Admiral Nelles right. But history would have to wait for May 1943.

The *danse macabre* played out across the unforgiving Atlantic and into Canada's heartland was more than one or one hundred and one engagements. It pitted steel mills and shipyards in Hitler's Germany and occupied Europe against the Allies's. Even the army of slave labourers Albert Speer and Dönitz deployed to build U-boat after U-boat into the hundreds never made up for the fact that Hitler unleashed the war in 1939, when the *U-Bootwaffe* totalled seventy-five boats, only one-third of which were operational, and not the three hundred Dönitz had told his *Führer* he needed to fulfill *Führer* Directive Number 9: the annihilation of the English economy.

To defeat England, Dönitz calculated, his *guerre de course* (war against trade) would have to sink 700,000 tons of shipping every month. His marksmen never quite reached that figure, though in 1942 they came close, averaging just over 500,000 tons a month. After the war Winston

Churchill wrote, "the only thing that really frightened me was the U-boat peril."

To transport the bread, cheese, powdered milk and meat that kept England and millions of Allied troops fed and the machines, guns and munitions needed to defeat Hitler, tens of thousands of North American men and women filed into shipyards, where they built more than 10,000 ships. The United States built 8,800 naval vessels, more than half of which served in the Pacific theatre. In mile-long production lines, Americans built 2,700 ten-thousand-ton Liberty ships, the majority of which braved the North Atlantic. Canadians built 121 corvettes, 60 Bangor minesweepers, 64 Algerine minesweepers, 16 Isle-class large anti-submarine trawlers, 70 frigates and 80 Fairmile motor launches. In addition, our yards built 402 merchantmen, 338 of them 10,000-tonners. Ninety of these were sold to the US, and 101 were given to the UK as part of Canada's economic aid to England, proportionately even greater than the more famous American Lend-Lease program. A special wartime Crown corporation sailed more than 170 vessels.[1]

For almost three years before the Battle of the Atlantic spilled over into waters that glide past Rimouski, Cap Sainte-Anne and Baie Comeau, it was also being fought in the manning halls of Quebec City and Halifax and at Montreal's Place Viger Hotel. Ships such as the Greek steamer SS *Anastassios Pateras* and the Belgian merchantman SS *Hainaut*, both of which were sunk on July 6, 1942, were manned by crews whose homelands had long been occupied by Hitler. Propaganda broadcasts naming ships and sometimes even crews made it clear that back in Bruges or Kosovokis or Bergen, families and friends could be endangered. *Agents provocateurs* tried to disrupt the finely tuned convoy system by whispering, "Britain is willing to fight—to the last Norwegian, Dutchman, Belgian, Greek, Pole, Dane or Free Frenchman." Field Marshal Erwin Rommel's victory in Libya in early 1941 sapped merchant seamen's morale, for the fall of Tripoli netted the Desert Fox huge quantities of munitions and equipment that merchant seamen had braved the wolfpacks to bring across the ocean.

Canadian authorities fought back with legislation and organization. An

Order in Council, PC 4751, passed days after the convoy system was set up on September 7, 1939, gave authorities the power to jail foreign merchant seamen who refused to sail on ships on which they had signed the ship's articles. The July 1941 conviction of three Greek deserters made it considerably less attractive for any of the thousands of Greek sailors who moved through Montreal to try to disappear into the city's large Greek immigrant community.

But it was the efforts of the Naval Boarding Service (NBS), established in June 1940, that ensured that thousands of men would sail. Led by Commander Frederick B. Watt, the NBS quickly moved beyond its original mandate to ensure that ships' crews were not a security threat (that is, that there were no *agents provocateurs* aboard) and that both the ship and its crew were sound enough to depart.

Watt's NBS won the confidence of tens of thousands of sailors by preventing unsafe ships from departing harbour and by adding to the NBS a social welfare role. Watt's officials took it upon themselves to provide sailors with books and magazines to read. Over the course of some 20,000 boardings in Halifax, the NBS distributed 78,000 ditty bags, 4 million cigarettes, 11,000 fur vests and 35,000 bundles of woollens, many knitted by society ladies. Watt oversaw the creation of professional manning pools and the institution of training programs; Montreal's NBS ran the empire's largest centre for DEMS gunnery training. Most important, Watt wrote in *In All Respects Ready*, the NBS killed rumours by giving the sailors "the facts—even the hard ones" about what was occurring on the North Atlantic run.

Of all the charts and figures that tell the tale of the Battle of the Atlantic, the NBS's is perhaps the easiest to read. Compared with the more than 27,500 ships carrying more than 166 million tons of cargo in some 2,750 North Atlantic and coastal convoys that sailed between 1939 and 1945, only a relative handful were unable to put to sea because of crew problems or sabotage.[2]

JULY 6, 1942

- Three thousand miles east, workers at Flensburger Schiffbau in Flensburger lay the keel for U-367.
- Three thousand miles east in Amsterdam, Anne Frank's family goes into hiding.

- Three thousand five hundred miles east in Berlin, Hitler gives orders to enlarge the Nuremberg stadium where the annual Nazi Party meetings are held "to accommodate a minimum of two million in the future."

At 6:23 p.m. on June 27, the radio operator aboard U-132 decoded the following message:

To Vogelsang.
   Proceed into ordered area QU BB 14 and QU 36 [the mouth of the St. Lawrence] in the period when moon is waning. Approach area unobserved. Remain submerged by day. According to report by Thurmann QU BB 14 and QU 36 in the major quadrant to the west is favourable attack area. Intercept shipping in the narrowest portion of the pipe [strait]. Traffic pulses occur particularly on Saturdays. Sundays are also a possibility. Surface forces are weak. It is probable that only aircraft will be encountered. Establish whether outbound traffic also proceeds via 22 [Strait of Belle Isle]. If the area proves unfavourable after careful and tenacious observation, you are granted permission to manoeuvre according to your own initiative.

   Three thousand miles away in Lorient on France's Bay of Biscay, Admiral Dönitz must have smiled to himself when he composed this order. Just over a week earlier, *Kapitänleutnant* Ernst Vogelsang had declined Dönitz's order to return to La Pallice, U-132's base on the Bay of Biscay, where the officers drank absinthe at the inaptly named Café de la Paix and ratings quaffed beer at the equally incongruously named Susie and Buffalo Bill bar. After learning of the damage U-132 had suffered during a mid-ocean encounter with HMS *Stork* and *Gardena*, whose shells damaged the submarine's periscope and whose depth charges cracked open diving tanks, resulting in telltale slicks, Dönitz ordered Vogelsang home for repairs. Vogelsang's reply, that despite the increased danger that resulted from the damage he and his men would "carry out the convoy task to the end," was not insubordination. Rather, for Dönitz it was proof of the mettle of the men who joined the so-called *Frei Korps* Dönitz, a name that harkened back to the ultranationalist troops who destabilized the Weimar Republic and who formed the backbone of Hitler's first storm troopers, the SA.

Despite Naval Service Minister Angus Macdonald's assurance that "long-prepared plans for the defence of the St. Lawrence" had been put into effect, the waters into which Vogelsang sailed, unobserved, in the early morning hours of July 2, 1942, differed little from those Thurmann had entered in early May. No doubt because of Thurmann's May 21 report "Cap Gaspé and other lights farther out extinguished," Vogelsang expected Canada's coasts to be blacked out and its radio beacons silent. Hence the surprise that comes through in his war diary entry for July 2: "Navigational radio beacons are operating as in peacetime according to the list of nautical radio stations."

As was the case on the US east coast, where lights from New York, Atlantic City, Savannah and Miami silhouetted ships, making them easy targets for U-boats, Canadian authorities resisted imposing a blackout. Unlike the Americans, however, who resisted largely because of pressure brought by tourist interests in Miami and Atlantic City, Canadian authorities resisted because without navigational lighting and radio beacons, shipping in the St. Lawrence would have been endangered. As Prime Minister King reminded the House of Commons on March 25, 1942, "These are some of the foggiest shores in the world, winds change direction rapidly, and the seas make themselves felt."

Resistance to imposing a blackout or dim-out (which is what Canadian authorities opted for, although it was still popularly referred to as a "blackout") did not, however, mean that Canadian authorities did not ready the Gaspé and the rest of eastern Canada for one should it become necessary. On November 12, 1939, just two months after the war began, instructions were sent to lighthouse keepers instructing them when to extinguish their lights. A year later, a more comprehensive system was developed that used the CBC's and Radio-Canada's broadcasts to signal lighthouse keepers when to turn off their lights. Rémi Ferguson, who kept the lighthouse at Cap-des-Rosiers, not far from Gaspé, told a historian the radio messages that were broadcast at 2:30 and 10:30 a.m. and at 2:30 and 10:30 p.m.: "'A notice to lighthouse keepers: execute instructions A for Alphonse,' and they repeated that three times. That meant to keep the lighthouse operating. B for 'bonbon' meant that there was the threat of a submarine offshore. That's when we turned off the lighthouse and stopped the foghorn until further notice." By the end of 1939, both the British territory of Newfoundland and the Free French islands of St. Pierre and Miquelon were incorporated into Canada's dim-out regimen.

Few aspects of the Battle of the St. Lawrence were as much discussed during the Battle or are as well remembered today as the dim-out. "Some people," recalls Lorraine Guilbault, who in 1942 was twelve years old, "said that the dim-out regulations were just part of the government's publicity campaign to support the sale of war bonds."[3] For most Gaspesians, however, the dim-out was serious.

The Fusiliers du St-Laurent enforced *l'obscuration*. Hundreds of men in uniform checking to see if houses and other buildings were properly blacked out and manned checkpoints at which cars that had more than a ¾-inch slit of their headlights unpainted were stopped and their headlights were painted. In response to fears about dangers to highway traffic, in 1943 the regimen was changed to painting out the "upper half of the headlights down to half-an-inch below [the] centre" of the headlights. Dozens of stories reported the preening of mayors such as Gaspé's Davis, who on February 27, 1942, declared that *l'obscurcissement* exercise held on the Sunday before February 27 was "a complete success. . . . Private homes, community and religious buildings, the harbour, everything was in total darkness for nine hours." The dim-out was one of the few aspects of the war that was openly discussed at school, recalls Guilbault. "When it came to the defence of the river, the thing we talked about most at school was the blackout. We were taught how to put up curtains to darken our houses and how to do the blackout at school."

On the whole, the dim-out regulations were well observed. When they were not and when that fact became widely publicized, the dim-out became a bone of contention between English and French Canada. In June 1943,

Brigadier-General Edmond Blais, the army officer commanding the Quebec military district, told the Canadian Press that "while the dim-out is fairly generally observed, in most of the fishing villages along the rugged coast many car headlights remain untreated." The *Halifax Chronicle Herald* wasted little time before editorializing, "It is true that last year dimout regulations were not fully observed but no attempt appears to have been made to enforce them." On June 9, the Montreal *Daily Star* applauded the government for a planned "campaign to enforce 'dimout' regulations," non-compliance with which it immediately went on to equate with "careless talk"—which everyone knew, from the ubiquitous posters warning against repeating shipping information, "costs lives"—and with "the circulation of sensation and inaccurate rumours." In other words, the *Daily Star* all but branded those who failed to paint out their headlights or who let light shine through their curtains as fifth columnists.

Nor were the air defences what Vogelsang might have imagined from Thurmann's having reported that in the days after the sinking of *Nicoya* and *Leto* defences were "very alert." Memoranda that declared where his planes were to be stationed aside, Air Vice-Marshal A. A. L. Cuffe, commander of EAC, was shuffling his planes around the gulf as bases at Gaspé and Mont Joli became available and, even more important, poor communication systems undercut Cuffe's men's effectiveness. Poor communications between EAC and the US Air Force in Newfoundland prevented Canadians from finding out about the May 10 sighting and bombing of U-553 by a B-17 flying out of Gander until late on the eleventh, far too late to launch their own planes for a follow-up attack.

But it was the sheer size of the river and gulf, some quarter million square kilometres, that posed the greatest challenge to communications. While the introduction of convoys with known routes reduced the operative area significantly, port-to-port coverage was beyond the ability of the RCAF and its American partner, the US Army Air Force. Late in the 1942 shipping season, the pressure of more than a dozen sinkings would lead EAC to undertake night escort flights. Such flights were good morale boosters, but without such innovations as the Leigh light or fully workable airborne radar, neither of which would be available before the end of 1942, night flights were less than effective in finding the U-boats before the U-boats found the ships. To find U-boats before they found the convoys, Canadian air defence authorities relied heavily on the civilian Aircraft Detection Corps (ADC).

Established in 1940, by the time Thurmann entered the St. Lawrence in 1942 the ADC numbered 1,320 volunteer observers in Quebec and across the Maritimes and Newfoundland. But the ADC proved problematic. The chief problem was not that the "thousands of additional eyes and ears" filed thousands of reports of which only a handful proved to be true; most of the reports were checked out by either RCMP officials or the Fusiliers du St-Laurent. Rather, the problem lay in the delay between the time of a confirmed sighting and the time EAC was informed of it. On the north shore of the St. Lawrence, there was one unsecured telegraph line (which, when broken, was repaired "by whatever passerby notices the need") strung precariously along hundreds of miles.

Communication systems on the more populated southern shore of the St. Lawrence were better, though nowhere near what they would have had to be for aircraft to be able to respond rapidly enough to catch a U-boat after a sighting. Observers made their reports through commercial telephone and telegraph companies, which routed them to a reporting centre. The reporting centres relayed the reports by wireless telegraphy to EAC in Halifax. EAC then dispatched whatever planes it could. In September 1942, this reliance on well-meaning amateurs and a Rube Goldberg communications system would fail catastrophically. Nevertheless, ADC served an important role as a morale booster and as a means of relaying unmistakable information, such as the crash of a friendly aircraft, to officials quickly.

The waters Vogelsang sailed into should have been stoutly defended. The Defence of Shipping—Gulf of St. Lawrence Memorandum for 1941 called for the deployment of at least twenty-nine ships organized into "hunting and striking A/S [anti-submarine] forces" to be placed at strategic points along the river. Six armed yachts, four or five corvettes and four Fairmile motor launches were to be based at Gaspé, with another ten ships slated for Sydney, Nova Scotia.

These plans were undone by shipbuilding delays and by the exigencies of war. Twenty-six RCN escort ships (nineteen corvettes and seven destroyers recently acquired from the United States) were assigned to the Newfoundland Escort Force, charged with protecting convoys leaving Halifax and Sydney. Operation Paukenschlag, the 1942 assault on US coastal shipping that began after the United States Navy transferred the bulk of its Atlantic Fleet to the Pacific, also undercut the RCN's plans.

Then, as now, although in gross terms self-sufficient in oil, Canada chose to sell oil pumped from Alberta's fields south to the US market rather than pump it across the continent to the industrial centres of Quebec and Ontario, the shortfall in the east being made up by imports from Venezuela, Aruba and Texas. Off the US coast between January 15 and May 10, 112 tankers, representing almost 1 million tons, were turned into infernos while Admiral Edward King kept his (denuded but still not insubstantial) Atlantic Fleet in port and refused to institute convoys, despite pleas from the British. By the end of April, as oil supplies in Halifax fell to just over a two-week supply (45,000 tons), Vice-Admiral Nelles responded to King's intransigence with a most un-Canadian outburst—"To hell with that, we'll get our own"—and with an order to establish convoys between the West Indies and the oil pipeline termini at Portland, Maine and Halifax. The four (later six) corvettes came from both the Gulf Escort Force and the North Atlantic run. On the Newfie–Derry run during the first half of 1942, Canada had 196 ships, fully 48 per cent of the escort fleet (the RN supplied 50 per cent and the Americans 2 per cent).[4]

Thus, instead of twenty-nine ships divided between two bases, the 1942 Memorandum on Defence of Shipping—Gulf of St. Lawrence refers to at most ten anti-submarine ships. The most hopeful sentence was "One and, if possible, two destroyers to be based on Sydney, N.S., and all available A/S Vessels sent to Sydney or Gaspé." The most pessimistic: "An armed motor-boat patrol will be commenced between Île Aux Coudres and the mouth of the Saguenay River." In the months that followed the sinking of *Nicoya* and *Leto*, Canada's defensive hopes were pinned on convoying through the St. Lawrence.

Although a gingerly affair made up of just one ship, SS *Connector*, and one escort, HMCS *Drummondville* (a Bangor minesweeper under the command of Lieutenant J. P. Fraser, RCNR), the first regular St. Lawrence convoy, SQ-1 (May 17, 1942), was a success.[5] According to James Essex, Commander

"Daddy" Woodward attributed success to *Connector*'s speed, which, at 10 knots, was a good 3 to 5 knots faster than could be made by most other merchant ships in the river.

By the end of May, Naval Service Headquarters had managed to scrape together five more Bangor minesweepers, three armed yachts and nine Fairmile launches. Six weeks later, after seeing four of its charges sunk, *Drummondville* became the first Canadian ship ever to engage the enemy in Canada's inland waters.

The chase that ended with the sinking of SS *Anastassios Pateras*, *Hainaut* and *Dinaric* wasn't long. At 11:05 p.m., while the lights of the U-boat beneath him were still turned low (internal U-boat lighting followed Berlin time, which was 0505), Vogelsang spotted a fourteen-ship convoy, blacked out by order of the convoy commodore but made visible by the phosphorescence of the sea. None of the convoy's lookouts saw U-132's conning tower, one of the few to be painted with a swastika, the symbol of the Nazi party and state.

Over the next fourteen minutes, as the night deepened in Gaspé, as dawn broke over Europe on the day that Anne Frank and her family went into hiding in Amsterdam, Vogelsang closed from some five miles away on the port side of the convoy. His target could not have been more inviting. Even the fine optical glass of his Zeiss binoculars could not help him distinguish one ship from another as they huddled together travelling in a straight line through the night 1,500 metres away.

Vogelsang watched the "overlapping steamers." He read off the attack information: "Target speed = 5 knots, angle on bow = 75. Computed lead angle = green 9.5. Range = 1500."[6] The numbers transferred through the lines to the torpedo's guidance system, which directed the fins behind the torpedo's propeller to turn so that by the time they'd travelled the 1,500 metres, they were almost on a dead 90° track.

As *Anastassios Pateras*, *Hainaut*, *Dinaric* and nine other merchant ships "steam[ed] along in quiet water and fog," their lookouts scanned the night. Eight hundred metres away, Vogelsang's men heard the familiar order: "*Offnen Sie alle Bugklappen.*"

"Bow caps open," came the reply a moment later. But Vogelsang and the other men on the conning tower already knew they'd been opened, for they'd felt the boat dip ever so slightly as water rushed into the forward tubes.

"Bereit! Eins!" ("Ready! Torpedo Tube One!")

"Bereit! Zwei!" ("Ready! Two!")

"Bereit! Drei!" ("Ready! Three!")

"Bereit! Vier!" ("Ready! Four!")

"Los! Eins!" ("Fire! Torpedo Tube One!")

"Los! Zwei!" ("Fire! Torpedo Tube Two!")

"Los! Drei!" ("Fire! Torpedo Tube Three!")

"Los! Vier!" ("Fire! Torpedo Tube Four!")

U-132 shuddered as four huge pistons, one behind each torpedo, shot forward, pushed by a blast of compressed air (which was vented back into the boat, preventing a telltale burst of bubbles). Each piston drove forward with the force of 24 atmospheres, pushing the torpedo in its tube out into the water at close to 30 knots. Just before exiting the tube, a tripping mechanism started the torpedo's electric motor. When the piston reached the end of its track, it triggered a mechanism that slammed the torpedo tube cap closed.

Seconds ticked by, counted off by Vogelsang's stopwatch.

At 11:20 p.m., the men on *Dinaric*'s bridge "heard a terrific explosion and saw a flash indicating that a ship not far off from ours had been hit," *Dinaric*'s captain, Marijan Zadrijevac, told the Canadian Press. Before Zadrijevac, who before the war had been a professor at the Nautical School of Yugoslavia, could order his helmsman to change course, "a new detonation on a second ship close to ours exploded" as a "burst of flames shot into the air."

The first torpedo hit SS *Anastassios Pateras*, a 3,382-ton Greek freighter. The wound in its starboard side was mortal.

Hit between the cross bunker (a passageway that allowed the ship's firemen to shuttle coal back and forth between the starboard and portside coal bunkers) and the stoke hold, the ship took an immediate 10° list. Her captain quickly ordered it abandoned. Two firemen, John Howard of England and Silvino Eugenio of Brazil, and a trimmer, Ham Karamm, a Free Frenchman, were incinerated by the flash that burned through the St. Lawrence fog.

Four hours later, the Greek ship's crew reached the shores of Cap-Chat.

Romuald Roy, who directed the local Red Cross office, told the Canadian Press "the first men out threw themselves down on their knees and scooped up handfuls of sand, which they kissed passionately while uttering incomprehensible cries of Greek delight."

The blast that destroyed *Pateras*'s buoyancy wakened an unnamed sailor on a ship also unnamed by the Canadian Press. "There was a terrible report—I thought it was us," he recalled. Then, strangely, the silence of the calm river night rushed back in. "Not a sound came from her" as she began to sink.

Another ship, *Hainaut*, now with a four-foot hole blasted in its starboard side at Hold No. 2, would never go home, nor would one of its stokers.

The force ripped upward through the starboard side of the ship, destroying the lifeboat lashed to the boat deck. The explosion caused pipes, fittings, bulletproof glass and reinforced concrete slabs that protected the map room to break loose; the slabs blocked the passageway to the map room.

Immediately after the explosion, Captain Léon Castelein ordered his men to their lifeboat stations. They used their hands as eyes to struggle through *Hainaut*'s darkened passageways and across the wreckage-strewn decks. The decision to abandon ship came a few moments later when the captain and his chief engineer, Charles De Landtsheer, found that water was pouring into the engine room.

Vogelsang watched as the convoy "dispers[ed] in all directions." Both *Dinaric*'s helmsmen and the one on the ship that followed it spun their helms four points to starboard. Ten minutes later, while his captain, Marijan Zadrijevac, was checking the ship's position in the chart room, *Dinaric*'s chief officer, Mr. Hayday, spotted "something ahead which looked like islands" and ordered an immediate hard turn to port to avoid them.

Vogelsang's war diary records none of these course changes, but he must have noted them, for he stayed with Hayday's ship.

*   *   *

Several thousand yards away, the last two acts of *Hainaut*'s drama unfolded. Worried that in the darkness of the night his men on the lifeboats and rafts would become lost, Captain Castelein ordered that once clear of their sinking ship, the lifeboats and rafts must stay close to each other on the flat waters of the river. Immediately after the boats and rafts cast off, *Hainaut*'s survivors heard one of the ship's stokers, Mokbel Mohammad, calling from a distance. After a short search, they found him, then realized that another stoker, Säid Nouman, was missing; he would never be found.

The search for Mohammad had taken the ship's survivors far enough from *Hainaut* that they could no longer see her. They were close enough, however, to hear her death throes. Out of the darkness of the night, forty men heard the sharp sounds of metal ripping, of heavy weights—perhaps the vehicles that had been lashed to the deck   splashing into the water, the scream of escaping steam and then, finally, the sound of boiling water when the air that had been within the ship broke to the surface as *Hainaut* plunged to the bottom. Moments after the last sound, their rafts and boats began to rock, at first gently, then more violently, as *Hainaut*'s death gurgle spread out on the quiet, still waters.

An airplane spotted Castelein and his thirty-nine men at dawn; they were picked up at 7:45 a.m.

At 11:58 p.m. and three minutes later, Vogelsang fired two more torpedoes. Each missed its target. His aim was better at 1:45 a.m. on the seventh, when, after an 800-metre run, a torpedo hit *Dinaric*, just as Zadrijevac was about to order a change in course.

Dinaric's chief officer, Hayday, who filed the report for his hospitalized captain, reported, "The explosion sounded to me like a dull thud. I do not think there was any flash or flame but a large column of water and debris were thrown into the air." By the time the spectacular geyser collapsed back into the sea, the four men on the engine-room watch—James Jameson, Henry Thomas, Herbert Walton and Slavko Ziganto—had been obliterated in a cauldron of burning, twisted steel.

The blast wrecked the bridge. The captain was blown off it and covered with debris. He was saved by one of his officers, who risked being trapped himself in order to get his captain to safety.

Hayday too was momentarily trapped. "I could not get out of the chart room for a few minutes on account of the falling debris and escaping steam from the engine room."

Once Hayday managed to get out of the chart room, he met up with Zadrijevac, a lookout and the second mate. Together, the four men climbed down first to the wrecked foredeck and then to the boat deck, where the crew had already gathered. The explosion had destroyed the starboard boat. The port and bridge boats were sound and were soon launched.

Anxious minutes ticked by as the ship continued to list, with the captain and chief engineer still on the deck.

"I told the Captain that he had better get into the [life]boat so that we could cast off because it looked as if the ship might overturn on to the boat," recalled Hayday.

Hayday's report made special mention of Wireless Operator MacHenry, who "was the last man to leave the ship and remained on board until the last getting his signals out."

Lieutenant Fraser and his eighty-three officers and men had seen two of the ships they were shepherding torpedoed. They'd fought the urge to turn, fire star shells and drop depth charges. Fraser's bridge knew that some men were dead, others in the water.

They wanted "kills." Men had been killed under their watch. But, as much as they wanted the order, as much as Fraser wanted to give the order to attack or to try to save men in the sea, in the deep dark of the all-encompassing St. Lawrence all aboard knew he wouldn't—couldn't.

They wanted kills. But their mission, the convoy escort's mission, was "to ensure safe the timely arrival of cargo ships." So when QS-15 scattered, *Drummondville* followed the largest group of ships to offer what protection it could.

Drummondville was a 581-ton minesweeper built by Canadian Vickers in Montreal. Like most of the sixty Bangor-class ships built during the war, *Drummondville* saw little service as a minesweeper, that threat being largely eliminated when Germany's surface fleet was swept from the Atlantic.[7] Instead, beginning in 1940, *Drummondville* served as a convoy escort out of Halifax to Mid-Ocean Meeting Point, almost 1,500 miles east of Halifax, beyond which the escorts based in Londonderry shepherded thousands of ships to safety in Britain.

The first counterattack in the Battle of the St. Lawrence began by chance. Apparently concerned that *Dinaric* might successfully make the coast (where it could be salvaged), Vogelsang ordered his helmsman to turn U-132 around *Dinaric*'s stern so he could fire at it again.

This time, however, it was his turn to be taken by surprise. "I turned to a new approach course when there is a muzzle flash on the port bow on bearing 160 degrees. A star shell lights the area astern of the boat," he recorded in his war diary.

Fraser didn't need the report from his lookouts to tell him that "dead ahead" was the U-boat that had torpedoed *Dinaric*. His bridge didn't need the order Full Speed Ahead—all knew that standard operating procedure called for ramming: in March 1941, U-boat ace Joachim Schepke's U-100 had been rammed by HMS *Walker* and *Vanoc*.

Now it was a battle of engineering—Fraser's engines running at full speed versus Vogelsang's tanks, propellers and dive planes.

For one captain's men there was the routine: the almost instantaneous slide down the two ladders into the control room. The closing of the hatch. The shouted order "*Fluten.*" The turning of dozens of dials, valves and controls. The flood of water into the forward tanks first, perhaps the order for men not on station to run to the bow to increase the angle of descent. The turning of hydroplanes. The quick and sure switch from diesel engines to electric motors.

For the other, there was the ringing of the ship's telegraph. Here too, the turning of valves and the rush of steam, not water. Flank speed and a helmsman's eye. Those who saw what they all wanted to see had time only to brace themselves. Others had already been ordered to the depth-charge racks.

Seconds ticked by.

At 16 knots, 1,000 yards can be covered in just over 120 seconds. A crash dive takes only 30.

Thirty-five seconds after spotting U-132, *Drummondville*'s bow replaced it on the surface plane of a little corner of grid square BA 3911.

Then, as the star shell faded, came the order: "Fire depth charges!"
Ten 410-pound canisters (more than 300 pounds of which was TNT)
rolled off *Drummondville*'s stern, and soon huge geysers shot out of the water.

In the months that followed this first skirmish, the asdic operators aboard
dozens of escort ships would have their asdics all but blinded by the bathyscaphe effect: the mixing of cold and warm water and of salt and fresh
water in the river and gulf creates layers that distort asdic signals, leading
to false echoes and even entirely hiding U-boats.[8] Now, at a few minutes
before 2 a.m., it was the German U-boat captain who cursed the water layers, for they prevented him from diving deeper than twenty metres without using special pressure and other settings—settings that his chief
engineer feared would not work because of the damage they'd suffered
before entering the St. Lawrence.

What Vogelsang recorded in his war diary as "three well-placed depth
charges" hammered on U-132's already damaged hull. The hull would have
been crushed instantly had any one of them exploded within twenty metres of
it. Inside the U-boat, lights flickered, circuit breakers snapped, pipes vibrated.

Vogelsang's war diary doesn't tell who suggested flooding the front torpedo tubes to take U-132 lower, but it doesn't matter. Desperate times
called for desperate measures. Vogelsang issued the order, but in all likeli-
hood he spoke only to his chief engineer, who then ordered the flooding.
And then came another "fall," to forty metres.

Three more blasts, these some 300 metres away, and Fraser's men thought
they'd got their kill.

Vogelsang's war diary says nothing about breaking surface during the
depth-charging, but both *Drummondville*'s log and the report submitted by
Fraser (and corroborated by *Drummondville*'s officers and other members of
the crew) to the Admiralty's Office of Assessment state that after the first sets
of depth charges, the U-boat surfaced astern, apparently badly damaged.
Fraser could not see its conning tower and assumed that the boat was "lying
on its side." At 2:19 a.m., two minutes after having "sighted [the] submarine
on the surface," Fraser "carried out a deliberate attack" by attempting to ram
it again, "the U-boat sinking before she [*Drummondville*] got there."

As he had earlier, Fraser ordered depth charges to be dropped over the swirl created by the vanishing U-boat. Fraser and his officers and men all stated that after the last depth charge, the "water gradually became covered with high smelling oil."

On October 8, the U-boat Assessment Committee ruled against awarding a kill to Lieutenant Fraser and *Drummondville*, citing among other things the "extreme unlikel[ihood] that a U-boat turned over on its side and conning tower down would come to the surface." In 1985, Michael Hadley suggested that perhaps "U-132 had broken surface during one of her destabilized buoyant lifts." What's beyond doubt, however, is that in the two hours beginning at 12:21 a.m. on July 7, U-132 received a severe mauling.

For some reason, perhaps because of the excitement of the battle, *Drummondville* didn't send a signal that she was attacking. Naval Command knew nothing about either the sinkings or the battle that raged for two hours twenty kilometres north of Sainte-Anne-des-Monts until 2:30 a.m., long after Vogelsang's quiet electric engines had pushed him out of danger.

On the night of July 6, 1942, the base at Gaspé was a more established operation than it had been in May. Now commanded by P. B. German, Fort Ramsay's personnel had expanded to more than two hundred men and officers. This growth caused a housing problem that was partially solved by a Mrs. Kruse, who agreed that some fifteen men, including James Essex, could be billeted in the hotel she ran out of her home. Four decades later, Essex could still recall the tunes of Cole Porter and George Gershwin that "pour[ed] forth" from Mrs. Kruse's parlour.

"The night shift, which usually ran from eight to eight," recalls Ian Tate, "was generally pretty quiet save for the odd administrative message from Quebec City or Halifax.

"At 3:30 a.m., there would have been five men or women on duty. The telegraphist on duty would have known immediately that the message he was getting was extremely important because it would have been sent with priority 'Immediate.' Seconds later he would have rushed the typed message down the hall to Operations. The Operations duty officer would have then immediately contacted Commander German in his home on the base.

Commander German in turn likely would have immediately contacted Eastern Air Command."

For some reason, however, Gaspé didn't hear the signal *Drummondville* sent at 2:30 a.m. Word came about a half hour later, by telephone, informing Gaspé that two Cansos based at Sydney had been ordered into the early morning light. But orders or no, Sydney's Cansos and those at Gaspé would stay grounded by fog for more than ten hours.

Two hundred miles to the east, around the coast of the Gaspé Peninsula at Mont Joli, the weather was better, though EAC's luck was worse.

Alerted at 2:30 a.m. by a phone call from the small naval station at Rimouski, ten miles away, Squadron Leader Jacques A. Chevrier ordered Mont Joli's technicians to ready Squadron 130's Curtis Kittyhawks for flight. An hour later, led by Sub-Lieutenant Chevrier, four single-seat fighter planes, each carrying 227 kilograms of bombs and armed with six 12.77-mm machine guns, the bullets of which could rip through a conning tower, were flying over the St. Lawrence at almost 250 miles an hour. Thirty minutes later, through the dim early morning light, Chevrier's squadron spotted an oil slick.

Chevrier ordered his squadron back to Mont Joli. He himself never made it. While flying over the river near Cap-Chat, his plane burst into flames. Witnesses reported seeing a long smoke trail before the plane, travelling at high speed, hit the water. One of the few French Canadian pilots in the RCAF, Chevrier was the first Canadian serviceman to die in the Battle of the St. Lawrence. The sorrow over his death at Mont Joli turned to bitterness two weeks later when, in a debate in the House, Charles G. Power, minister responsible for the RCAF, rose to squelch the rumour that the reason it took an hour for Mont Joli to get its planes in the air was that the pilots "were all drunk and out with women at the time of the sinkings."

Other flights launched from Sydney and Mont Joli over the next few days would be no more successful. Two would bomb what their aircrews thought were submarines.

In 1975, then air marshal C. R. Dunlap and Murray Lister, the air vice-marshal, recalled in a letter to historian W. A. B. Douglas the second of these flights, which took place on July 8, 1942:

Neither Wing Commander Lister nor Dunlap was stationed at Mont Joli. They were there because two days earlier Dunlap had ferried a Nomad bomber to the Bombing School at Mont Joli, and Lister had volunteered "to pick him up." Just before Dunlap and Lister were due to take off for their return to their base in Mountainview, Ontario, Mont Joli received a telephone message "that a submarine had been spotted on the surface a few miles up river from Sept Iles, and that members of the crew were seen diving and swimming underwater near the ship's hull," apparently investigating damage to the hull. Dunlap recalled: Naturally one's first thought was "Let's get something into the air and carry out an attack." . . . After all Sept Iles was only 135 miles away on the other side [the north shore] of the St. Lawrence. The first act was to relay the information to Eastern Air Command . . . but alas their nearest base was so far removed from Sept Isles that it would take hours for one of their aircraft to arrive.

Dunlap and Lister convinced George Godson, one of the base's armaments officers, and Flight Lieutenant Taché to install several 250-lb. bombs and a bombsight; this last was abandoned because it would have taken several hours to install. After gathering maps and weather information, Dunlap and Lister plotted their course in the Operations section, and then boarded their Bolingbroke for an unauthorized mission. "We made no move to communicate with our Headquarters in Toronto, i.e., No. 1 Training Command [or Air Services in Ottawa], for there seemed no point in doing so," recalled Dunlap.

With Lister at the controls, the Bolingbroke took off at around 1 p.m.; they were over the search area about a half hour later.

Squinched in the bomber's "glass house" in the nose of the aircraft, Dunlap felt "somewhat naked"; there had been no time to install the machine guns that he would have used to defend the plane as it approached the U-boat.

Tension built as they neared Sept-Îles. Neither man had ever seen combat. Training with live ammunition? Yes. But in training, the man with the gun isn't trying to hit you. Flight training with windsocks and tracers? Yes. But not German-engineered bullets fired by marksmen who know it's either you or them.

Dunlap recalled the "thrilling prospect of perhaps being able to do something about destroying the enemy craft responsible for the recent disastrous sinkings."

Their plan was textbook: skim along at treetop level, low enough so that they could see the U-boat before it saw them, and then, "by a quick change of course . . . , complete [a] shallow dive attack before it could submerge, or indeed before the submarine, if still on the surface could get a full blast of gunfire off in our direction." But "would it still be on the surface, or would it be at periscope depth, or would it be completely beyond view?"

They reached the Sept-Îles lighthouse.

Nothing.

"We knew the elapsed time since the sightings and that underwater a sub wouldn't make more than five or six knots, so we had a rough search area which we covered in a series of parallel sweeps [trying] to see the periscope," recalled Lister.

Square after square, flying right angles. Making ever-larger squares.

Each time nothing.

"We then searched all the bays and shore line of the river in that area, finally returning rather deflated to base."

While Lister and Dunlap searched the waters off Sept-Îles, U-132 was over one hundred miles away, between Anticosti Island and Gaspé, fixing the periscope and pump damage sustained in the first depth-charging of the Battle of the St. Lawrence.

Three days later, on July 10, Brigadier-General Georges Vanier, district officer commanding Military District No. 5, which encompassed the Gaspé, wrote to National Defence Headquarters in Ottawa that rumours of additional sinkings and of the possibility of landings by Germans to either kill Canadians or kidnap them as hostages were sweeping the Gaspé: "Although I am not responsible for its [the Gaspé's] protection and security"—responsibility lay with the General Officer Commanding in Chief Atlantic Command in Halifax—"I feel bound in conscience to recommend that a motorized column, not necessarily large in numbers, should be established at once in some centralized place of the Gaspé Peninsula from which it could radiate to the long stretches of the coast which are completely open and without railway communication. This motorized column could send out patrols, particularly at night. "

On the tenth, while authorities suspected that U-132 was still in the river because there had been no transmissions to BdU, the defence of the Gaspé spilled over into Parliament and into the perennially dangerous waters of Quebec–Ottawa relations. About the time Vogelsang saw, 800 metres away, "four motored land-based aircraft clos[ing] from bearing 220 degrees," the member of parliament for Gaspé, Sasseville Roy, rose on a point of privilege and told the House that "three more ships forming part of a fourteen ship convoy were torpedoed last Sunday night opposite Cap-Chat in the St. Lawrence river," and asked, "Is the minister disposed to make a statement to the House or to arrange a secret sitting to inform the people's representatives as to the seriousness of the situation?"

Incensed at Roy's breach of parliamentary privilege to override the censorship rules announced in May, the prime minister himself responded none too subtly. He began by reminding the House that "the minister [for naval services] made it quite clear [in May] that there would be a proper time for the government to make an announcement of any event of this kind," and then added, "Premature announcements were only serving the ends of the enemy and would not help the ends of Canada's defence."

The Speaker of the House refused to recognize Roy's supplementary question.

Over the next three days, during which time Vogelsang continued to prowl the Strait of Belle Isle and adjacent waters of the gulf, evaded at least five planes by emergency dives and tried to press at least one attack, the political storm worsened. The Saturday edition of *L'Action Catholique* (the second most important paper in French Quebec, which, according to historian Eric Amyot, had decidedly Pétainist leanings) carried an editorial not only repeating the information Roy had revealed in the House, but also stating that the same facts were known by "half the people in Quebec City before Roy spoke in the House on the 10th." Without repeating what Roy had told the House, even the *Montreal Gazette* asked, since what had occurred on the St. Lawrence was an "open secret in the whole countryside and beyond," why did the government of Canada believe its silence amounted to a "withhold[ing] of information from the enemy"?

When the House met on Monday the thirteenth, Roy attempted to repeat the line of questioning he had begun the previous week but was prevented by the Speaker, who recognized Defence Minister James L. Ralston; Macdonald was out of the House at the time. Ralston picked up where King had left off the previous Friday by repeating that Roy's question of the tenth was "a gift to Hitler's men because it meant that the U-boat if it is still in the St. Lawrence does not have to surface to send a message and thus reveal itself."

With Roy effectively silenced, other members of the opposition felt it was time to attack the government for its handling of the St. Lawrence situation. Obviously still smarting from the dressing-down Minister Macdonald had given him in May when he said that the U-boats that attacked *Nicoya* and *Leto* had come from St. Pierre and Miquelon, Richard Hanson, House leader of the opposition Progressive Party, rose and said, "Reports were widespread in the Province of Quebec and that he [Macdonald] himself had received letters to the effect that U-boats were freely operating both at Matane and at Cap Chat and that everyone knew it." Hanson continued by telling the House that "precise statements would have a reassuring effect. What is the position with respect to convoys in the St. Lawrence? Are there any? Should we not know the position in a general way? What is the [navy's] position with respect to protection?" Ralston refused all comment, which led the House leader of the Co-operative Commonwealth Federation to echo Roy's call for a secret session: "This is a means that not only the British Parliament has resorted to but also our sister dominions."

Later, Naval Services Minister Macdonald returned to the House and, in a long speech, explained the government's position with regard to both censorship and protection of the shipping for which Canada held responsibility. "Information," he began by admitting, "as to the sinking of these ships was in the possession of many people early last week. . . . Many people knew of it; it was known along the waterfronts of the country, it was known to the press by Monday or Tuesday. The press refused to publish it . . . until an official announcement was made. It was in the possession of the Leader of the Opposition, because he had heard the story on the train and spoke to me about it."

Macdonald continued, taking aim at the complaints made by the Quebec press: "But there is a tremendous difference between Canadians knowing about it. The entire people of this country might know of a sinking . . . , but so long as it was not made public in our papers or broadcast over our radio, the chances of it getting to Germany are small. . . . Once it is broadcast it . . . speedily finds its way to Germany and is used there for propaganda purposes." The rules established by the chief censor "are made [therefore] for the sole purpose of keeping from the enemy information which may be of great value to him in directing the movements of ships."

Macdonald then turned to upbraiding Roy for misusing his privilege as a member of parliament:

> There is very little use, there is very little purpose, in censoring the press . . . if any Honourable Member of this House can stand in his place and by asking a question or by making a direct statement, as the Honourable Member for Gaspé did, undo the efforts of those who are endeavouring to ensure the safety of allied ships and allied seamen. . . . "Guard your tongues" we are telling the people in French and English all the time. How can we expect the average citizen of this country to guard his tongue if Honourable Members of this House do not guard theirs?

Macdonald, who had been absent from the House the previous Friday, now spoke to what the government believed was Roy's abuse of privilege. A measure of Macdonald's anger is the fact that his words skirt the parliamentary rule that statements in the House are to be addressed to the Speaker and not to individual members. "I will say this to the Honourable Member for Gaspé; had I been in the house on Friday I think I should have felt constrained to rise and ask this House to expunge from the record the statement which he made. Thereby it would not have become a public statement."

Aware that the King government, even though it held a majority of seats from Quebec, could not afford to alienate public opinion—especially having just seen a great majority of French Canadians refuse to release the government from its 1940 campaign pledge not to bring in conscription—

Macdonald briefly held out an olive branch to Roy and Roy's supporters in the House. Recalling what he had said earlier in his speech about the leader of the opposition's having come privately to him to discuss what he had heard on the train, Macdonald said, "My Honourable friend could have asked his question privately if he had wished. . . . Then he would have been given the information on his honour as a member of the House. But I do not understand how asking the question or making the statement in this House is going to add to the protection of my Honourable friend's constituents."

The olive branch extended, Macdonald quickly retracted it, with his strongest attack on Roy. The attack took the form of an explanation of how the defence of the St. Lawrence fitted into Canada's strategic thinking:

> If he [Roy] thinks for one moment that the whole of the Canadian navy is going to line up along his shores and defend those shores only, letting the convoy system we have and the protection we have for all the rest of Canada go to the dogs he is making a tremendous mistake. I am not ready to change the disposition of one ship of the Canadian navy for him or all the questions he may ask from now until doomsday.

The sinkings in the St. Lawrence may have excited MPs because the carnage was occurring within sight of the nation's towns and villages, but Macdonald was telling the House—and, since his comments were published in Hansard, all Canadians—that the way to stop the sinkings was not to withdraw the Canadian navy from the North Atlantic (still less from the Caribbean oil run), but rather to continue all possible efforts to defeat Nazi Germany.

On July 15, while Vogelsang spent the day diving to avoid detection by eight different aircraft, Quebec's Liberal premier, Adélard Godbout, a nominal ally of King's federal Liberals, wrote the prime minister expressing his concern about public opinion in the Gaspé: "I am convinced that a perilous situation exists, one which contained [sic] additional and incalculable elements of danger to the safety and security of Canada." The local population, Godbout asserted, "is bewildered and nervous." And he claimed that twice during the past week two "reliable sources" had told him "that the wireless station in Sainte-Flavie airport [Mont Joli] was recently attacked by two men who had either landed from a submarine or were saboteurs still roving about our country."

It would be several months before Canadian authorities would learn of a spy being landed by U-boat.⁹ And King knew that there had been no damage at all to the wireless station or any other military or civilian installation on the Gaspé. Still, pressure in the House and from Godbout led him to reverse the government's position and hold a secret session to discuss the situation in the St. Lawrence.

At 3 p.m. on July 18, 1942, the Canadian parliament met in its first secret session since the Great War.

The notes prepared for Minister Macdonald make clear that unlike the public debates that preceded the calling of the secret session, the secret session itself was an orderly affair in which the government shared both operational and other details with the elected members. The notes covered seven areas, the longest of which pertained to the dim-out. The minister sought to impress on the members the difference between a full blackout of both navigational lights and broadcast beacons, which the government judged to be too risky, and the dim-out, which "prevent[ed] the dangerous silhouetting of ships against bright lights." Extinguishing navigation lights would not, he argued, "materially increase the navigational problems of the submarines."

The second issue on which Macdonald briefed the House concerned whether supplies had been hidden in the St. Lawrence. As he had done in May, he told the House that it was all but impossible for this to be the case since such supplies would have had to have been brought by surface ship "and it would be almost impossible for them to escape detection." He gave MPs information regarding the operating period of U-boats ("6 to 8 weeks without refuelling or reprovisioning") and their range ("12,000 to 19,000 miles") that was not shared in open session.

Macdonald also provided a rather detailed disposition of ships in the St. Lawrence and explained how that disposition affected Canada's other naval requirements, including the all-important oil stores:

Twelve Fairmiles have been brought into the St. Lawrence area to provide additional protection for convoys in the River and Gulf. It has also been necessary to send a number of Corvettes into the Gulf; these were found by taking off escorts from ocean tanker convoys bringing oil to Canada. This has involved a decrease in the shipments which can be imported in a given time and is causing Naval Staff and the Oil Controller some concern. It may be necessary in the near future to take these ships out of the Gulf again in order to assist in bringing oil supplies to Canada.

At the time of the incident forty-nine vessels were escorting twenty different convoys. Twenty-six vessels were at sea on patrol. These figures do not include local patrol vessels.

The government was considerably less forthcoming about EAC. The minister was prepared to say only that "Air Protection is considered adequate. It consists of long range flying boats, landbased bombers and landbased fighter bombers at Rimouski and Mont Joli."

Surprisingly, the notes say nothing about the army's decision to act on Brigadier-General Vanier's letter of July 10. On the seventeenth, Major-General William Elkins responded to Vanier's request for a "motorized column" by ordering the 4th Canadian Armoured Division, then based in Debert, Nova Scotia, to dispatch a motor platoon to Mont Joli. Tasked with operating between Bic Island and Cap-Chat, the platoon arrived in Mont Joli on July 18.

Hours after the secret session of the House ended, Prime Minister King recounted the session in his diary:

Attended from 3–6:19 secret session of H of C. Took up statements by Roy and others about conditions in the gulf of St. Lawrence off Gaspe, and the St. Lawrence generally,—out of the sinking of three convoy ships some days ago. All kinds of rumours have been afloat.

A.M. [Angus Macdonald], with aid of map, showed how our Navy was employed. I thought he refuted completely all the rumours. [Air Force Minister] Power was able to tell of the exploits of the A.F. and the probable sinking of a submarine in the St. Lawrence; [and] the death of young Chevrier.

No doubt while writing these last words, Canada's prime minister thought that, as he believed he could with his own mother, Chevrier's family would be able to communicate with their departed loved one.

JULY 20, 1942

- Three thousand five hundred miles east in Kleck, Belorussia, German forces murder one thousand Jews.
- Five thousand miles east in Russia, German forces continue their drive toward Stalingrad.

- Four thousand miles east, deportations begin from Kowalek Panskie, Poland, to the Chelmno death camp, where the first gassing occurred in 1941.
- Four thousand five hundred miles east in Poland, Treblinka is readied for its July 22 opening.

"We heard the explosion in the mess," recalls Roy Woodruff, who in 1942 was a nineteen-year-old able seaman aboard the Q-074, one of the two Fairmile launches that (along with HMCS *Chedabucto*, a Bangor minesweeper, and HMCS *Weyburn*) was escorting the five merchant ships that made up QS-19. After the disaster of QS-15, the detachments of the Gulf Escort Force had been increased, albeit at the cost of less frequent sailings.

"Zero-Seven-Four was *my* ship," he says with a voice that even sixty years later emphasizes "my." "I was on her from the day she was commissioned [April 21, 1942] in Midland, Ontario, took her out into Georgian Bay and then down through the locks to Toronto where her gun—the gun that was my action station—was installed, then down to Kingston, where they put in her electrical system, and on to Montreal, where her radar and asdic were installed. I was in her three years, three months, through three captains, through terrible storms that tossed the little ship around like a cork. She was a short ship and would pitch and toss as she rode up and down waves."

And Woodruff was with Q-074 at the end when, her engines cold, she was towed from Quebec City to Sorel, Quebec. There, on June 29, 1945, she was turned over to the War Assets Corporation for disposal.

"We only heard the sound once on Zero-Seven-Four, but I knew that dull thud from my days on the North Atlantic run before I was drafted off the corvette HMCS *Prescott*," recalls Woodruff.

The explosion Woodruff heard that sent him running up from the Fairmile's mess deck was caused by *Kapitänleutnant* Ernst Vogelsang's twelfth torpedo, fired in his most daring attack in Canadian waters to date.

Peering through his periscope shortly after 1 p.m., Vogelsang "sighted smoke plumes bearing 260," almost perpendicular to his port bow. Soon he was able to distinguish the "steamers" from the escort ships, one (probably Woodruff's) "at inclination 0,700 m distant," well within visual sighting range, especially during sea state O.

To avoid detection, Vogelsang dove to twenty metres.

Would the sound of propellers stay constant?

It did, signalling U-132's crew that the "anti-submarine vessel pass[ed] ahead" of his bow. As the swish, swish of the screws faded off to his starboard, Vogelsang ordered his hydroplane operators to turn their wheels, and moments later his electric motors pushed his boat to periscope depth (13.5 metres).

U-132 was now "inside the convoy," a position described by U-boat captain Herbert Werner in his memoir *Iron Coffins*: "Our distance from the shadowy monsters ranged from 400 to 700 metres. It was a stunning situation, sailing undetected amid an Armada of enemy ships, selecting at leisure the ones which had to die."

Vogelsang settled on the thirty-year-old, 4,283-ton SS *Frederika Lensen*, then travelling in ballast 800 metres away.

At 1:39 p.m. on July 20, while cruising off Cap-Chat, Vogelsang fired again. Less than a minute later, *Frederika Lensen* was opened to the sea and four men were dead.

The explosion, that followed when the crosshairs of the torpedo's warhead touched as it sped into *Lensen*'s starboard side, killed four men, Englishman Robert James Spence and three lascars: Abudul Rajack, Ali Edris and Ali Mossadden. The 18 × 20 foot hole blasted beneath the bilge keel wrecked the engine room. The force was enough not only to burst the boiler but to rip it from its anchor bolts.

Vogelsang correctly guessed that the "muffled explosion" he heard was the boiler. He never knew, however, that the explosion blasted it fifteen feet upward. The salvage crew that later boarded *Lensen* found that the "boiler [had] landed on top of the engine."

Action Stations rang across the convoy as *Lensen* began to spew steam and smoke from its side and tons of water poured in.

"As steam burst from the stricken ship, our Bangor-class escort," wrote Harold Freeman in an article entitled "Daring Mid-Day Sub Attack Hits Freighter in St. Lawrence," which the Censor Office allowed to be published on October 13, "leaped ahead from her position half a mile astern of the freighter, a little Fairmile came cutting in on the starboard side and a corvette turned on a dime from her position ahead of the convoy to help."

Breaking convoy rules, the captains of SS *John Pillsbury* and *Meaford*, two Canadian lakers, and one of Canada's new 10,000-ton ships, rang for Full Speed and set their own courses out of the convoy's lines.

"When I heard the detonation," Woodruff remembers, "I ran from the mess deck to the companionway, and as I climbed up the Action Stations alarm sounded. When I exited on deck, I was facing aft and a glance (*Lensen* was on our port side) showed me the large, gaping hole."

Woodruff then immediately turned left and ran up the starboard side of the ship toward the gun at the bow. "As I passed the bridge, I saw the bridge lookout, Georges Desrochers from Montreal, pointing down to a line of bubbles—the wake of the torpedo—coming to the surface just ahead of the wheelhouse."

By the time Woodruff had covered the last few feet to his action station, his captain, Thomas Denny, RCNVR, who before the war was a British Columbia businessman and yachtsman and later became Commander in Charge of Fairmiles, East Coast, ordered a hard turn to the starboard.

"Our asdic man had gotten an echo, and the captain was running it down. We ran it down and dropped a set of depth charges off both sides of the ship and the stern. Then we turned around and dropped another set and then another.

"I was in the bow, so each time we came around I could see what the explosions had brought up. I remember seeing a circle of diesel fuel and large black oily lumps."

Sixty metres below, U-132 rode out the storm, Vogelsang recording only that he'd been forced under and had been depth-charged. As he waited on the bottom, Vogelsang could hear the propellers of warships suddenly turn away as they went to rescue *Lensen*'s crew.

"After we had exhausted our depth charges," Woodruff recalls, "we circled round and went to the lifeboats. We took one in tow—I'd been in gunnery training with the DEMS gunner who threw me the line—and brought the boat to HMCS *Weyburn*. After throwing the line to them, I noticed another guy I knew, Lieutenant Pat Milson, and waved to him."

Then, while Vogelsang watched through his periscope, Denny ordered his helmsmen to steer a course for the listing—but not sinking—ship. Vogelsang's war diary records its list as being 20° to the starboard.

"Commanding Officer Denny asked for volunteers—a seaman and a stoker—to board her with her officer in order to secure a tow line," recalls Woodruff. "I volunteered along with Gabriel Canuel, a strong guy who was an enthusiastic amateur wrestler from Rimouski. We climbed up the ladder that just a few minutes earlier *Lensen*'s men had used to leave her. We asked the officer if there were any casualties, and he told me, 'Four lascars went out the bottom.' I'll never forget the expression on his face when he said it. One minute they were there and the next, he said again, 'They were blown out of the bottom of the ship.'[10]

"Then, while the officer went to get a hawser [a thick towing rope] and two axes, Gabe and I were to stand ready to cut the rope if the *Lensen* began going down, so it would not take Zero-Seven-Four with it.

"While he was getting the rope, I went to get some paint. We were always looking for paint, and when I asked him if he had any, he said, 'Take what you want, she's going down.' We also took life jackets. Theirs were better than the navy's. But we didn't take anything personal," recalls Woodruff.

When the *Lensen*'s officer returned with the hawser, Canuel and Woodruff secured it to the stricken ship's stern and then threw the other end over the side, where it was picked up by Denny's ship.

"Zero-Seven-Four then headed straight for the beach," says Woodruff, "pulling the *Lensen* stern first. Her list didn't increase, but Gabe and I stood ready with the axes. The creaks and groans we heard were awful, like pain from deep within the ship."

Q-074's draught was only a few feet; *Lensen*'s was 26.1 feet. *Lensen* beached long before Q-074 would hit the beach. Once he'd beached the bigger ship, Denny ordered a course for Sydney.

Vogelsang too turned away, noting in his war diary that "the steamer sinks steadily by the stern, only roughly 1 m of freeboard remains."[11]

"We arrived in Sydney the next day," recalls Woodruff, "and there heard for the first time about Lord Haw Haw, who mentioned the torpedoing of the *Lensen*."

On July 22, the day on which six thousand miles away mass deportations from Warsaw to the Treblinka death camp began, U-132's swastika-adorned conning tower broke the surface. Vogelsang signalled Lorient asking permission to begin his homeward passage. Permission was granted. Six days later, off Sable Island, Vogelsang sank SS *Pacific Pioneer* before suffering another ferocious depth-charge attack.

Three days later, only two days from the pens at La Pallice where U-132 would be refitted, Vogelsang's radio officer handed him the following message from the Flag Officer Submarines in Lorient:

> Well carried out operations.
> The decision by the commanding officer to continue his patrol after being damaged by depth charges [while still in European waters] and his tenacity in the operating area in the St. Lawrence River paid off well and resulted in a nice success.

Woodruff's war continued, and the sinking of *Frederika Lensen* became a memory. Early in 1943, he was promoted to coxswain. In 1944, the last of Q-074's original crew, he heard that a logbook had been seized from a sub captured in the Mediterranean and that the log recorded that a submarine had attacked and torpedoed *Frederika Lensen* and was in turn attacked by 074 and had been destroyed.

"It was a strange feeling," Woodruff recalls. "You hated to think that you had put some out down there without them seeing the sky again, but I felt good that we had put them out of action, maybe even preventing another attack like the one on the *Lensen*."

CHAPTER THREE

THE ORDEAL OF QS-33

AUGUST 27–28, SEPTEMBER 3 AND SEPTEMBER 6–7, 1942
USS *Laramie*, SS *Chatham*, *Arlyn*, *Donald Stewart* and *Aeas*, HMCS *Raccoon*,
Mount Pindus, *Mount Taygetus* and *Oakton*

> *Till over the deep the tempests sweep of fire and bursting shell,*
> *And the very air is a mad Despair in the throes of a living hell.*
>
> —JOHN ROONEY

The breaking of radio silence was enough.

It meant another attack.

The details would follow—the ships, positions, counterattacks, pleas for help. HMCS *Arrowhead*'s signature, which came across at 11:35 p.m. on September 6, 1942, told the four men in the signals room on the second floor of the grey clapboard building all that mattered. Out on the broad stretches of the St. Lawrence, ships were under attack—as SS *Donald Stewart* had been three days earlier, as SS *Arlyn* and *Chatham* and USS *Laramie* had been three days before that. All four had been up in the Strait of Belle Isle. Now the signal came from 150 miles up the river, within sight of the lighthouse at Cap-Chat.

Had the signal come six hours earlier or even four hours later, help could have been sent quickly. The small squadron based at Mont Joli may have been partly staffed with trainees whose planes were not equipped to drop bombs, but the U-boats didn't know that. Air cover of any type might keep them at bay. Heavier planes were farther away, at Sydney, Gander, Chatham. Whichever aerodrome the pilots of the Hudsons or Digbys called home, Eastern Air Command's pilots had a score to settle. Not forty-eight hours earlier, U-517, which sank *Donald Stewart*, had used up one life when it crash-dived to escape bombs dropped by J. H. Sanderson's Digby. But for now, and for hours to come, air cover was out of the question.

"We waited for the signal," recalls then sub-lieutenant Ian Tate. "We recorded the messages, and we sent them next door to the operations centre, where they were plotted on the map that covered the far wall. Commander German asked for news. We relayed what we knew—nothing—to Ottawa and Eastern Air Command in Halifax, and we waited."

The waiting was the toughest part. Perhaps they'd hear of a "kill." Perhaps they'd sit with rapt attention as they decoded a message like this one, received a few days earlier from HMCS *Raccoon*:

FIRST TORPEDO PASSED 25 FEET AHEAD OF ME. SECOND TORPEDO PASSED UNDERNEATH ME FORWARD OF BRIDGE. BOTH WITHIN 3 SECONDS AT 0240 3RD AND TRACKS CLEARLY VISIBLE DUE TO PHOSPHORESCENCE MY POSITION 1500 YARDS ABREAST OF LEADING SHIP PORT COLUMN COURSE DEGREES 240. COURSE OF BOTH TORPEDOES 285° FIRE FROM MY PORT QUARTER. RAN UP TRACK 6000 YARDS DROPPING DEPTH CHARGES BUT NO CONTACT. AFTERWARDS I STEERED CLOSING COURSE ZIGZAGGING AND RESUMED STATION

The little armed yacht was out there now, part of an escort force led by the corvette HMCS *Arrowhead*, the Bangor minesweeper HMCS *Truro* and two Fairmile launches.

Hopes for a kill vanished as September 6 gave way to the seventh, and those hopes were replaced with worries about *Raccoon* itself. Why had it not reported in? Nor would daylight end the ordeal. By late morning, Commander German sent the minesweeper HMCS *Vegreville* to reinforce QS-33's defences. Before dark, not fifty miles from the map that showed movement of every ship between Quebec City and the east coast of Newfoundland and as far south as New York, SS *Mount Pindus*, *Mount Taygetus* and *Oakton* were sent to the bottom.

They'd all been part of small convoys—three ships, five ships, nine ships, as against the sixty-five that routinely sailed from Halifax and soon would from New York.

SEPTEMBER 6, 1942

- Four thousand miles east in Russia, elements of the 17th German Army capture the Black Sea port of Novorossisk.
- Four thousand miles east in Russia, heavy house-to-house fighting continues in the centre of Stalingrad.
- Five thousand miles east in Egypt, German troops under Field Marshal Erwin Rommel retake Alam el Halfa.

- Four thousand miles east in Warsaw, Poland, more than one thousand Polish Jews are killed in the Warsaw Ghetto uprising; deportations of 48,000 Jews to Treblinka death camp begin.
- Two thousand five hundred miles south, off the coast of Colombia, U-164 sinks the Canadian ship SS *John A. Holloway*.

Just before 6 p.m., the convoy QS-33, led by the corvette *Arrowhead*, passed into what German navigational charts designated as grid square BB 3836.

Three years earlier, *Arrowhead*'s asdic operator Geoffrey "Jock" Smith's biggest worry was getting the Upper Canada College student newspaper out on time. Then came the invasion of Poland and, on the same day, the torpedoing of the passenger ship SS *Athenia*, the flagship of the Anchor Donaldson Steamship Line, managed by Smith's uncle. Now the tall, thin Smith was cramped in a three-sided asdic hut perched on the starboard side of Captain Alfred "Iff" Skinner's bridge, listening for the telltale "ping" that would signal one of *Grossadmiral* Dönitz's U-boats.[1]

The southern border of grid square BB 3836 corresponded to the coastline just yards away from the winding road that ran through the sleepy village of Cap-Chat and then on through the rest of the rugged coast of the Gaspé. Several hundred yards from the southwest corner of the square, at 49° 05' 20" N, 66° 44' 27" W, 133 feet above the river, stands a lighthouse, the beam of which shone out into the inky darkness.

At 11 p.m., the light caught Smith's attention, causing him to look up from his asdic set and over his right shoulder. Not a thousand yards away, he saw the silhouette of a small Greek freighter, SS *Aeas*, laden with 1,824 tons of lumber and 1,490 tons of steel, and thought, "What a target that would make."

Smith wasn't alone in this thought.

Several hundred yards to *Arrowhead*'s port, farther out on the river, hidden by the darkness of the night, low in the water, rode U-165, commanded by *Korvettenkapitän* Eberhard Hoffmann.

On his first patrol, Hoffmann, at thirty-five, was older than most U-boat commanders; his career stretched back to the tumultuous days of the Weimar Republic, when the *U-Bootwaffe* was a shadow force. In 1932, Hoffmann was sent to Torpedo Boat Flotilla school, which doubled as a U-boat training school. Four years later, after Germany had regained the right to openly build U-boats, Hoffmann was appointed *Kompanieführer* and then *Kapitänleutnant*.

From 1936 until 1942, Hoffmann taught at the school, likely training the other U-boat commanders who attacked Canada as well as those who in 1942 savaged the shipping off the US coast. Until February 1942, Hoffmann's war was confined to training runs in the Baltic. Thus the obvious relish in his war diary as he entered Canadian waters on August 25: "According to Thurmann and Vogelsang, an especially good operational area as the adjoining grid squares to the west and southeast. Average air cover, relatively inexperienced defences." Hoffmann would have occasion to alter this first judgment but not the second.

Ten days earlier (August 27), Hoffmann, who had been lurking near the Strait of Belle Isle, had attacked SS *Arlyn* and USS *Laramie*. Both ships had violated their convoy sailing orders and steamed ahead of the United States Coast Guard cutter *Mohawk*, which had been escorting convoy SG-6 since it had left New York bound through Canadian waters for Greenland.

Later, researchers awarded the sinking of *Arlyn*, laden with 400 tons of explosives, gasoline, trucks, army supplies and food, to *Kapitänleutnant* Paul Hartwig (U-517) because he fired the *coup de grâce* at the still-floating derelict six hours later. Still, the "3 heavy explosions" Hoffmann saw at 11:30 p.m.—his report to BdU doesn't distinguish between the two ships— destroyed and killed on the blacked-out ships, which had failed to take the elementary precaution of zigzagging.

*   *   *

The torpedo that hit *Arlyn*'s port side demolished its engine room, killing twelve men instantly. Although the blast brought down the radio antenna, *Arlyn*'s master, Eyolf Wennesland, told naval authorities that distress signals were sent. *Arlyn* immediately began to settle by her stern but then, instead of sinking, levelled off, her decks awash.

Behind large clouds of steam and smoke, the ship's company broke in two. Before Wennesland gave the order, some men rushed to the ship's davits, lowered the lifeboats, jumped in and pushed off, rowing the ten miles to shore. Others, including the fourteen navy gunners who were on station at the ship's one 4-inch and four 20-mm guns when the torpedo hit, waited at their guns for twenty-five long minutes but had "no opportunity to offer a counter offensive," as E. D. Henderson, a US Navy ensign, put it in the confidential report on the sinking of *Arlyn*. On Wennesland's order, they finally abandoned ship and swam to rafts and lifeboats that had moved away from the ship in expectation of its sinking. The next morning, SS *Harjurand* picked up Wennesland and the crew that had stayed with him, later landing them at Sydney.

Seconds after *Arlyn* was hit, *Laramie*, a US Fleet oiler that in 1940 had been in Montevideo harbour when the German pocket battleship *Graf Spee* scuttled itself, sounded General Quarters—"All hands man your battle stations."

Within seconds, her captain had ordered Right Full Rudder. Six decks below in her engine room, Carmello "Chuck" Roberto heard the ship's telegraph ring Full Speed, as he felt the 14,500-ton ship begin to respond to the turning of its huge rudder.[2] One hundred feet from the ship's bow, Arthur Alvater, the ship's pharmacist mate, who was already on watch at the ship's forward gun, watched the flames leap from *Arlyn*.

"I was on the bridge next to the helmsman," recalls Dick Powell, *Laramie*'s supply officer, who had overseen the stowing of not only the tons of meat in the ship's newly installed 4,000-cubic-foot refrigerated holds, but also the tons of mines and high-test aviation gasoline, some of it in steel barrels lashed to the deck. "First we saw the *Arlyn* get hit. There was just enough time for General Quarters. Then we got hit. There was no flash, thank God, or the aviation gasoline that spilled out of the storage tanks holding 500,000 gallons would have gone up. But there was a tremendous thud and tremendous force; we were turned 180° from our true course."

The torpedo struck *Laramie* ten feet below the waterline, between frames 7 and 8 on the port side, some hundred feet from the bow. The explosion, which blasted a 42 × 26 foot hole in the ship's side, pushed halfway into the 58-foot-wide ship, collapsing five decks upward and killing four men who were asleep in their quarters.[3]

The bulk of *Laramie*'s crew, however, were lucky. The blast breached the ship's No. 2 gasoline tank, sending thousands of gallons of aviation gasoline upward like a geyser, drenching the boat deck (at one point the gunners were standing ankle deep in gasoline) and flooding the forward hold. "Had a fire started, its results would have been disastrous," noted Rear-Admiral Wilson Brown in the final damage-control report. He credits the fact that "the flame and heat subsided almost instantaneously" and that there were "no secondary fires" to the fact that the torpedo hit the refrigerated hold: "Certainly, considerable energy was absorbed in their demolition, and a mass of cork and frozen provisions must have provided some insulation against the initial blast of heat and hot fragments, holding them back until the water rushed in to quench the flame." Had the torpedo hit five feet or so lower, the damage-control report would not have said, "No general flexural vibration of the ship was noted"—the engineer's rather dry way of saying that the keel wasn't bent or broken by the blast.

Oscar L. Lusby, James Curtis Voorhees and Jamie D. Wells were asleep in the forward crew's quarters when the torpedo hit. Awakened by the explosion, Wells ran onto the deck. Once there, he realized that his mess mates had not also come up. He ran back into the ship. When he got to their quarters, the water, already knee deep and "covered by a heavy coating of aviation gasoline," was rising quickly. While helping Lusby down from his bunk and "through the tangle of debris to the escape ladder," Wells saw Voorhees, pinned by debris. After getting Lusby to the ladder, Wells turned to help Voorhees. With the water within two feet of the overhead, he pulled the collapsed bunk away from Voorhees and then took "Voorhees' arms around his neck [and] pulled himself [and his severely shocked crewmate] through the water to the escape ladder," wrote W. S. Keller, *Laramie*'s executive officer, in his report that recommended Wells receive a commendation.

On deck, discipline threatened to break down. According to Captain P. M. Moncy, following the call to General Quarters "someone, probably one of the new draft of seamen recently received on board, called 'Abandon Ship.'" Before officers and experienced petty officers throughout the ship got control of their local situations, Carmine J. Aloia, Elmo W. Boone and Robert A. Mills abandoned the stricken, but not sinking, Fleet oiler.[4]

As water poured into *Laramie*, her list to port increased from 15° in the moments after the explosion to 30° and threatened to worsen because of the large volume of liquid cargo in her holds. Ensign "Judy" Garland Casey, who along with other members of the ship's Forward Damage Control Party received citations for meritorious conduct, led the efforts to right the ship. He ordered that the port main cargo pump be placed in the cargo tanks and that the oil be pumped over the side. Two hours into the operation, one of the pumps stopped; disregarding atomized diesel oil, steam and gas fumes—and without breathing apparatus—Casey climbed into the tank to restart the pump. In four hours, Casey's party pumped 11,800 barrels of diesel oil and 171,000 gallons of aviation gasoline over the ship's side.

Though a Fleet oiler, *Laramie* was a warship, ready, even in a damaged state, to fight back. Despite the ever-present danger of fire, within minutes Captain Moncy ordered a star-shell search. The aft 3-inch anti-aircraft guns fired fifty-three rounds at a point 1,000 feet high and 5,000 yards away. Instantaneously, as shells burst in the sky, releasing magnesium flares suspended by parachutes, a large arc of night vanished. Even through the measured prose of the operations report, it is easy to feel the crew's disappointment that the 5-inch and other guns remained silent: "To the deep regret of all hands, no enemy was sighted."

The crisis and the night passed. And, under its own power, *Laramie* made Sydney on the afternoon of August 25, burying five of its American sailors in Canada's inland sea.

Ten days later (September 6, 1942), as Jock Smith looked out at *Aeas* from his asdic hut aboard *Arrowhead*, Hoffmann aimed even more carefully. Between his tubes and the ship he'd chosen to attack steamed what he rather grandiloquently called a "destroyer." Moments later, he saw not only that he'd accurately predicted where *Aeas*'s hull would be, but also that he'd accurately predicted that "destroyer's" draught. Seconds before the torpedo struck *Aeas* amidships, killing two men instantly, Hoffmann's "eel" passed directly under *Arrowhead*, sounding to Smith like a subway train.

For seventeen-year-old Edward Read, who was just stepping out of SS *Oakton*'s galley, the intense quiet of a windless night on a calm sea was shattered. From his distance and angle (*Oakton* was ahead and to *Aeas*'s starboard), it was not the kind of explosion the newsreels showed. "There was no great flash, and there was no towering geyser. All we heard was an extremely loud dull thud. But we knew that a torpedo had gotten a ship over to our port," recalls Read.

The shockwaves that hit the shore were louder and longer, echoing off the hills, the highest of which was topped by a large cross. By the time the residents of Cap-Chat got to their windows, they could see the light from the burning ship out beyond the little harbour.

The blast that ripped through Smith's headphones caused him to jump out of the three-sided asdic hut; he landed at the foot of *Arrowhead*'s exposed bridge. Captain Skinner, a veteran of the merchant navy who'd been in command of *Arrowhead* since January 1941, rushed to Smith. Deafened by the blast, Smith could see but not hear his captain's questions. As Action Stations was called, Arthur Crockette, *Arrowhead*'s anti-submarine officer, took over from Smith.

As Smith's hearing returned, he heard Skinner through the megaphone asking *Aeas*'s master what had happened. He thought he'd hit a mine.

Still stunned, Smith immediately told Crockette that he "thought that the ship had not hit a mine but had been torpedoed, that I'd heard the torpedo run under our ship."

Barely had the men on the bridge had time to digest what they'd just been told—that their convoy was under torpedo attack—before Skinner ordered a hard turn to port, rang for Full Speed and set off at 15 knots to run down the torpedo's track. *Arrowhead*'s lookouts, now wearing red goggles to protect their eyes against night blindness as sixteen star shells made day out of night, scanned the waters looking for an untoward ripple, the wake of a periscope. Across the bridge from Smith's asdic hut, "Dutch" Davey, *Arrowhead*'s leading radio directional finding (RDF, or radar) rating, watched the blips of the Fairmiles—HMCS *Raccoon* and *Truro*, SS *Oakton*, *Mount Pindus*, *Mount Taygetus* and *Benacas*—fade in then out of his screen as the radar antenna rotated. He counted the blips and plotted them against the positions of the ships he had in his head. Davey knew that the chance of seeing a blip from a periscope was close to nil, and nil again if the U-boat itself was only partially surfaced but within a half mile of his antenna, for each burst of radio waves emitted by the kite-like antenna connected by coaxial cable to the magnetron left a dead zone in the immediate area around the ship. Still, one extra blip, just one extra blip, and they'd know where to start fighting.

Truro too reacted, setting a course that cut across the convoy. A dangerous manoeuvre at the best of times, *Truro*'s run almost turned tragic when her steering broke down as she steamed into the heart of the small convoy. Only quick work on the part of a stoker, sent to the auxiliary steering cabin in the stern, avoided a collision between the escort, on her first mission, and one of its charges.

Once out of danger, *Truro* continued its course toward the assumed path of the torpedo and carried out its own star-shell and asdic search. Finding nothing, *Truro* returned to the convoy, which had slowed almost to a halt, to find that two ships had scattered and that her asdic had malfunctioned; for the rest of the voyage *Truro* would be able to use only her hydrophones.

As *Arrowhead* closed on the U-boat's suspected position, the blare of the steam signals sounding Action Stations across the convoy was drowned out. A second, louder explosion rent the night. Caused by the cold river water washing over her boilers, this explosion ripped out *Aeas*'s bottom; four minutes later, she was gone.

The action aboard *Arrowhead* and *Truro* was matched by the merchantmen. "For us, the scream of the steam whistle was nothing new," recalls Read. "Captain Brown had us practise often. As soon as we heard it, each of us knew what to do. My job was to go around the galley aft, climb up a ladder on the side up the ship and take the axe that was there and be ready to cut the rope that was holding the lifeboat in; when cut, it would swing out on the davits. One of the men standing next to the davits would then secure the seacock—the drainage hole kept open when the boat was secured on deck—then they would see her down to the water before they shimmied down the ropes to the boat. Once in, they'd ship the oars and hold the lifeboat close so the rest of us could get in. The *Oakton*'s first officer's job was to pull the pins that held the Carley floats in place, before heading aft himself."

At 15 knots, it took *Arrowhead* less than two minutes to be over the torpedo's tracks, perhaps a thousand yards. Smith and the bridge listened for
the slightest ping. And if they heard it, they would hope it wasn't an echo
caused by either a long-forgotten wreck or the devilish waters of the river
and gulf, where the mixing of fresh and salt water created gradients that
could render asdic all but useless.

Nothing.

Without an asdic contact, Skinner had to drop his depth charges by feel.
No doubt he hoped that today he'd be as lucky as he'd been a quarter century earlier when he escaped from a German POW camp. "The captain,
who had been a member of the Newfoundland Regiment," recalls Smith,
"had been working on a prison farm near Kiel. One day he was able to grab
a pitchfork, and he stuck it through a guard's chest. He then escaped and
managed to get back to the UK."

Skinner ordered one pattern over the point where he suspected the U-
boat had been when it had fired the torpedo. Then another, a little farther
away. His tactics, learned while on the North Atlantic run (on which
Arrowhead once spent twenty-one straight days at Battle Stations), were
sound. But U-165, rigged for silent running, had already moved on, continuing to stalk the convoy from a distance.

Breaking off the search after dropping four sets of depth charges,
Arrowhead returned to *Aeas*. Screened by the armed yacht *Raccoon*,
Arrowhead began the emotional and dangerous task of taking oil-soaked
men aboard. The men in the water were endangered both by the debris and
choking and by *Arrowhead*'s hull, which could push men under to their
deaths. Though screened by the waters of the river that played havoc with
asdic, had Hoffmann chosen to fire, *Arrowhead* was a sitting duck.

Even sixty years later, Jock Smith's voice is tinged with horror and sorrow
when he recalls the plight of the men covered in oil, many burned by steam
from bursting pipes, others with limbs broken by flying debris, floating in
wreckage-strewn waters. "It was the first time I'd been involved in something like that," he recalls. "It was the first time for most of us. All I felt was
that I had to try to do the best I could for everyone. We dropped the rope

net, and those men who were strong enough to climb up did; others we had to help by us climbing down the ropes and pulling them out of the debris-covered water. So many of them were so badly burned.

"Once we got them up on the ship, we gave them a tot of rum. We cleaned those who were burned the best we could. And then we sprinkled a powder on them; it was tannic acid, which we later found out was no longer the approved treatment for burns.

"I remember one man. He was about fifty and badly burned. He asked me, 'Do you know my son?' What does he do, I asked, as I cleaned him and poured powder on his burns. He told me he was Johnnie Johnson, the RAF ace. I didn't think it was true, but he took out of his pocket a laminated article about him."[5]

Just over an hour after Hoffmann destroyed *Aeas*, *Arrowhead* steamed back to the front of the convoy while *Raccoon* returned to its screening position astern its port side. Their zigzagging courses meant *Raccoon* was often out of sight of the other two escorts, but their constant speed and predictable bearing meant that at regular intervals they closed to relatively near quarters—close enough for *Raccoon* to appear as a back trace on *Arrowhead*'s primitive radar screen. Just before 2:12 a.m., Hoffmann, who on September 3 had missed *Raccoon* twice, fired at her again.

With the escort back to full strength, Captain Brown called an end to Action Stations on *Oakton*, and Read and the first cook, Douglas Wilkinson, headed for their cabin to catch what sleep they could before the next watch had to be fed. Just before reaching the cabin, Read recalls, "something lit up the night sky behind us. We heard something too, but it wasn't like a depth charge."

Once again Smith heard it—this time, however, not through his headphones but through the steel plating of *Arrowhead*'s hull. "Down in the forward mess, we didn't just hear it. We must have been awfully close because we felt it so clearly that we ran up thinking we'd been hit." Above deck, Gaétan Chaput, who manned *Arrowhead*'s 4-inch gun, heard two explosions and "saw the water go up . . . from the port quarter."

Scant seconds later, Skinner, who had gone to his cabin leaving his first officer in charge, returned to the bridge to find Anti-Submarine Officer Crockette in a heated argument with the ship's asdic and radar operators.

The two operators argued that *Raccoon* had been hit. The asdic rating, Frederick Dive, later told the board of inquiry that investigated the loss of *Raccoon* that he had "been carrying out my given sweep when I heard the report on my phone. This report did not sound like the report of a depth charge. It wasn't sharp. After the first report, I slid the phones off my ears after which I heard the second one and possibly a third." Even more ominous were the words of Skinner's radar operator, Theodore Burton, who told the board of inquiry, "I saw the *Raccoon* for less than one minute after the explosion, then she seemed to fade away, and was not picked up again."

Crockette, however, was adamant, later telling the board of inquiry, "As nothing was heard on the radio/telegraph and no visual signalling [of being under attack] was seen, it was assumed that the *Raccoon* was carrying out a depth charge attack, and we maintained our station on the convoy in accordance with the Standing Operating Instructions issued previous to sailing. Visibility was very poor, about a half mile, and because of this, and her earlier actions, it did not appear strange not seeing the *Raccoon* during the rest of the dark hours."

Officially, Skinner sided with Crockette, though his actions indicate his doubts. For he once again ordered Action Stations and then a course change that took him down past the convoy to *Raccoon*'s last known position.

Once again, star shells. Flashes of day in the night, revealing nothing.

Once again, a pattern of depth charges. Once again, asdic searches, showing nothing.

The mission of the convoy escort took precedence. Skinner broke off the search and steamed back to the merchant ships, which had headed north into the middle of the river.

Through the night, the question hung on Skinner's bridge: was *Raccoon* still out there somewhere? Perhaps with a total power failure, unable to communicate?

SEPTEMBER 7, 1942

- Three thousand five hundred miles east, workers at Bremer-Vulkan in Bergen lay the keel for U-288; in Hamburg, workers at Blohm & Voss lay the keels for U-983 and U-984.[6]
- Five thousand miles east in southern Russia, the German Sixth Army begins an advance, planned to take Hitler's troops the last four miles through Stalingrad to the Volga River.
- Five thousand miles east in Egypt, the British Army, under General Montgomery, stabilizes its defensive line at Alam el Halfa.
- Ten thousand miles southwest in Java, the government of the Dutch East Indies flees as the Japanese advance.
- Nine thousand miles southwest in the Solomon Islands, six hundred US marines attack the Japanese base at Taivu. The raid succeeds in damaging the base and disrupting the Japanese preparation for an attack on the main US position at Guadalcanal.

As dawn broke over Gaspé, the tension became palpable.

Already one ship had been sunk, and now *Raccoon* had missed her appointed time to report in.

Commander German waited, wondering if the second U-boat that NSHQ had signalled to him as having been HF/DF'd in the St. Lawrence was closing in on QS-33. He ordered the signals officer to send a coded message to *Raccoon* telling it to report in.

Other attempts were made to raise *Raccoon*. Men looked at their watches and at the clock on the wall. They smoked Sweet Caporal cigarettes. Each time Commander German asked, the rating listening intently through his headphones gave the same response: "No signal from *Raccoon*."

Worried too, Skinner altered his course, moving toward the quarter where *Raccoon* should have been.

Nothing.

Perhaps *Raccoon*'s radio rigging had been damaged. Perhaps she could not receive messages from as far as Gaspé. Commander German's men sent the signal "I Method," which required Quebec City to repeat the message back, thus ensuring that, wherever *Raccoon* was, if its wireless was working she would be able to pick up the signal. Signalmen monitored all frequencies.

Still nothing.

The speculation in Gaspé ran the gamut. Had *Raccoon* been blown up by a U-boat? Perhaps her wireless transmitter had been hit by a U-boat trying to fight it out on the surface? Or had she been boarded by the Germans? If so, what of their fellow officers and ratings? What of her secret code books?

Finally, Commander German ordered that the signalmen send the message "Report forthwith" in plain Morse code.

Poor weather on the morning of September 7 prevented a planned air search. In an ironic foreshadowing of its own fate over two years later, the corvette HMCS *Shawinigan* carried out a sea search. On the tenth, because of the lack of radio contact and the absence of reports of survivors coming ashore (indeed, the only onshore report corresponded with the explosion heard aboard *Arrowhead*), Commander German was forced to conclude and to report to the naval authorities in Ottawa that *Raccoon* "was presumed lost with all hands."

The Board of Inquiry that sat in Gaspé on September 18, 1942, agreed with the asdic and radar officers' belief that the evidence pointed toward the finding that "the explosions heard . . . were direct hits by one or more torpedoes." Knowing the limitations under which Commander Skinner laboured as a convoy escort, the board of inquiry concluded its short report with the sentence, "We do not consider any negligence can be attributed to Commander Skinner."

Raccoon's loss did not become public until September 13, when *Le Soleil* published an article entitled *"Cinq navires ont été coulés"* ("Five ships have been sunk"), six days before concrete evidence of the sinking was found. The following day, September 14, the RCN issued a two-page press release announcing that *Raccoon* had been "lost through enemy action while guarding a convoy of merchant ships." In order to hide the whereabouts of the action, the release spoke of "an increase in the tempos of enemy activity on Canada's side of the Atlantic." As well, the release purposely misled by trying to separate *Raccoon*'s loss from the other sinkings: "He [Angus Macdonald, minister of national defence for naval services] regretted to have to report that four merchant ships had been lost by enemy action, with ten of their officers and crew. The remainder of their personnel were rescued."

The stories that built upon the release were even more fictive. Both the headline splashed across the *Ottawa Daily Journal* and the first sentence of the article "Canadian Naval Vessel Lost in Battling Subs"—"Fighting one or more enemy submarines in defence of a convoy of merchant ships, the Canadian patrol vessel *Raccoon* is presumed lost with all hands on board"— suggested a specific action at sea far beyond what actually occurred.[7]

In keeping with the guidelines established after the first St. Lawrence sinkings, no press release announced the September 21 discovery of small pieces of wreckage and clothing on the western end of Anticosti Island. The navy was equally quiet about the gruesome discovery some weeks later, also on Anticosti Island, of the badly decomposed body of Russell McConnell, a star hockey player at McGill University and a well-liked graduate of Royal Roads, who helped found the servicemen's theatre in Gaspé.

When dawn broke over *Oakton* on September 7, it was alone, sailing toward the tip of the Gaspé.

"I was the second cook on the *Oakton*, so I had the early morning mess," recalls Ted Read. "It was dark when I came out of the galley. When I left, I was surprised. Not only was the sea as smooth as a plate, but we were alone. It was like the days before the *Nicoya* got hit, before they had to start the convoys." Read didn't know it then, but after the second explosion Captain Brown had ordered his helmsman, Laurent Marchand, to "get the hell out of here; go south, we'll take our chances with the shoals."

"The *Oakton* wasn't a fast ship," recalls Read, "and we were carrying a full load of coal from Sandusky, Ohio, to Corner Brook, Newfoundland, so we were heavy and low. Like this normally we'd make 5 knots. But the engineer—he'd been with the ship and Captain Brown for years—must have known how to get more from her old engines. We were making tracks, going maybe 9 knots—anything, I guess, to get as far from where the shooting was and as close to Sydney as we could." Before the afternoon was out, Read, Brown, Wilkinson and a few dozen other men would escape Paul Hartwig's torpedoes with their lives; another seven wouldn't.

Perhaps only war could have brought Read's and Paul Hartwig's lives so close. Nine years younger than the U-boat captain, whom historian Michael Hadley aptly refers to as the *enfant terrible* of the Battle of the St. Lawrence, Read was born in Montreal of Newfoundland parents. His father, C. H. Read, had served with the Royal Newfoundland Regiment under Sergeant-Major "Alf" Brown, who years later did his old friend a favour when he took the young, tall, thin, sandy-haired Edward aboard his ship as a deckhand.

"I'd had other jobs since finishing high school when I was sixteen. Odd jobs at first, then, as the war got Montreal humming, I got a job as a riveter at Fairchild Aviation down in Longueuil. I didn't like working inside much, though. I remembered what it was like when my father lost his good job at Eatons; he'd been a manager. During the Depression we spent years without regular money coming in. Later, my father told me sometimes we survived on my paper route. So I jumped from it to a better-paying job that was outside and came with room and board too.

"I'd always wanted to go to sea. I'd grown up next to the Lachine Canal, seeing all those boats and those men going all over. And here was my chance.

"My father wouldn't sign the forms allowing me into the navy at seventeen. And I wanted to do something for the war effort. He told me this was something I could do."

Before *Oakton* sailed from Montreal, Read had talked his friend Nelson Puddester, also from a Newfoundland family, into signing on with him. When seasickness quickly put an end to Puddester's career as second cook, Captain Brown told Read, "'It's easy to find a deckhand, but you can't find a second cook everywhere.' So I started doing dishes for nineteen men and peeling potatoes. Sufferin' Jesus," added Read when he recalled this story.

A flat-bottomed scow, designed to fit into the small locks of the Welland and Lachine canals, *Oakton* didn't rise up and then slam down on waves during storms. "She didn't have the V-shaped keel that could do that. Instead, she corkscrewed up and down, first toward port, then toward starboard, riding over the waves, but you never thought she was going to turn." Captain Brown, Read recalls, was the gruff old type, but his bark was worse than his bite. "Sometimes when we were passing through the Lachine Canal he'd tell me to grab a cab to see my mother and father."

*   *   *

About the time Read's ship was making its final passage through the Welland Canal, U-517 was passing through the Strait of Belle Isle.

Like so many other U-boat captains, Hartwig was from Germany's interior. Born in Saxony in 1919, Hartwig grew up in a Germany that extolled the *U-Bootwaffe* (the U-boat Arm) of the First World War. The *U-Bootwaffe*, not the battleships and cruisers of the blue-water navy, almost brought England to her knees. Even more important, the *U-Bootwaffe* remained clear of the twin stains of the Kiel Mutiny, when the kaiser's imperial flag was struck and the Red flag flew in its place, and of the blue-water fleet's ignominious end, its self-scuttling at Scapa Flow.

When Hartwig was in his teens in Hitler's Germany, books like *Alarm! Tauchen! U-Boot in Kampf und Sturm* (*Alarm! Dive! U-boat in Combat and Storm*), which extolled the chivalry of the U-boat forces and called for scrapping the limits placed on Germany by the Treaty of Versailles, were popular. According to Hadley's *Count Not the Dead: The Popular Image of the German Submarine*, a year before Hartwig joined the *U-Bootwaffe*, one of the most popular pulp paperbacks was *Torpedo Achtung! Los!* (*Torpedo Away!*), which raised a paean to the new era: "The seed is sown! We, the war generation, see it rise with our own eyes; it's a magnificent feeling to be here and to be able to help it happen. *Heil* to our *Führer*"—lessons that seem to have taken, for according to the Report on Interrogation of Survivors from U-517 (Hartwig's boat was bombed to the surface on its second patrol on November 21, 1942), Hartwig was a "cold and calculating young Nazi, filled with ideals of false heroism and unyielding devotion to his Führer."

Hartwig was two years older than Read when he decided to go to sea. He did not, however, join the German merchant marine. Instead, in 1935 he joined the *Kriegsmarine*. He volunteered for the *U-Bootwaffe* on September 9, 1939, the day Hitler's troops invaded Poland, starting the Second World War. After the standard several months of submarine training, Hartwig served as first lieutenant on Günter Kuhnke's U-125; Kuhnke was a highly regarded commander who won the Knight's Cross in September 1940. Hartwig was then sent for two months of commanding officer training and to the command of the then-unfinished U-517.

Hartwig's next few months would have differed little from those described by Herbert Werner in his memoir *Iron Coffins*. At that point in the war, captains (and chief engineers) were assigned to their boats when they were still abuilding so that they would know every gauge, rivet and bilge pump—the guts of their ships. Launched in early January 1942 and commissioned on March 21, Hartwig's U-517, a 740-ton Type IXC U-boat, passed its silent running test at Rönne on May 12 and her measured mile, crash-diving and speed tests three days later off Danzig. On May 20, Hartwig led his crew through torpedo-firing tests at Gdynia, and then gunnery trials at Pillau during the first week of June. During these weeks, Hartwig's crew came to view him as "an efficient, if not very popular, captain," in the words of the Allied officers who interrogated U-517's crew.

Returning to Hamburg for final adjustments, Hartwig spent some time, before leaving Kiel on August 8, studying the charts of Canadian waters. More than a few of those charts would have been German. German naval ships explored both the British Columbia and the Atlantic coasts in 1904–5 and scouted anchorages as far as Montreal. In 1937, German agents, operating behind a dummy Dutch forestry company, surveyed Anticosti Island and its anchorages.

At times, Hartwig's war diary, his actions and the banter reported to historian Michael Hadley belie the portrait of a hard-drinking, jealous martinet contained in the interrogation report. The report notes that Hartwig was apparently so jealous of his first first officer, *Oberleutnant zur See* Gustav-Adolf von Dresky, that he arranged to have Dresky transferred from U-517 before its first patrol. According to the interrogation report, "when von Dresky went ashore for the last time, the ship's company gave him three cheers, which infuriated Hartwig."

Indeed, even in translation, parts of his war diary betray a poetic mind. Upon entering the Strait of Belle Isle at 4:39 a.m. on August 27, he wrote, "Bright moonlit night, vis 30 nm winds freshening slightly. Steered toward land on Westerly course. Encountered fishing vessel showing navigation lights moving between Hare Bay and Anthony. She proceeds toward Anthony."

This impression is strengthened by two stories. The first, told to journalist Warren Moon in the 1970s, is of his taking his "boat close to the shore in fog so that his men could hear the music coming from a bar." The second, told to Hadley, is of an early Sunday morning when, from their conning tower, Hartwig and his men saw a tiny village and, in that village, "a

shack with lights on and smoke curling invitingly from its chimney."
Hartwig and the officer of the watch, engineer and lookouts then took time
from looking for ships to torpedo to reminisce about home, about "freshly
baked crusty rolls"—so far from the mould-covered food eaten within U-
517. Hartwig told Hadley of their "half-earnest, half-whimsical banter about
launching a dinghy for a trip ashore."

Whatever Hartwig's attitude toward poetry, his war diary also makes clear
that by the time he shaped a course through the Canadian waters, his was
a finely honed military mind that could spot and capitalize on his opponents' errors.[8]

Just hours after entering the Strait of Belle Isle on August 27, Hartwig
saw two ships that were running ahead of both the main body of SG-6F
and its air cover: the US Coast Guard cutter *Mojave* and *Chatham*, a passenger ship outbound from Montreal carrying 562 men, 428 of whom were
US Army troops bound for Greenland. At first they presented a textbook
anti-submarine defence, *Mojave* conducting a zigzagging sweep ahead (and,
by virtue of the zigzag, both a bit to starboard and a bit to port) of *Chatham*,
and on it, "9 trained lookouts stationed 1 on the forecastle, 2 on bridge
wings, 2 on wings fantail, 1 aft at the gun, 2 on the pilot house [and] 1 on
top of the pilot house." In theory, *Chatham*'s odds (one ship, one escort and
one U-boat) should have been better than they were for the ships on the
Newfie–Derry run. On those convoys, sixty or more ships could be spread
out as much as 50 square miles, protected from as many as twenty U-boats
by as few as five escort ships.

But Hartwig quickly noted the flaw: "The escort is zigzagging at regular
[that is, predictable] intervals. The other ship is rigidly steering 052."

In the moments before he fired his salvo of two torpedoes, he manoeuvred his 77-metre U-boat into the opening on *Chatham*'s starboard side.
Years later, Hartwig told Moon that all the while he kept up a running
commentary that "painted a picture of what was happening" as U-517 made
its first attack. His "quiet commentary" was whispered from man to man
throughout the U-boat. "As soon as we heard it hit [one torpedo missed]
there was a great cheer from the crew," Hartwig recalled.

Just under one thousand yards away, the death cries of fourteen men went
unheard, lost in the roar of the torpedo's exploding charge, which blew her

boilers fifty feet upward, through five decks of hardened steel. Across the length of the ship, deck after deck was ruptured. Transverse bulkheads designed to hold back tons of water were torn. Metal shards moving at hundreds of miles an hour cut through still more steel, wire, flesh. The crew's dining room, which at 8:45 a.m. was filled with men eating reconstituted powdered eggs, black coffee and toast, was now filled with the acrid, choking fumes of burning oil, ship's stores and melting lead-based paint. Only exemplary rescue work by *Mojave* and USS *Bernadou* kept the death toll from reaching horrifying proportions.

The obvious pride Hartwig took in telling Moon about the address to his crew after the sinking of *Chatham* shows that he was no simple villain sent from central casting: "I told them they should always remember that it could easily be the other way around—that they themselves could have been killed. I said they had to live in a kind of humility—that they would not necessarily be victors all the time. And that while we had a duty to *our* country, so had the other side to *their* country. I said that while we had to be successful, we did not have to hate the enemy." Courtliness aside, however, Hartwig was a professional warrior commanding a state-of-the-art warship on a mission to attack men plying the river and gulf of what to him was a foreign land.

Hartwig's torpedo brought the war home to the small fishing village of Battle Harbour, recalls Dudley Crowther, then a twenty-three-year-old member of the Newfoundland Ranger Force who organized relief efforts for the injured men coming ashore. "I commandeered a wooden one-room school that, like every building in Battle Harbour, was still lit by oil lamps. We put out mattresses, blankets and everything else the men needed. We cared for 160 men for the better part of a week until an American warship came to pick them up. But a number of them were badly burned and we couldn't care for them.

"There was a Grenville Mission school in St. Mary's Harbour, about a few miles away in the bay. We used the same lifeboats the men used to come ashore to take them to St. Mary's Harbour. Luckily, the weather was good so it was not a difficult trip to the hospital.

"Of course we'd been following the war and we'd seen many convoys. But when they came ashore, the war suddenly struck home to us."

Three days later, Hartwig was almost undone by the image he tried to create within the cramped pressure hull of U-517. There—amid the stink of sweat, diesel fumes, oil, fungus, mould, gases given off by the lead-acid batteries, and semen—Hartwig strove, like all U-boat commanders, to create a world in which the hard realities of life were dissolved not just by the mission *Grossadmiral* Dönitz had handed them but, more immediately and more symbolically, by the men's own part in Hartwig's command. Each man knew that more than any other captain, their captain was alone; alone among naval captains, U-boat captains aimed the weapons at their targets. Each man relied on others more than did crewmen on surface ships, so that the captain's will must be theirs. According to Hadley, "Hartwig's approach was a deft combination of that consciously understated image making and calculated tactics common to many navy leaders. It always remains important for a crew's *esprit de corps* that a captain demonstrate he can indeed perform, for that above all else inspires confidence. If he can carry it off with style, so much the better."

On September 1, following Dönitz's sailing orders, which listed the small North Shore bay as "an anchorage for steamers," Hartwig entered Fortuna Bay at night. Throwing caution to the wind, he pushed as close as fifty yards from the pier. "We could see the buildings and the lights quite clearly. There was nobody around to see us and, unfortunately, there were no freighters. So we turned around and left," Hartwig told Moon.

The U-boat captain escaped by the skin of his teeth.

Out of the dark of night, suddenly, Hartwig's lookout saw some 500 yards away the telltale sign of a warship, the corvette HMCS *Weyburn*: the glowing water piling in front of the bow as it cut through the water, a moving phosphorescence coming straight at them. The warship saw him too, Hartwig quickly realized. For when he tried to escape on the surface at full speed, his diesels driving U-517 at 12 knots, the warship not only followed but began gaining on him. To avoid being either rammed or shot from behind, Hartwig crash-dived.

But Hartwig was not out of danger. Either his soundings or his charts were wrong. Instead of the safety of deep water, he hit bottom at 120 feet.

"It was," Hartwig told Moon, "a very bad situation. We were scraping on the bottom making a lot of noise. All we could do was keep absolutely quiet and listen to the vessel approach us and pass overhead," hoping that neither the ship's asdic nor its hydrophones gave it a fix.

They didn't. And after several anxious minutes, Hartwig escaped.

Two days later, while sinking *Donald Stewart*, a 1,781-ton laker with concrete in her hold and tons of aviation fuel in 55-gallon drums lashed to her deck, Hartwig again played chicken with the RCN. Hartwig's war log for September 3 reads,

> 1:30 a.m. [local time] Grid 2273. Starboard astern shadows. Convoy in sight. Screen on port side. Convoy moving in echelon starboard. Place myself astern of convoy and prepared to attack from starboard.
>
> Just before firing, I passed along the starboard side. Guard ship 600 m away. When he is on my beam, I go into the attack at full power, firing two single torpedoes.
>
> The guard ship then turns sharply, heading toward me. The torpedo hits and a steamship goes up in flames. I try to go around the burning steamship in order to sink the second freighter.
>
> The guard ship is now 300 m away.
>
> Crash-dive.

"I figured," Hartwig told Moon, "that the lookouts would be watching only the dark side of the convoy where they would expect a submarine to attack from. I thought I would take them by surprise. So I decided, against all the rules, to attack."

Hartwig's decision to hold his bearing even after the "guard ship," HMCS *Weyburn* (which had seen the wash produced by his conning tower), veered toward him, surprised Captain Tom Golby—and sealed *Donald Stewart*'s fate. Had Hartwig been spooked by the star shell now illuminating his hull and had dived or even ordered a hard turn in the hopes of repeating the *pas de deux* of the day before, his war diary would have recorded that the angle of attack was "hopeless." Instead, he waited until *Weyburn*, closing from 1,000 yards at better than 15 knots, was just seconds away before issuing the twin orders to fire and crash-dive.

One torpedo ran harmlessly into the night. The other hit *Donald Stewart* forward of her stern, blowing a hole in the hull, which was weighed down by tons of cement, and igniting the gasoline. Within moments, Romeo Gaudet, Harry Kaminsky and Harvey Sutherland were dead. The blast lit the Strait of Belle Isle and was seen by Donald Murphy, a leading stoker aboard HMCS *Clayoquot*, more than twenty miles away. The men on *Stewart*'s bridge and in the aft house above the engine room survived the fireball that raced up and down the foundering, burning 250-foot ship. Ironically, the best description of what the men who survived these explosions and fire went through comes from Hartwig himself: "We were so close [before diving] that I could feel the heat of the burning ship on my face and there was so much noise from the explosions and the fire that the helmsman could not hear my orders," he told Moon.

Hartwig's crash-dive saved him from being shot at by *Weyburn*'s guns. But this time, the gulf's waters did not hide him from asdic. Captain Golby knew where he was. Then, just as Golby passed over the swirl left by the crash-dive, *Weyburn*'s depth-charge launchers jammed. What would ordinarily have been a brace of four or six depth charges—two set at 50 feet, two at 100 feet and two at 200 feet—or even eight, with the final two dropped with the safety still on but with the knowledge that as they touched bottom they too would explode, was cut to two. Those two must have been close, for Hartwig's lights shorted. Four or even two more might have caught him.

As *Weyburn* attacked U-517, the men on HMCS *Trail*, which was escorting another small convoy through the strait, witnessed still another tragedy. They saw a crewman realize he was trapped by the burning sea on the burning ship. "White faced and horrified," James Lamb later recalled, he "calmly turn[ed] to face the flames before the inferno consumed him."

Life in the merchant marine, on ships like *Donald Stewart* or its sister ship, Read's *Oakton*, should not, of course, be romanticized. The work was hard.

Long periods of boredom were interspersed with strenuous, repetitive activities and unending chipping of paint. But, as many who have written about them have noted, merchant seamen see themselves as being the last of a breed: free men who freely sign the ship's articles. The articles may bind them to a ship and to a captain's command, but only for a specific period of time.

The pay was low, conditions often poor. Captains or first officers could be stupid and tyrannical, but surprisingly few merchant seamen view these types as the norm. They stand out in their memories because they are so rare. "The old man knew how to take care of his crew" is a phrase much more commonly heard when retired merchant sailors speak of their captains than the salty language for which sailors are famed. Even sixty years later, Robert Pike, who served aboard SS *Waterton*, a British freighter sunk off Cap-de-la-Madeleine on October 11, 1942, fondly recalls his captain, William Lutjens: "He was a good captain. Looked after the crew. He made sure that we had what we needed."

Read served under two captains and speaks highly of both. His experience may be coloured, he admits, by the fact that one of the captains was his father's old friend. Still, neither he nor Marchand recalls Brown treating Read all that differently than he did any new hand. "He did it for me, but he did it for the other young fella; when we were on lookout watch, sometimes he'd take us up on the bridge and give us a turn at the helm. Boy, did we feel big then."

Some twelve hours after the sinking of *Donald Stewart*, Read lifted the hawser that had held *Oakton* to the stanchion on the side of Lock No. 1 of the Lachine Canal and then jumped aboard. A short time later, just before slipping under the railroad bridge that connects Montreal to Halifax in the southeast and the rail lines that run to Halifax or New York, *Oakton* passed the busy Port of Montreal. Among the ships berthed in the inner harbour near the huge concrete Red Rose flour silos and downriver toward the city's financial district, then the economic heartbeat of Canada, were three weather-beaten, rust-stained Greek ships.

A reluctant ally that entered the war only after Mussolini invaded in 1940, in 1942 Greece was occupied by Hitler's troops, which had been dispatched when Mussolini's invasion force broke. Along with hundreds of other masters, including *Aeas*'s, the masters of SS *Mount Pindus* and *Mount Taygetus* refused orders to return home, putting themselves instead at the service of Britain and its allies. A few days later, after the *Oakton* steamed by them, these three ships weighed anchor and steamed first to Quebec City for a convoy conference, then to Île d'Orléans, where they were degaussed, and finally another 170 miles downriver to Bic Island, where convoy QS-33 firmed up.[9]

"For us, the most important thing about Bic Island had nothing to do with the convoy or the escorts," recalls Read. "It meant another full dollar a day, the war risk bonus." The men on *Mount Taygetus* must have felt the same. Like Read, they knew of the U-boat risk, but for them especially, when in the St. Lawrence, the threat must have seemed small beer indeed. The storms of the North Atlantic hadn't sunk *Mount Taygetus*, and neither had Dönitz's wolves, though two years earlier they'd come close when *Mount Taygetus* was part of SC-42, a convoy that included SS *Joannis* and *Inger Elizabeth*, which Hoffmann and Hartwig, respectively, would sink within a fortnight.

Two hundred miles east of Bic Island, the Gulf of St. Lawrence and the part of the river that the U-boats were known to be operating in totals hundreds of square kilometres. Huff-duff bearings and locations of recorded attacks may have narrowed Hartwig's area of operations considerably, but the lag between getting a fix and the arrival of air cover was still measured in hours—time enough for Hartwig to become the proverbial needle in the haystack. Were he to have surfaced soon after the attack and then run on the surface for five hours after attacking *Donald Stewart*—and despite the obvious dangers, even during the day, Hartwig preferred to travel on the surface both because of the speed he could make and because it allowed him to air out his fetid boat and charge his batteries—Hartwig could have been anywhere along the edge of a 200-square-kilometre box. Had he spent these five hours cruising underwater, the box would have been 50 square kilometres. In addition, of course, he would have been underwater and thus invisible to planes and all but invisible to asdic.

Eight times in the days after sinking *Donald Stewart*, Hartwig ordered Alarm after his lookouts spotted RCAF patrol planes The young pilots, products of the Commonwealth Air Training Plan, which trained 150,000 pilots in bases across Canada, tried everything. Cutting their engines and gliding silently. Skimming low over the water with the sun at their tails, hoping to blind Hartwig's lookouts. Dropping out of the clouds.

J. H. Sanderson, flying a Douglas Digby out of Gander, got the closest. Eleven hours after Hartwig sank *Donald Stewart*, Sanderson put his twin-engine Digby into a power dive that took him directly over U-517. He was— just—too far away. The brace of four depth charges he dropped from 150 feet hit the water twenty seconds after Hartwig crash-dived. Twenty seconds translated into 30 metres, a scant but sufficient margin of safety. The blasts shook Hartwig up but left him undamaged.

Daybreak on the seventh gave way to the morning, and still Read's *Oakton* was alone on the south side of the St. Lawrence. "Some time near 11 a.m., a plane came over and signalled us to rejoin the convoy. Using a lamp and my boy-scout Morse code, I told them we didn't know where the convoy was."

A few hours later, a Fairmile launch appeared and its captain told Brown to take *Oakton* into the middle of the river. By midafternoon, Captain Skinner had reassembled QS-33 with *Oakton* on its starboard. By 3 p.m., rain had cut "visibility to one mile or less," forcing the convoy's air cover back to base.

Skinner didn't know it, but earlier in the day, before the convoy re-formed, his charges had dodged a bullet. At 7:06 a.m. on September 7, Hartwig took aim at "three fat steamers" as they entered QU BA 3693. After taking aim, however, he realized that the "inclination was hopeless." Rather than risk a torpedo—which cost 24,000 Reich marks (about the cost of a small house in Germany) and took 3,720 man-hours to build—by firing when the angle was beyond that angle at which torpedoes would run truest, Hartwig decided to reposition himself in front of the convoy, running ahead of it until late in the afternoon.

Shortly after 4 p.m., eighteen miles off Gaspé point, QS-33 steamed directly over U-517. Again Hartwig resisted the first chance to fire when the inclination would have been 70°. He risked being caught in the asdic beams, trusting that the same temperature and salinity gradients that made holding trim difficult would hide him from what Joseph Schull calls the "searching fingers of Asdic."

Following a flagged order from the convoy commodore aboard SS *Benacas*, *Oakton*'s helmsman, Laurent Marchand, turned the wheel as the convoy cut another angle, designed to protect them but putting Hartwig between the "1st and 2nd steamers."

Still the angle was not perfect, so, according to his war diary, Hartwig "proceeded between the 2nd and 3rd steamers at right angles to the convoy course" and then turned 180° so that he could fire from both his forward and aft tubes. From where he was, all his "eels" would have to do to sink three ships at once was to run simple and true.

As Hartwig manoeuvred between the convoy's columns, Jock Smith's asdic watch came to an end.

"It was a beautiful sunny day and I decided to go for a walk around the ship," he recalls. "When I came to the stern, I met one of the torpedo ratings I knew. We reminisced about the sinkings during the night and expressed relief at the bright sunny day we were experiencing."

"A perfect day at sea," Smith remembers. "Bright sun, blue sky. On the *Arrowhead*'s starboard side, three small merchant ships slowly ploughing their way along the Gaspé coast," looking not all that different from the ships that a century and a half earlier had left New France carrying beaver pelts by the ton. Smith's memory of running fairly close to the heavily wooded shoreline is the same as Read's; since the second sinking the night before, "we'd been running for the shoals."

Four hundred yards away and twenty feet below the dappled surface, while peering through one periscope, Hartwig pushed the button that fired a torpedo from his one functioning aft tube. Peering through the other periscope, Karl Brandi, his thirty-year-old first officer, pushed the two buttons that fired the torpedoes in the U-boat's forward tubes.

A perfect day at sea. Small whitecaps and even the streaks of those playful porpoise so beloved by sailors.

Then, horror.

Instead of a jumping porpoise, Smith and the rating saw white streaks in the water shoot past their stern.

In an instant, a picture-postcard afternoon had turned to war.

"*Torpedoes passing astern!*" Smith yelled. This last word was barely heard as sea breeze and the low throb of the ship's engines were replaced by the ringing of Action Stations.

Seconds later, Captain Brown saw that his commodore had hoisted the black flag, which signalled Enemy in the Vicinity, and three others. "Captain Brown turned to the code book to see what the other flags meant," recalls Marchand, who was at the helm. "He didn't have time to finish before we could see a column of water rising from the *Mount Taygetus*. Brown ordered a hard turn to port."

Wilkinson ran aft, yelling for Read in their cabin. "Get the hell out here, something's going on!"

Hartwig watched through his periscope.

The torpedoes, driven by 100 hp motors powered by lead-acid batteries and guided by gyroscopes made by Siemens, sped onward through the calm, sunlit sea.

Smith ran to the bridge. Before entering it, he turned and took a quick glance to starboard in the direction of the three small ships.

Read, too, ran—first to the hook on the wall to get his life jacket, then through the cabin door.

"Just as my eyes focused on the ships," Smith recalls, "there were three large clouds of smoke, one arising from each of the three ships." He looked at his watch as soon as he realized they'd been hit. By the time he looked up, scant seconds later, they were starting to disappear below the sea.

Aboard *Oakton*, time unrolled.

"Before I could get out on deck," Read recalls, "I heard the first one get it. Seconds later, as I got out on deck, I felt the *Oakton* . . . it was like it missed a beat. A deep rumbling thud, coming from beneath us. I ran, but the deck wasn't where my feet expected it to be. The explosion of the torpedo didn't destroy the deck. No, it drove the ship down—the entire length of the ship down—into the water. The water that poured over the deck pushed me head over heels into the garbage cans. She struggled to lift herself, as she did when a wave broke over her bow in a storm. She did, but it wasn't the same; she was heavier, being pulled. You could feel her going down."

As Read got up and ran to his action station, Smith glanced at his watch again and realized with horror that what he'd just witnessed had taken less than thirty seconds. "One minute there were three small merchant ships pushing their way along the Gaspé coastline, and suddenly there were none."

Hartwig almost missed his chance to observe all three hits. Just before he ordered "*Los*" [fire], he thought he'd been sighted. Immediately after the torpedo tube cap clanged shut, U-517 dived. But the escort veered away a mere 200 metres from his periscope. Hartwig commended Watch Officer Lieutenant Rolf Pingel's operation of the ship's hydrophones, which allowed his bridge crew to hear the hits. His entry laments the fact that he had been able to fire only three torpedoes because Tube V was "unserviceable."

The nineteen men aboard *Oakton* were now running for their lives, doing for real what they had done so many times in practice. Read cut a corner when, instead of climbing up the ladder to his action station, he climbed up on the rail and hoisted himself up to the deck by his arms. Before Read axed the rope that held the starboard lifeboat in, he saw the ship's first officer pull the pins that had been holding fast the Carley floats.

"Thirty seconds later, the lifeboat was in the water and I had shimmied down the monkey rope," recalls Read. "The ship was settling quickly. Before we got hit, the drop would have been something like twenty feet from the lifeboat station to the water. Now it was more like fifteen and dropping fast.

"Before I shimmied down, I could hear the water rushing into the ship. There hadn't been a big blast, but some of the hatchways had been blown off and coal dust had been blown into the air. I could see water shooting out of No. 2 hold."

Marchand recalls, "There was no panic, but everyone moved quickly. Captain Brown was the last man down into the boat."

In just over a minute, *Oakton* had been hit and her men had abandoned her. Now they were sliding into lifeboats that their shipmates were struggling to keep steady, for though dying, *Oakton* still had enough forward motion to swamp the lifeboats.

Before another minute was out, the lifeboats were filled. Then men were rowing as fast as they could away from their ship and from the vortex they knew would form with its sinking.

"We hadn't gone more than fifty or sixty yards," recalls Read. "It was maybe two or two and a half minutes since she'd been hit when, suddenly, we saw her break clean in two. We were dumbstruck.

"The two halves were just about equal. The bow rose up on one side, and the propellers rose up on the other. Everything that wasn't bolted down on the deck slid down, the hatchways broke off and just for a second we could see the coal the stevedores had so carefully shovelled into her in Sandusky begin to spill out. When we saw that the propeller was still turning, one guy said, 'Jeez, she's still trying to go somewhere.'"

They watched as the funnel, still belching smoke, and the monkey deck (which was above the bridge in the forward part of the ship) came together. Then the funnel smashed through the monkey deck.

"Together, the two halves then sank in water that was boiling like a cauldron as all the air in them came to the surface, along with everything that wasn't bolted to sinking steel. Then we heard the muffled explosions of her boilers and one last great bubble," recalls Read. "The other two, the Greek ships, were off on our starboard side. They went down awfully fast too. We were too far to hear their boilers explode, but we saw their boats go out, and then they were gone too."

Hartwig and his crew also heard the sounds of all three ships' boilers exploding and of their bulkheads breaking.

The signals officers in Gaspé heard *Arrowhead*'s signature and again knew that men were dead and dying and cargo was sinking.

Another turn and 15 knots put *Arrowhead* over the rapidly fading torpedo tracks. Then, despite the temperature gradients and the mixing of salt and fresh water, a ping, a good ping. Clear enough to give Skinner's depth-charge men something to go for.

One pattern.

Then another, as *Truro* joined the attack.

And more, now from the Fairmiles.

Beneath the roiling sea, lights flickered, crackled and shorted out. Sparks flew around the ship as insulation around the wiring wore thin. Pipes squealed against their braces; some broke.

The ping of the asdic continued, the sound both bouncing off and penetrating Hartwig's hull. The closeness of the next depth charge told the men in U-517 that this time the water wasn't hiding them.

Steel squealed. Gauges gyrated and burst. Water seeped into the bilges. Ten minutes.

Another blast, and plates bent as the U-boat, now in darkness—surrounded by darkness, the water that would be instant death—vibrated, but not as Hollywood or even the producers of the movie *Das Boot* would have it. Unless a depth charge explodes within twenty feet and blows a hole in the pressure hull, depth-charging has little effect on U-boats.

Though only 77 metres long, U-boats like Hartwig's have a mass of 1,500 tons. This mass is immersed in an infinitely larger mass of water, which to an unbreached hull is almost solid. "Depth charges don't move boats even an inch," according to Werner Hirschmann, chief engineer on U-612 and U-190, "but, rather, are like a blow with a giant hammer on an immovable object."

"It's that pounding which breaks the glass of lights and gauges, which bends the metal of the deck plates where, either from the time they were cast or welded into place, there is a pre-existing weak spot," says Hirschmann. "It's the thousands of tons of pressure generated by the outward movement of the pressure bubble formed by the detonation that is transmitted by the water directly through the hull and into such things as shafts. Shafts and their housings bend because the force exerted on them is not equally distributed along their lengths, both because the explosions occur in one specific place and because by their very nature shafts and their housings have pockets—the gap between the shaft and its house—that are irregular."

Twenty minutes, and still more.

Had the outer hull held? Was oil leaking from the bilges? If so, would the Canadians above see it as proof of a hit? Would they drop more, or would they think the boat had gone to the bottom?

More blasts. Perhaps these were the ones that damaged the ship's water-distilling plant, cutting its output from fifty gallons of drinkable water to ten; a jury-rigged system would later produce just another ten gallons.

More sounds of propellers. Hartwig and his crew were scared, terrified or resigned; he and his men had to be as silent as possible. They'd long ago taken off their shoes and donned the special socks that dampen all sound. Orders were whispered; damage-control reports were whispered. If caught by a hydrophone, a cough, a sneeze, a dropped tool could mean a better-aimed spread.

Hartwig commanded, but when the U-boat was underwater, even when being depth-charged, it was his chief engineer who was in charge of operations. It was he who interpreted the damage control for his captain, who told him what the boat could withstand—a deeper dive? Once told to keep it at, say, 75 metres, it was he who had to determine if the boat was becoming lighter (because of leaking oil from the bilges) or heavier (because of water pouring into a ruptured bilge tank). If lighter, even by a small percentage of its total weight, it would rise, and valves had to be opened to let in just enough sea water. If heavier, water had to be blown out of the tanks by releasing compressed air into them. So that this would not become a calling card to the depth charges, the release had to be timed exactly to the rhythm of the blasts raining down from above.

Thirty minutes.

Still more hammering on the welded steel hull. Every decibel crashed into the crew's ears. Hartwig and his bridge crew listened to the hydrophones. They could make out different propellers. Another blast. Another ping. Another blast.

U-517's hull still held. But for how long? The real danger, Hartwig knew, was not the charge now pounding the boat, but the next one. Would it be closer?

After almost forty minutes of being pounded, Hartwig decided to use a secret device called the *Pillenwerfer*. Launched from a torpedo tube, it did not explode, killing men. Rather, it burst into millions of bubbles that hid the U-boat from the asdic operator.

Aware that his force's supply of depth charges was rapidly diminishing, Skinner broke off action and ordered his ship and the others to save the men in the lifeboats. Their last depth charges burst only the *Pillenwerfer*'s bubbles, as U-517's silent electric motors pushed its hushed crew away and out of danger.

Read and his shipmates watched as the Fairmiles cut past them on their way to depth-charge the U-boat. Then, after one of the men took a count, he heard him say, "Captain Brown, there're eighteen of us here—the chief's missing."

"That silly old bugger went back for his glasses," said an oiler, as Captain Brown realized his penny-ante poker buddy, the chief engineer, was last seen going into the *Oakton*, now just tons of wrecked steel perhaps a thousand feet below.

" 'We'd better go look in that mess,' said Captain Brown, pointing to the flotsam and jetsam that marred the sea where *Oakton*'s two pieces sank," Read recalls.

"I don't really remember us being worried that we wouldn't find him," says Read. "It wasn't that kind of a moment. Someone passed around cigarettes—we smoked a lot of them back then. We heard the explosions of the depth charges and watched the great domes of water they shot up. At one point we even thought we'd seen the submarine rise up like a cigar. We'd heard that sometimes when being depth-charged they did that."

"The escorts kicked up quite a ruckus. The Fairmiles were flitting all over and all around us," Read remembers. "There were depth charges going off every which way.

"We rowed into the floating mass of broken hatch covers, coal dust, splinters, still some clothes that had boiled up from inside the ship, paper, paint chips, oil that had once lubricated the engine, and insulation. It wasn't long, less than five minutes, before one of the guys spotted a large section of wooden hatchway, and holding on to it was the chief. As soon as he saw us, he yelled, 'For Christ's sake, get me out of here, it's cold!' "

The crews aboard *Mount Pindus* and *Mount Taygetus* were not as lucky. Together they lost seven men, and many with flash burns, adrift in lifeboats or Carley floats, didn't receive proper medical attention for hours. According to *Arrowhead*'s log, Captain Skinner ordered the Fairmiles to pick up the survivors at 4:55. The last surviving merchant ship of QS-33 was sent on to Sydney, escorted by *Truro*. *Arrowhead* and the Fairmiles turned to Gaspé, arriving there close to 8:30 p.m.

"When we got into port, they marched us into a barracks, where we were given clean, dry clothes and something to eat," recalls Read, who slept that night in a barrack requisitioned from one of the servicemen assigned to Gaspé. Other men, who lived at Mrs. Kruse's hotel, gave up their beds so that the survivors of QS-33 could sleep between two clean sheets. The dead were buried immediately.

Two days later, when they arrived by special train in Montreal, Read and his shipmates and the men from the three Greek ships that had been sunk were taken to the Queens Hotel, across from where Bonsecours Market stands today.

"Once they got us there, we were taken into a large reception room, where we were sat down. There were both civilians and naval personnel, with lots of gold rings on their cuffs," recalls Read, a memory he shares with Marchand.

"They congratulated us on surviving and then impressed on us the importance of keeping these sinkings secret. We understood why," recalls Read.

"But they never did tell us how we were supposed to explain to our families why we got home so soon and why we came home without our kit. And why there was no ship for us to ship out on in a week like we normally did. Jeezes Murphy," says Read.

On September 8, while Read's train chugged through the Quebec countryside toward Montreal, an announcer in Berlin read the following war report:

> The loss of twelve merchant ships totalling 80,144 tons in the month of August led Britons and the English to take desperate defence measures. Now, for example, the Canadian navy, which is nine-tenths composed of requisitioned fishing boats, coastal ships and luxury yachts, is obliged to create an escort system . . . with these third-class ships. This service comprises a third of the threatened maritime route between Canada and the British Isles.[10]

Two weeks after the sinking of *Oakton*, *Mount Pindus* and *Mount Taygetus*, the nuns of a small convent in Gaspé opened their door to find that someone had left the body of Georgeios Triantafyllarous on their doorstep. Later that day, he was buried in the corner of a cemetery not far from the tip of the Gaspé Peninsula, where today stands the Musée de la Gaspésie.[11]

CHAPTER FOUR

THE LIFE AND DEATH OF
HMCS *CHARLOTTETOWN*

JUNE 7, 1941–SEPTEMBER 11, 1942

The steel decks rock with the lighting shock, and shake with the great recoil,
And the sea grows red with the blood of the dead and reaches for his spoil

—JOHN ROONEY

Officially, only the captains of the escort ships of SQ-35 that put out from Sydney for Quebec City on September 8, 1942—the corvettes HMCS *Charlottetown* and *Weyburn*, the Bangor minesweeper HMCS *Clayoquot* and the two Fairmiles—and the convoy's commodore knew of the mauling of QS-33. Unofficially, the seamen's messes were awash with talk of the battle that had claimed men they knew on *Raccoon* and men they didn't know, men who had sailed on the four freighters now on the bottom.

"The mess was abuzz with it," recalls Donald Murphy, *Clayoquot*'s leading stoker. "We'd heard that the *Raccoon* had gotten it. And we knew that we were about to sail into the same waters. We weren't scared, though. We were sailing as part of a large escort: two corvettes, us and the Fairmiles. But we had no illusions. Ships were being torpedoed since May. We knew we'd have to be careful."

For most of the ratings, being careful meant straining their eyes as they stood watch. Each of the endless hours—two of every eight on watch—spent staring across the ever-changing canvas of light, reflection, shadow and moving mist was one more hour passed safely, one more hour closer to Bic Island, where it was too shallow for U-boats to operate.

For others, such as nineteen-year-old Allan Heagy, *Charlottetown*'s newly minted radar operator, who joined the ship only hours before it left port on September 8, being careful meant sitting for four hours at a time in the small radar hut on the port side of the bridge turning a crank that rotated his ship's radar antenna on the main mast and staring into a ten-inch-diameter oscilloscope watching for an unexpected jagged line—a reading that would trigger Action Stations.

"Radar then," recalls Heagy—who, after joining the navy in London, Ontario, in April 1941, volunteered to be trained on a new secret weapon, the cover for which was a radio-repair course at the University of Western Ontario—"wasn't anything like it is today. It wasn't even as good as the radar—then called radio directional finding (RDF)—then in use on British ships, which were equipped with 271 or centimetric radar, which rotated automatically and operated on a shorter wavelength that allowed them to 'see' both trimmed-down U-boats and even periscopes, and at closer range.[1]

"We rotated our 286 radar by turning a crank that was connected by a series of rods to the antenna (called a Yagi), which was shaped like two of those old TV aerials that used to be on top of houses. As we rotated the Yagi, we watched for jagged lines. Unfortunately, as we rotated it, we picked up as many back echoes as true readings. Figuring out what the oscilloscope was telling you took a lot of guesswork."

SQ-35 was a milk run, just like the other ten patrols telegraphist Fred Rush recalled in a 1993 interview: "Looking back, it was quite a time. We were a bunch of green kids. I was an old man of twenty-three or twenty-four. It was a holiday with pay, with no thought of war. We ate good—navy style—and slept good. One day up the river to pick up our small convoy, three or four days back to Sydney and then back to Gaspé for a layover. A real holiday with pay."

Amidst the endless cleaning and painting, there was time for baseball and swimming, "a very gentle time."

SQ-35 would be *Charlottetown*'s last patrol.

Across the St. Lawrence and even in Ottawa, action swirled.

A HF/DF report on September 8 placed one U-boat north of Anticosti Island, squarely in the middle of the Jacques Cartier Passage, one of the convoy routes. The next morning, Heagy's opposite number on *Charlottetown*'s sister ship, HMCS *Summerside*, called out Contact Co-ordinates.

Captain F. O. Gerity chased the U-boat for six miles and fired star shells, but his lookouts saw nothing. On the ninth, after Flight Officer R. S. Keetley returned to his base at Chatham, the following signal was sent to Naval Service Headquarters, on the second floor of a building on Sparks Street in Ottawa:

> At first [the pilot] did not think it was a submarine [twenty miles south of the eastern end of Anticosti] but mistook it for [a] sail boat due to its excellent camouflage. The conning tower was painted white and the hull sea green, [giving it] the same appearance as water. It was extremely difficult to distinguish the U-boat from a small sail boat. Recognizing it to be a U-boat the pilot brought [the] aircraft [into a] dive from 4000 feet to 800 feet and noting that the enemy machine gun was mounted and directed at [the] aircraft the pilot open[ed] fire.

The U-boat, identified as Eberhard Hoffmann's U-165 by historian Roger Sarty, escaped Keetley's depth charges by seconds. Several hours later, two corvettes and a minesweeper ordered by Commander German to search the same waters off Anticosti dropped four depth charges after having gained asdic contacts. Hartwig spent most of the same day under, spotting either escorts or patrol aircraft at 6:30 a.m., 3:35 p.m., 5:15 p.m. and 7:46 p.m.

While Hartwig was lying low, King's war cabinet was meeting in Ottawa to consider Churchill's request of a "loan" of escort vessels for Operation Torch, the amphibious assault on North Africa planned for November 1942. Macdonald reported that Canada could supply up to seventeen vessels but that doing so would mean denuding the Gulf Escort Force of twelve corvettes and would thus require the closing of the St. Lawrence to all but essential coastal and ferry traffic, which would be escorted by the few ships left at Gaspé. Later in the day, after Rear-Admiral Nelles sent a signal closing the river and the gulf to transoceanic shipping, Naval Control of Shipping in Halifax ordered the immediate diversion of all inbound shipping to Halifax, Saint John or Sydney; new convoy schedules were drawn up to allow ships at Montreal or Quebec City to sail as soon as was practicable.

Although the possibility of closing the St. Lawrence had been discussed as early as 1939, doing so created an immediate communications problem for King's government. Official naval documents state the obvious: closing the St. Lawrence "undoubtedly represents a severe moral and physical defeat to Canada's war effort." Hard truths from a military pen, however, did not square with rules laid down by the censor's office after the sinking of *Nicoya*. Accordingly, there was no public statement announcing the closure of the St. Lawrence.

JUNE 7, 1941

- Three thousand five hundred miles east in Kiel, Germany, workers at Howadstwerke lay the keel for U-375.
- Five thousand miles east in Egypt, German bombers bomb Alexandria, killing 230.

- Five thousand miles east, British and Free French troops prepare to invade Lebanon and Syria.

Shortly after 7 a.m., Foreman Duncan McCorquodale and some two hundred other men walked out of the warehouse-like building that housed the Kingston Shipyards offices and the machine shops that fashioned steel into any of ten thousand parts of a ship. They stopped some hundred yards away, in the middle of a 300- by 60-foot slip that just a few days earlier had been filled by Hull 19, shortly to be called HMCS *Prescott*—the third corvette built by Kingston Shipyards. Soon the gentle rustling of the breeze coming off the narrowest part of Lake Ontario, which lapped the US shore a few miles south and which less than two miles east formed the headwaters of the St. Lawrence itself, was drowned out by the ear-splitting sound of pneumatic hammers driving rivets into I-beams and plates. The beams formed the keel and the plates formed the hull that Hartwig's torpedoes would destroy on September 11, 1942, 361 days after Naval Service Headquarters in Ottawa received a one-sentence signal from the naval officer in charge in Quebec City: "H.M.C.S. 'CHARLOTTETOWN' COMMISSIONED THIS DAY."

"The men," recalls Francis MacLaughlin, who in 1943 worked at the yard while other corvettes were being built, "took their cue from General

Manager T. G. Bishop." Tommy Bishop was from the old school, as were McCorquodale and even Donald Page (who at twenty-five was almost forty years younger than the other two), who headed the Design Office. "They were no-nonsense men, very much aware, and made us very much aware, how important our role was."

The controlled mayhem of the shipyard was their battlefield. Beyond the smoke and glow of braziers that turn cold plugs of steel into red-hot rivets was an endless ballet in which one strong, sweaty man tossed one, then another, red-hot rivet up twenty, thirty, forty feet to another man standing on a staging plank, who caught it in a cup and plucked it out with tongs. Before it could cool and lose its red heat, he held it straight, and a third man drove it through a narrow hole in three-quarters of an inch of steel. Sixteen rivets, and one more plate was held in place—one small contribution to the defeat of the U-boats that prowled the North Atlantic.

For weeks, even as astute an observer of the Kingston yard as young MacLaughlin would not have been able to tell Hull 20 from the previous two corvettes built on the same slip. HMCS *Napanee* and *Prescott* belonged to the Flower class, so named, it was said, because a wag in the Admiralty looked forward to the propaganda value of the headline "HMS *Pansy* Sinks U-Boat." Hull 20 belonged to the revised Flower class. Originally slated to be inshore patrol vessels, the first corvettes were built with short fo'c'sles and noticeably unflared bows. Once forced onto the North Atlantic run, they were admired by the British Admiralty for their ability to weather the heaviest Atlantic gales "without material damage." They were, however, notoriously uncomfortable ships.

At 205 feet 1 inch long, corvettes of the first building program were too short to straddle the North Atlantic's waves; at 905 tons, they were too light to cut through the rollers. Instead, they climbed over them, bobbing like corks. Their short draught, 13 feet 5 inches, made them roll violently in the heavy seas of the North Atlantic. Men who sailed in them proudly said "they'd roll on grass in heavy dew." This short draught also accounted for their extraordinary manoeuvrability. *Charlottetown* and its sister ships could turn a complete circle in a hundred seconds, much faster than either a surfaced or a submerged U-boat.

"They corkscrewed all over the place," recalls Max Korkum, who late after the war commanded HMCS *Sackville*, the "last corvette," now berthed in Halifax. "But what really wore the men down about the first corvettes was that they were a wet ship. Because of their short fo'c'sle (the short raised deck at the bow of the ship), water poured over the deck, running down in torrents onto the boat deck (behind the fo'c'sle but in front of the superstructure). From there, water ran onto the main deck, and could run into the ship itself via ventilators and hatchways. Inside the ship, water shorted out electrical equipment and made for hellish living conditions."[2]

Frank Curry, who joined the RCN in 1940 when he was twenty years old and who served on an original Flower-class corvette, HMCS *Kamsack*, remembers that sea water was constantly backing up into the mess deck. "When they [were] not floating in dirty salt water on the deck, loaves of bread were soggy and almost always mouldy because of the mess's dampness."

"Our clothes too," Curry says, "were always wet and so were our hammocks, because we had to crawl into them in our wet clothes. During the winter runs on the North Atlantic, the watch going on duty had to put on the ice-covered and chilled duffle coat of the watch coming off duty.

"The battering of the ship in the North Atlantic—and remember, these ships rolled in even the slightest seas—took its toll on our bodies. Our hips were constantly being wrenched by the ship's roll and the fact that we had to hold on to the stanchions while we walked and she rolled. The battering also took its toll on our dishes. I remember leaving port time and again with a full set of dishes for the crew and that by the end of the patrol we were eating out of empty jam tins because every one of our dishes had been smashed."

The addition of 3 feet 3 inches to the corvettes' length (to 208 feet 4 inches) and 2 feet 2 inches to their draught (to 15 feet 7 inches) in the revised program begun in late 1940 did not materially alter either their manoeuvrability or their sea-keeping ability. The first change to appear was an increased flare to the bow (which drove water away from the ship's deck). Even more important was the extension of the fo'c'sle, which made the ships drier, quite literally because there was more ship between the deck and the sea.

"The extension of the fo'c'sle did one other thing," says Korkum. "It changed the rolling of the ship. They still rolled a lot, but the ones with the extended fo'c'sle didn't pitch and yaw with the same speed or ferocity."

Ensuring that over the 373,000 man-hours it took to build Hull 19, shipwrights, boilermakers, platers, riveters, coppersmiths, steam- and pipe-fitters, and chippers and caulkers had the pieces they needed took, wrote Lesley Roberts in 1944, 55,000 phone calls. *Part IV—Machinery (Steam—Reciprocating) Including Electrical Generators of the Specifications for an Admiralty Single-Screw Corvette of the 1941 Programme* ran to more than fifteen pages. Whatever supply bottlenecks Bishop faced while overseeing the building of Hull 20—and the National Archives contains more than a dozen pages of correspondence pertaining to the Kingston Shipbuilding Company's requisitioning of a ship's telegraph from Marine Industries in Montreal and to Marine Industries' demands for payment of $1,850 for the "telegraph and fittings"—they would be far easier to overcome than those he had faced just eighteen months earlier when Kingston began building HMCS *Napanee*.

When on September 13, 1939, Canada received from the Admiralty the plans for what was originally called "patrol vessel, whaler type" (a variant of *Southern Pride*, a whaler designed by William Reed of Smith's Dock Co., Ltd., in Yorkshire), the country hadn't built a significant ship in almost twenty years. The dockyards that undertook to build what Churchill dubbed "the cheap, but Nasties" (*Charlottetown* cost $532,000) had barely survived the long dark years of the Depression by doing repair work.

Though slightly revived by the small rearmament program begun in 1936 when the King government more than doubled the Naval Estimates to $4.8 million (funds that ensured that when war broke out in 1939, Canada possessed six modern destroyers, enough to mount a credible defence against surface attacks on the east coast), the Canada that undertook to build and launch twenty-eight corvettes before the end of 1940 hardly possessed either the industrial plant or the experienced personnel required for such a project. Of the Great Lakes yards that built dozens of corvettes and minesweepers, the "History of the British Admiralty Technical Mission in Canada" (1946) wrote, "Without having dealt with them, no one brought up to Admiralty practice could begin to appreciate the primitive nature of all these yards. . . . In one there was no drawing office at all." Of Canada's machine-tool industry, the *sine qua non* of a shipbuilding industry, the "History" wrote that it was "relatively small, and that tooling of plants largely depends on U.S. and U.K. sources: this applies particularly to the specialized tools required for fire [gunnery] control"—sources that were hard-pressed to meet their own demands.

Valves—or, to be more precise, the lack of valves—caused the "most serious bottleneck in production, owing to the small number of firms manufacturing them and the very large requirements of very varied sizes and designs." This bottleneck was broken by the Canadian Pulp and Paper Association, which "set up an organization for producing them in the workshops of their numerous subsidiary companies." Fan motors, cabling, electrical fittings and a hundred other components were difficult to get or were not being manufactured to the specifications required for a warship. The size and diversity of the electrical industry, the "History" concluded, corresponded to Canada's small population:

Practically all the manufacturing firms are off-shoots of American concerns. . . . One effect of this is that most of the firms, particularly the smaller ones, are not as fully staffed on the engineering side as they would be if they had to depend on their own resources. . . .

When difficulties over the development of small motors for fans were under discussion, the Chief Engineer of the Canadian Westinghouse Company stated that he did not have the staff of engineers qualified to design a direct current machine, and therefore had to use a standard design from the Westinghouse Company.[3]

In 1940, every one of the hundreds of thousands of tons of steel that thousands of men and women turned into corvettes and minesweepers had to be imported from the then-neutral United States. Until the Parker Fountain Pen Co. began capitalizing on its experience with small tubing to build hundreds of thousands of electrical fuses, few could be found. The same was true for ignition switches until the Renfrew Electric and Refrigeration Company stepped in. Cansfield Electric designed and built marine electrical equipment. Boilers and triple-expansion steam engines capable of producing 2,750 BHP and 185 rpm, enough to drive a corvette at 16 knots but rarely ordered during the 1930s, were manufactured by Dominion Engineers.

In 1940 stocks of building materials were so low at the Kingston yard, recalled Page in a 1990 interview, that he had to send a crew to scour the farms outside Kingston to find the planking needed to build staging for the riveters and welders working on Hulls 17 and 18. Naval guns were in such short supply that the first of the fourteen corvettes to sail for England crossed the Atlantic with grey-painted wooden dowels sticking out of their gun turrets. By the time they reached the English Western Approaches, the "guns" were drooping, a sight that prompted an admiral to exclaim, "My God! Since when are we clubbing the enemy to death?"

McCorquodale's men began where shipbuilders since the Phoenicians have begun—with the keel. In the 1860s, when Kingston Shipyards built 1,223-ton sailing ships, the phrase "her keel was laid" was literally true. Cut from huge trees, keels were rough-hewn timbers hundreds of feet long laid in the middle of a slipway.

The materials McCorquodale's men worked with were considerably less romantic. Scores of angle bars, similar to T-brackets, were riveted to steel plates, which were then riveted to still more, L-shaped angle bars called channels to form the 208 foot 4 inch keel.

To a layperson, riveting resembles nothing so much as nailing, with all the attendant possibilities of pieces working loose. However, according to Francis MacLaughlin, "riveting not only joins plates and bars but also squeezes them together. They are squeezed so tight as to form a watertight bond. There are two reasons that rivets are red hot when driven into the hole. The first is so it is malleable. The second is because as it cools and shrinks, the bulbous head and flattened end are pulled closer together, therefore pulling the two pieces of steel (plates and/or bars) closely together."

The riveting never stopped. Once the keel was in place, the frames that form the skeleton of the ship were erected and fastened—with rivets—to the keel. Next, the bulkheads (solid transverse walls) were placed wherever watertight divisions were needed.[4] And they too were riveted into place. Then the prefabricated pieces of decking were put in place and riveted. All the time this was going on, McCorquodale's men were riveting hundreds of steel plates onto the outer lip of the frames to form the ship's hull.

The pounding of pneumatic hammers flattening out the stems of thousands of rivets wasn't the worst noise. "Riveting was noisy," recalls

MacLaughlin, "but even worse was the chipping. Red-hot rivets were pushed into the hole and then a backer would put a heavy backing hammer against the head while the riveter would use the pneumatic hammer to flatten and spread out the end.

"Chipping was necessary when overlapping plates made a watertight seal impossible. Chipping was done with a high-speed pneumatic-driven chisel, similar to a riveting gun. Instead of the staccato sound of a riveting gun, chipping guns caused a high-pitched screech. The metallic screech of metal on metal was awful. Only the man with the chipping gun had any ear protection. The rest of us simply had to put up with it."

In the days leading up to the scheduled launch date of September 10, McCorquodale's men put down their pneumatic hammers, electric arc welding guns, asbestos blowers and cutting torches, and reverted to the same techniques used to launch Drake's *Golden Hind* three centuries earlier. For eighty-five days, Hull 20 had been sitting on 12 × 12 × 4 inch building blocks, one line running directly under the keel and four others running six and nine feet out toward each side.

The process of lifting the ship from these blocks and sliding her into Lake Ontario began with the installation of a series of ropes that anchored her on her starboard side. Then launching ways were placed under her keel. Each long, well-worn timber sloped from under her keel into the waters of Lake Ontario. The installation of the butter boards came next. Slightly wider than the gap between the launching ways and the keel, these heavily greased boards were driven by sledgehammers into the gap between the ways and the keel, lifting the hull from the building blocks.

The launch itself was a civic affair. People gathered. Military bands from Fort Henry played. Dignitaries gave speeches praising the men of the Kingston Shipyards and appealing for people to purchase more war bonds. Then, at the appointed time, the trigger was thrown and the ropes anchoring the hull were cut.

"For a moment," recalls MacLaughlin, who in 1944 rode a later corvette down from the ways, "nothing happened. And then she started to slide sideways towards the open lake, gathering speed as she moved. At the end of the ways, she tipped into the water, portside bilge first, with a gigantic splash that resembled a tidal wave moving away from the ship."

Over the next eighty-five days before "No. 20" sailed from Kingston to Quebec City for commissioning and final outfitting, McCorquodale's men worked on it day and night. Thousands of feet of wire and piping were snaked through her. Fuel tanks, which held enough oil to travel 4,000 miles at 12 knots, were constructed; to save weight, and thus fuel, the outer wall of the fuel tanks was the ¾-inch plating of the hull. Messes, storerooms, wardrooms and ammunition lockers were formed by welding bulkheads in place. The frames for the watertight doors, one in each transverse bulkhead, were riveted in place. Above her deck, a bridge arose that would hold the asdic hut, radar and steering. Two racks from which depth charges could be rolled were welded to her stern. On each side, 100 feet from the stern, depth-charge throwers were riveted and welded into place. Ahead of the bridge, a raised round steel plate was readied to receive a 4-inch gun. Work went on continuously all over the ship except for several hours on the day her power plant was installed: two huge Scotch boilers and a three-stage reciprocating steam engine, which had taken 10,000 man-hours to build.

"The day the boilers were hoisted from the railroad siding that ran close to the berth where the hull was brought after the launching, all other work on her had to stop. We never had an accident," recalls MacLaughlin, "but moving it was dangerous work. If one of the cables of the Shear Legs snapped, it would have cut a man in two.

"We didn't lift the boilers and engines with a crane like the ones you see today building skyscrapers. Instead, we had something called a 'Shear Legs.' The Shear Legs consisted of two heavy steel posts that pivoted on the ground and were joined at the top by steel beams. Their only movement was from the vertical to overhanging the water (and thus over the corvette's hull, into which the Shear Legs could lower engines and boilers). The movement was controlled by a steel cable going to steam-driven winches well back on the dock. The railroad siding came under the Shear Legs," recalls MacLaughlin.

"And, of course, we didn't have walkie-talkies to communicate with the drive house. Instead, the foreman directing used hand signals. After making sure that everyone was clear, he'd twirl his fingers and the hoisting would begin; he used the baseball safe signal for 'stop.' If he wanted a bit more height, he'd tweet his thumb and forefinger together."

"Once the boiler or engine was hoisted, the winch man paid out the steel tackle, and the top of the Shear Legs would begin to pitch out over the hull of the ship. The hoist tackle would be paid out and the engine or boiler would start to sink into the hull. After it disappeared from view, men down in the hold manhandled it until it was over the fittings that had been drilled in huge blocks of steel. Then the word came up from below to lower it again. Their aim had to be perfect—there was maybe an eighth of an inch leeway," recalls MacLaughlin.

DECEMBER 13, 1941

- Three thousand five hundred miles east in Hamburg, workers at Blohm & Voss lay the keels for U-607 and U-608; U-600 is commissioned.
- Three thousand five hundred miles east in Hamburg, workers at Howadstwerke lay the keel for U-661.
- Three thousand five hundred miles east in Berlin in the German Reichstag, Adolf Hitler declares war against the United States of America.
- One thousand miles south in Washington, DC, US president Franklin D. Roosevelt asks Congress for a declaration of war against Germany.
- Eight thousand miles west, the Japanese attack Wake Island.

The cold wind whipping off the St. Lawrence carried away the last words of the centuries-old invocation, "May God bless this ship and all who sail in her," spoken by Commander L. J. M. Gauvreau, the naval officer in charge at Quebec. Led by their captain, Lieutenant John Willard Bonner, RCN, the officers and ratings who would serve on the newly commissioned HMCS *Charlottetown* marched onto the cold and darkened ship. It was a solemn moment, recalls Ray MacAuley, then an eighteen-year-old able seaman. He had joined the navy two weeks before work began on *Charlottetown*'s keel. "We knew that these same words had been spoken before thousands of American and British sailors, men just like us, men killed at Pearl Harbor and just two days earlier when Japanese dive-bombers sank HMS *Prince of Wales* and *Repulse*."

As the last member of the crew stepped off the gangplank, Bonner's ship came alive, throbbing as his engineers engaged her triple-steam reciprocating engine, powering the dynamos. Then lights—up in the bridge, above the hatchways, down the passageways. Moments later, the coxswain stationed at the mast ran up the commissioning pennant and the White Ensign. Two days later, fearing that *Charlottetown*, its equally new sister ship HMCS *Fredericton* and the Bangor minesweeper HMCS *Vegreville* would be locked in by the ice accumulating in the basin beneath the heights of Quebec, Commander Gauvreau ordered Bonner to lead the other two ships to Halifax.

The forty-six-year-old Bonner was a most unlikely warrior. He was a former RCMP captain who had spent not a little time pursuing "Uncle Iff" Skinner—Skinner, before becoming captain of HMCS *Arrowhead*, was a rum-runner from Newfoundland. And, like Lieutenant Commander Norman Smith of HMCS *Raccoon*, Bonner spent years commanding United Fruit ships. Ready to retire the year the war broke out, he entered the navy instead, taking command of *Charlottetown*'s sister ship, HMCS *Rimouski*. Bonner was also a devoted family man. His daughter, Marilyn Whyte, recalls the story of a physical exam during which Bonner was asked to remove his false teeth; Bonner replied to the stunned medical corpsman that the perfect teeth in his mouth were his own.

Bonner was a leader of the Presbyterian church in Halifax, where on occasion he preached. Though none of his sermons survive, they must have been somewhat unusual, for in addition to having an interest in Biblical prophecy—hardly in the mainstream of Presbyterian thought—Bonner was a Mason. As well, recalls his sister-in-law Grace Bonner, he was learned in the Scottish heritage of Cape Breton and was able to read and write Gaelic. A tantalizing inkling of the quality of Bonner's mind and temperament lies at the bottom of the last page of *Charlottetown*'s second logbook, which was taken off the ship sometime before its last escort patrol. After twenty-four lines of standard naval information—"15:15—Fog clearing slightly"; "21:00—98 revs"—in a cursive hand is the following:

And now, dear reader, turn to Book III to see what happened next

—a sentence that bespeaks a man very much at home in the genteel traditions of the eighteenth-century novel.[5]

The chain of command exists on small ships like corvettes as much as it does on great battleships. Bonner's orders were rarely issued directly to the ratings. Rather, if they concerned general operations of the ship, they were given to Lieutenant George Moors—who, like every other first lieutenant, was called No. 1—or to whichever other officer was the officer of the watch. Moors would then relay the order to the coxswain, who would then detail the ratings. If the order concerned either the engine room or the boilers, the captain spoke directly to the engineer, who then detailed ratings to carry out the order.

"But it wasn't the chain of command," recalls MacAuley, "that made *Charlottetown* a good ship. We had faith in Moors; he was a fair man. Mind you, we ratings knew we weren't in it for fun. We joined the navy to do a job, and we were serious about it. Still, there were times when Moors had to discipline, had to show he was a fair man.

"*Charlottetown* was a good ship because Bonner was a good captain. He set the tone. The rules were there and he expected us to follow them. He had pride in his ship and, though we hated all the chipping and painting he ordered when we were in port, we could tell from the fact that it was important to him that he had pride in it and us. While we were working-up in Halifax, Bonner took every opportunity to give us gunnery practice. The first few times it was kind of fun; after that we hated it. Gunnery practice in Halifax in January is a pretty cold experience, but he didn't just order it, he took an interest in it and complimented us when we improved.

"The captain was always 'the Captain.' He had the experience. Before the war he was a captain in the merchant marine, while most of us were only in our late teens or early twenties. But—and this is important to understanding how a ship actually works—Bonner took the time to know his crew. He had good people on the bridge. I was just an able seaman, but I had put in to train at the helm. Moors chose me. The first time I was up there I remember being very nervous. Neither Bonner nor Moors said anything, but they showed their confidence in a scared young kid by giving him the helm.

"Captains have to be stern, but we saw a sense of humour. After a local paper wrote that we were Unlucky 13—because there are thirteen letters in *Charlottetown* and we were commissioned on the thirteenth—Bonner told the crew that 'it would be the U-boats who were unlucky because of number thirteen.'"

After several short patrols immediately outside Halifax during the first days of March 1942, MacAuley's war began in earnest on March 13, when Bonner ordered the rudder hard to starboard and called for Slow Speed Astern. Immediately, even before the engine-room artificers began turning the large handles on the valves that would let more steam flow from the boilers to the engines, the engineer on duty grabbed the telegraph's handle and moved it forward until the arrow pointed to "Slow Speed," which instantaneously rang and registered "Slow Speed" on the bridge. Then a rating opened the steam valve, which let more steam into the engine. The increased steam pressure caused the eccentric crank, which ends with the propeller, to begin to turn. After some thirty seconds—maybe twenty revolutions of the propeller—*Charlottetown* was two or three feet off the jetty and Bonner called Full Stop and Let Go All Lines. Then, with his ship free from land, he called Slow Ahead, the start of eleven uneventful days escorting HMS *Severn*, a British submarine, to Delaware, picking up two others at New London, Connecticut, and bringing them back to Halifax.

At 6:40 a.m. on April 24, 1942, while escorting ON-84 on the North Atlantic three days out from Halifax, Bonner's asdic operator thought he heard a ping. Seconds after that, four men, including MacAuley and Able Seaman Léon-Paul Fortin, the *Charlottetown*'s sole French Canadian, were running for the 4-inch gun twenty feet from the ship's bow. MacAuley, the gun's layer rating, quickly climbed into the gunner's seat on the gun's port side; at the same time, the gun's trainer climbed into the seat on the starboard side. Together they aimed the gun, MacAuley's dials controlling its elevation and the other's its horizontal position. Fortin stood at the ready, awaiting the captain of the mount's order to put a shell and charge into the breech.

As they waited nervously for orders from the bridge, they added their eyes to those of the lookouts scanning the water in front of the ship.

One hundred and twenty-five feet behind MacAuley, *Charlottetown*'s torpedo ratings manned the depth-charge racks. Since depth charges weighed over 300 pounds and had to be manhandled onto the racks from storage lockers some thirty feet away, there were always ten unarmed depth charges on each rack, one each on the port and starboard throwers. As soon as Action Stations was called, the torpedo ratings undid the strap that held the depth charges in place. Then they waited—first for the order that would tell them at what depth to set the fuses, then for the order to fire them.

Even on the calmest days, the swells of the North Atlantic off Sable Island are more than enough to hide a trimmed-down U-boat; a periscope is nearly undetectable.

Then, at 7:05 a.m., the 14-kilocycle beam produced by the transducer housed in a dome in *Charlottetown*'s hull bounced back. Bonner ordered his helmsman to change course. Moments later, he ordered the torpedo ratings to fire.

Developed during World War I, the depth charge was an inexact weapon. The problems lay not so much with the hydrostatic fuse or charge as with the way it was fired and with the spread that could be achieved. Like a torpedo, an exploding depth charge produced a gas bubble that pushed outward with a force of 50,000 atmospheres—more than enough to rip through the U-boat's outer hull and then crush its protective pressure hull. When they failed to do so it was largely because they exploded too far from the U-boats they were aimed at.

In 1942, Canadian corvettes fired depth charges off their sides and from racks on their stern. Thus, unlike the most advanced RN corvettes, which were equipped with a "hedgehog," a mortar-like device that fired mortar-like pistols in front of the ship, RCN corvettes lost precious seconds as they manoeuvred over the U-boat by running over the wake left by the diving submarine. Once under, U-boats took vigorous evasive action by moving in any direction and by diving as deep as 700 feet, well below the 500-foot maximum depth setting of the depth charges available to the escorts in the St. Lawrence.

The geyser formed by the water pushed upward by the expanding gas bubble may have been spectacular, but from a tactical point of view it was worse than useless. The quickly moving gas caused innumerable perturbations that threw off asdic readings, making aiming the next spread even more difficult. Unseen shockwaves did more than simply ripple around the attacking ship. If the depth charge exploded shallowly enough and if the attacking ship was not moving fast enough, the shockwaves meant to destroy the U-boat could damage the ship that launched the depth charge; on September 6, 1942, *Truro*'s depth charges knocked out its asdic.

Bonner secured the ship from Battle Stations moments after the last geyser died and he saw the water littered with hundreds of dead fish—fish that moments earlier had been swimming in a school that had been picked up by the asdic unit.

Twenty hours later, at 2:48 a.m. on April 25, Action Stations rang out again after the asdic operator reported an echo bearing N 60 E, range 3,000 yards—fully 2,000 yards beyond the normal range at which a firm contact could be established. At 1,000 yards, the target was roughly 45° off *Charlottetown*'s port bow, at a right angle to Bonner's ship. Bonner ordered a hard turn to port. Moments later, as His Majesty's Canadian Ship steamed through "heavily churned" water that had been left as the U-boat dived, two depth charges set for 150 feet rolled off *Charlottetown*'s stern.

Seconds ticked by as the depth charges sank at a rate of 10 feet per second. Every 15 feet, the air in the fuse was compressed by the equivalent of 1 atmosphere of pressure. At 105 feet, the air was compressed by a factor of 7, effectively pushing the fuse toward the critical point. At 150 feet, the equivalent of just over 10 atmospheres of pressure, the fuse ignited, setting off 396 pounds of amatol or minol, generating an explosion equivalent to a torpedo.

By the light of the not-yet-set moon, Bonner's crew saw the geysers burst from the sea. Before the geysers collapsed, *Charlottetown* was plunged into darkness.

The ship's log—"The Asdic then went out of order, the steering jammed and the dynamo went out"—hardly captures either the tension or the fears that gripped the sixty men as damage-control parties fanned out across the ship. Bonner's mission was now no longer "the safe and timely arrival of the convoy," but survival.

Knowing that the U-boat's captain would soon come to periscope depth to see if the search had been broken off, and that if he caught *Charlottetown* dead in the water he'd undoubtedly torpedo it, Bonner ordered the manning of the auxiliary steering, located in the tiller flats in the stern between the depth-charge racks. He set a course for a mile away, hoping the darkness of the night would cloak *Charlottetown* while repairs were carried out.

The repairs took something less than an hour, for the ship's log reports both an asdic sweep and the dropping of another pattern of depth charges before 4:00 a.m. At 4:06 a.m. was still another pattern, this time over what the log records as a "doubtful echo." This second pattern was, however, incomplete: "One thrower failed to operate, due to a jammed impulse cartridge," and "the rails jammed after the second charge had been dropped." By 4:12 a.m., both "had been put in good order again."

Thirty-three minutes later, Bonner almost got another fix. "At 4:45 a voice speaking German was heard on the D/F set." Unfortunately, "there wasn't sufficient time to D/F the voice before it ceased." At daylight, Bonner recorded in his log, "nothing further being sighted[,] a course was set to rejoin the convoy" that had been guarded during the night by *Charlottetown*'s consort, the corvette HMCS *Kenagoni*.

The Board of Inquiry that sat in Halifax to investigate the engagement credited *Charlottetown* with having saved ON-84 from a U-boat attack. It reserved special praise for the asdic team for picking up the target at such a long range; 3,000 yards was at the far outside of the range expected from the *Charlottetown*'s 123 asdic.

Rear-Admiral G. C. Jones and Captain G. R. Miles (D), in charge of anti-submarine warfare, also made two criticisms, though. First, given the short interval between the initial sighting and the dropping of the charges, they wrote, "the initial pattern was set much too deep." They also criticized Bonner for going it alone: "No enemy sighting report either by rocket or radio was made until 2 hours after the initial attack. . . . Had *Kenagoni* been advised of the sighting and joined *Charlottetown* in a combined offensive, the chances of a 'kill' would have been much greater."[6]

SEPTEMBER 11, 1942

- Three thousand miles east in Hamburg, workers at Deutsche Werft AG lay the keel for U-533.
- Three thousand miles east in Bremen, U-196 is commissioned.
- Two hundred miles off Nova Scotia, the Canadian freighter SS *Cornwallis* is sunk by U-1230.

- Eight thousand five hundred miles southwest in New Guinea, Allied soldiers halt the Japanese advance at Owen Stanley Range.
- Four thousand five hundred miles east in Poland, 5,000 Jews are deported from the Warsaw Ghetto to the death camp at Treblinka.

When war came to their generation, James L. MacAuley's two eldest sons knew they'd have to fight. From their father, who had been so badly wounded in France that he could not take over the family farm after the Great War, they learned the horrors of the trenches. Ray's older brother, Horace, enlisted in the RCAF, serving most of the war as a radar technician in England.

For generations the MacAuleys had lived near Sussex, New Brunswick, a part of the world where neatly kept graveyards tell only part of a family's story. As often as not, the memorial for a young man gone is a name carved in a granite wall facing the sea.

As September 11 dawned, MacAuley had been in the Navy nine months, six of those at sea, and already he had his able seaman's papers and was training to be a helmsman.

Scheduled to take the helm at 8:00 a.m., he entered the bridge a few minutes early and was told by the officer of the watch that because *Charlottetown*'s consort, *Clayoquot*, was low on fuel, they wouldn't be zigzagging on their way back to Gaspé. After taking the helm, it took a moment for MacAuley to get the feel of the ship; the river, alternately lit by bright sunlight and shrouded in misty fog, was a little choppy as they passed six miles off Cap-Chat, the radar's oscilloscope confirming the dead-reckoning sighting taken by the officer of the watch. His legs splayed, his hands on the large polished wooden wheel, MacAuley looked ahead, listening for orders, slowly moving the helm an inch or two in response to the gentle roll of the ship as it steamed at 11 knots; moments later, like so many thousands of other men who fought their war by going down to the sea in ships, he was running for his life.

Ten minutes before MacAuley's duty began at eight bells, U-517's commander, Paul Hartwig, who had been cruising at periscope depth since first light, "sighted [a] steamer in BA 3911" off his port beam. Neither *Charlottetown*'s starboard lookouts nor her radar operator noticed the periscope between their ship and the shore off to the ship's starboard side; the devilish waters of the river also hid Hartwig from the ship's asdic. Three minutes later, U-517 "closed up action stations." Then, the order *"Los!"* and two torpedoes sped toward the "steamer."

As soon as he heard the clang of the torpedo doors closing, Hartwig began counting down the seconds, nervously waiting for the impact. At the same moment, *Leitender Ingenieur* (Chief Engineer) Helmut Martin moved to counter the effect on U-517 (a perceptible rise toward the surface) of the sudden loss of 4,800 kilograms of weight. Barely had the echo of the clang ended before he ordered the opening of the compensation ballast tanks closest to tubes I, II and VI. Four thousand eight hundred kilograms may not seem like much when measured against the U-517's 1,500 tons, but even the smallest loss, gain or change of weight distribution within a U-boat affected its trim and buoyancy. The cook made daily reports on both the weight of stocks used and from where in the boat stores were used. Even the weight of the garbage expelled through the torpedo tubes had to be precisely recorded. Martin ensured U-517's buoyancy by simultaneously blowing the main compensation of 4,800 kilograms and taking on an equal amount of water in the ballast and trim tanks closest to where each torpedo had been stored.

A scant fourteen seconds after Hartwig started his stopwatch—as Heagy made his way to the bridge to begin his radar watch, as Fortin began to settle into his watch on the gun platform, as Coder Russ Duff slept in his bunk, as Lieutenant W. A. Johnston slept in the sick bay, as P. Miller in the engine room noted that the ship's propeller was turning at 118 revolutions per minute, as Telegraphist Gerald Martin settled into the ship's wireless shack, as Leading Telegraphist Edmond Robinson made his way to the mess, as Able Seaman John Kinch asked for his plate of sausages— the steel plates McCorquodale's men had riveted into place on *Charlottetown*'s starboard quarter were torn asunder, first by one torpedo and then by another.

The first torpedo hit well behind the engine room. The blast literally lifted the 1,050-ton ship by the stern. The coxswain and two other men who were in the tiller flats died before the shattered hull dropped down, 30° to port from its true course. Seconds after the white-hot gas bubble that lifted the ship decayed, the second torpedo detonated and another gas bubble was born. The blast destroyed the engine room, killing Engine Room Artificer (ERA) Donald Todd, the chief engineer and one other man, and ensured *Charlottetown*'s quick fate: it destroyed the ship's aft watertight bulkhead.

"No one on the bridge saw a thing. The first we knew of it," recalls MacAuley, "was when a tremendous shudder ran through the ship. We all felt it—felt it move with our bodies. But I could also feel the destruction of the stern through the helm. One moment we were steaming, the helm answering, and the next moment we shook and a tremendous roar washed over us from behind and the helm went dead and all power [was] lost, including the telegraph to the engine room. It's hard to separate the two hits. For a split second, we could tell that the ship had been shoved off her course and was pulling toward the stern as tons of water poured in. And then another blast, this one from our right, and then everything began sliding toward the starboard and we saw the steam shooting up from the hole in the side of the ship."

The second torpedo struck immediately beneath Fortin's watch station on the starboard gun platform. The first shockwave blew him off his feet. The second sent him flying off the gun platform. Before he fell onto the hard steel deck—a fall that broke his arm—his boots flew off his feet.

Seconds after the explosions, Captain Bonner, who was in his quarters off the ladder to the bridge, came running onto the bridge. Immediately he instructed Moors to lead the Abandon Ship operation.

A mile to MacAuley's port, farther out on the river, *Clayoquot*'s crew watched in horror. Within seconds of hearing the first explosion, the captain, Lieutenant H. E. Lade, ran to his bridge, arriving in time to see debris still falling. As the men on *Charlottetown* ran for their lives, Lade rang Action Stations and ordered a hard turn to starboard. Then he rang for full speed and began a zigzag course designed to take him beyond *Charlottetown*'s port quarter—to where he suspected the submarine was.

Aboard the dying ship, Heagy struggled through the steam and debris to his evacuation station at the starboard boat. By the time he got there, an officer had taken charge and was handing out lifebelts and loading men into the boat, which had been swung out on the davits.

Bewildered by being thrown across the deck, Fortin soon realized that his ship had been torpedoed, that it had taken a dangerous list and that he'd left his lifebelt in the mess deck. He started to run for his Abandon Ship station, the portside lifeboat. As he ran past the funnel, he remembered an old locker filled with an older type of life preserver than the one he'd left in the mess deck. He took one and continued toward the portside boat.

"I found the group I was assigned to desperately trying to push the lifeboat outward so that they could lower it into the water," he recalled years later. "As I rushed forward to help them, I realized that my forearm was fractured."

Precious seconds ticked by. Tons of heavy fuel oil spread out from the stricken ship, covering the water. Thousands of tons of water flooded in, dragging *Charlottetown* down by the stern. Two minutes, and the boat deck, normally twenty feet above the water, was awash.

Realizing he'd never get the second boat launched as the oily water surged over their feet, Bonner ordered the launching of the Carley floats and told his men, "The hell with it, everybody in the water." Fortin and the other men at his station, Bonner excepted, then jumped into the oil- and wreckage-strewn water. As he tried to swim away from the boat, which he knew was about to plunge to the bottom of the St. Lawrence, Fortin first had to struggle out of the duffle coat that was weighing him down.

"We needed to get the Carley float closer," recalls MacAuley, "so Lieutenant Moors asked for a volunteer to swim for it. I was a pretty good swimmer, and with my lifebelt on, I dove into the oil-covered water—it was sickening—and swam to the Carley float so I could get out the paddles and stabilize it for the other men. Everyone too moved quickly. The ship was going down and we didn't want to get caught in the whirlpool we knew would follow.

"I must have been on the float for a minute. I had time to ship the paddles and a few other men had gotten onto the float's ring. There were also a few men in the webbing in the water in the middle of the float. And then there were six huge explosions in the water."

The explosions were not from Hartwig's eels. Rather, they were the last moments of six bubbles, each pushing out at 50,000 atmospheres, caused by *Charlottetown*'s own depth charges. The exact reason why they exploded is unknown. Since *Charlottetown* was not at Action Stations, the depth charges on the depth-charge rack should have been set to safety; those in the locker would not have had their hydrostatic fuses in place. Lieutenant Moors was in the water when the depth charges went off, and the force crushed a Ronson lighter in his jacket pocket (Ronson replaced the lighter). Moors told the board of inquiry that he thought the torpedo that destroyed *Charlottetown*'s stern may have fractured the pistols (fuses), causing them to detonate even though they were set to safety.[7]

"I went right up and down," Frank Dillon, who was swimming toward a Carley float, told a reporter. "How high? It could have been 5 feet or 500 feet. I doubt that it was 500. It could have been 25 or 30 feet, dear knows. When I came down, I naturally went under and then came up. I swam up, I remember that. I did not lose consciousness for some reason. I did feel the pain. And I swallowed a lot of oil."

"Our float was a few hundred yards away," recalls Heagy. "It was a hideous sight. The ship was going down, the sea was covered with oil, men were swimming for the Carley floats, and then all of a sudden the sea erupted beneath the men when the depth charges went off. We felt the tremendous vibration and saw the men in the water. After the roar of the explosions died down, we could hear the men yelling.

"The water started to boil. I was on the float, not in the water, so I felt the ripples and heard the explosions, but I wasn't injured. Some of the men must have been blown out of the water. Others were bleeding from the mouth. Those that I was able to get into the float were hurt inside. Of course we were all covered in oil and we were choking from the fumes and the oil that got into our mouths."

Dillon was one of the first to get to Heagy's float after the depth charges exploded. Dillon "helped me get men onto the float and made a point of trying to keep up our morale by telling everyone that 'there's better days ahead,'" says Heagy.

Fortin was in the roiling water. One of the lucky ones, the blast broke one of his legs but didn't injure him internally. Somehow he continued to swim.

Hartwig heard the blasts and watched the agony unfolding in the waters off the small village of Cap-Chat. "It's a poor ship indeed. A lot of their sailors were killed by their own depth charges. Nobody could help them," he told his crew.[8]

In the last moments before *Charlottetown* plunged to the bottom, still another tragic scene was played out. Able Seaman Charles "Judy" Garland, who, according to Moors's report, "showed especial gallantry in standing by and passing out life jackets from the locker, giving them all away when he himself could not swim," found himself trapped on the wreck. Having refused to leave the ship without Screech, the ship's mascot (which, ironically enough, was safely on a Carley float), Garland clawed his way toward the bow as the ship heeled up before its final plunge. He vanished from sight when, just before the plunge, another explosion—probably caused by cold river water washing over the boilers—opened the rest of the shattered hull.

"Once she heeled up," MacAuley recalls, "she just blew apart and vanished beneath the waves. The final explosion killed Captain Bonner, blowing his body far enough away from the vortex that it was not pulled to the bottom of the St. Lawrence."

"As long as there is life, there is hope," recalled Fortin. He yelled for help. But none came. "It seemed I was alone in the whole Gulf of St. Lawrence. This solitude was frightening."

His arms and legs began to go numb, and so did his mind, as he struggled in the 40°F (4°C) water, where survival time is counted in minutes.

Just as those minutes ticked away to an end, Moors's overloaded boat found him. "Take me aboard. If you don't take me aboard, I'll let myself go." His mates took him aboard.

Hartwig's laconic entry in his war diary—"1300–1600 [hrs.] continual depth-charge explosions or ammunition exploding on board the steamer"— gives little indication of the action that swirled 120 metres above him.

At 8:15 a.m. Lade's hydrophone officer gave him the information he wanted: a submarine bearing 150°, range 300 yards. Seconds later, three depth charges were fired, each set for 150 feet. Too shallow to damage U-517, the explosions damaged *Clayoquot*'s wireless transmitter, which delayed the sending of an attack report but did not materially alter the counterattack.

Six minutes later, Lade's anti-submarine officer reported another echo: bearing 340°, range 1,400 yards. Although he lost contact 100 yards from his target area, which led him to incorrectly assume that the U-boat was 50 to 100 feet below the surface, Lade pressed the attack, firing five depth charges.

Then, after sighting *Charlottetown*'s rafts and lifeboat, Lade ordered his helmsmen to steer a careful course into the heart of the floating wreckage. Before cutting his engines, Lade circled the rafts so that his asdic operator could perform the widest possible sweep. Assured that there was no contact, he ordered Full Stop, and the men on his boat deck readied to climb down the grappling nets to help the oil-covered survivors aboard.

A moment later, Lade's asdic operator gained another contact. Immediately, the anti-submarine officer ordered that the depth-charge throwers be readied. Realizing that, where they were, the charges would explode too close to *Charlottetown*'s already blasted survivors, Lade belayed that order and instead ordered Full Speed and a course designed to take him around the survivors.

"Despite our disappointment at not being picked up," MacAuley recalls, "we cheered *Clayoquot* when we realized she was going back into the fight against the German boat that sank us."

Whether because of the bathyscaphe effect, the turbulence caused by *Clayoquot*'s own propellers or Hartwig's decision to lie still a hundred metres below, Lade's asdic lost the contact shortly after *Clayoquot*'s propellers drove the ship away from the wreckage-strewn waters.

Shortly before 11 a.m., Lade called off the search when, through the fog, his lookouts spotted *Charlottetown*'s rafts again.

"We were in pretty rough shape by then," recalls MacAuley. "The water was cold, so we kept switching men from the wooden sides of the raft to the basket in the middle and to the sides. We tried to keep the worst-injured as stable as we could. But we were all shivering. The oil covering our faces stopped us from seeing it, but I'm sure that all of our lips had turned blue."

"The water was covered in thick oil and wreckage," recalls Murphy. "The men were on Carley floats and some were in the whaler, most covered in thick oil. To get them, we had to throw a Jacobs ladder over the side. Some were able to climb up themselves and some had to be helped by men who climbed down the ladder to help the most injured aboard. It was a horrible scene—we'd been together with those men many times.

"I knew one of her stokers, a guy called John Grant, from Halifax like me. He'd been injured from the explosions. He was covered with oil and badly injured internally from the depth charges. The sick-berth attendant treated him and gave him morphine to ease his suffering. I found out later that he'd died. It was hard to hear about because he was a stoker like me," recalls Murphy.

Not far away, though hidden by the fog that had gathered, Lieutenant Moors's lifeboat made a gruesome discovery amidst the wreckage that bubbled to the surface after the ship went down: their captain's body, floating upright in his life jacket, his face horribly distorted from the detonations beneath him. Years later, James Lamb, who commanded *Charlottetown*'s sister ship HMCS *Trail*, recounted the awesome moments that then played out amidst stunned and dying men:

With a gentleness surprising in a big man, George [Moors] lifted the slight body into the boat, where it was laid out with awkward reverence along the bottom board by youngsters awed at the nearness of their dead captain. They set out again then, rowing as best they could for the distant shore, but it quickly became apparent that something would have to be done if the oarsmen were to find room to row in the overcrowded boat. Accordingly, George lifted Bonner's body back over the side, and others helped him tie the dead man's life jacket to the rudder of the boat by a piece of rope. Now that room had been made, the oars could be worked properly, and course was resumed for the shore with the captain's body towing astern at the end of its line.

The corpse, floating upright, proved a difficult tow; the men strained at the oars to move the boat, ever so slowly, determined to save themselves and the body of their captain.

Bonner, in death as in life, proved mindful of the traditional captain's dictum that put the welfare of one's men first. After an hour of ever more difficult towing, the rudder was pulled right off the boat, and with its attached body, floated off astern. Willard Bonner, his last service done, disappeared in the mists forever.

Shortly afterward, Lade found Moors's boat and, after running down one last echo and firing a pattern of five depth charges (the blast of which damaged Lade's own asdic and gyrocompass), *Clayoquot* set a course for Gaspé, carrying fifty-eight survivors of the second of His Majesty's Canadian Ships to be sunk in four days.[9]

By the time *Clayoquot* reached Gaspé at 2:40 p.m. on September 12, men like MacAuley and Heagy, though still stained black with oil, were able to walk the gangplank back to land unaided. The ship's leading telegraphist, Edmond Robinson, collapsed on the jetty and died several days later from his injuries. Others, such as Fortin and Thomas Macdonald, ERA, were carried off and taken first to Commander German's house on the base. There German's wife, Dorothy, cared for them on the floor of the living room. Later, James Essex recalls, Commander German ordered that the men whom he knew to be dying from their internal injuries be taken to Hôtel-Dieu hospital in the town of Gaspé. One, Able Seaman Donald Bowser, was carried off dead.

Bowser's funeral, the first for a Canadian serviceman killed in Canada since the Riel Rebellion in 1885, was the one to be held in Gaspé, the home port of four Canadian warships sunk during the Battle of the St. Lawrence.

St. Paul's Anglican Church, where the fifty-four survivors of Hartwig's torpedoes and more than a hundred of their fellow sailors and soldiers from the bases that dotted the tip of the Gaspé Peninsula gathered on a beautiful mid-September day to pay their final respects, shares none of the ornateness of its more famous sister in London, the capital of Bowser's native England. Almost Calvinist in its simplicity, St. Paul's is located on the western arm of a spit of land that juts out from the town of Gaspé. At fifty feet, its spire had been used by three generations of fishermen as a sighting point.

When MacAuley and his shipmates entered the church, the sun was streaming in through the twenty-foot-high windows. At the end of the nave, before the pulpit, under the cupola beneath the spire, was their shipmate's casket, draped with the White Ensign. At each corner of the flag-draped casket was a sailor dressed in regulation blues—a sharp contrast with the dungarees and civilian jackets that had quickly been gathered up to clothe *Charlottetown*'s survivors. Each of the sailors in the honour guard stood three feet away from the casket's corners, their heads bowed, their polished rifles barrel to the ground, their white-gloved hands clasped over their rifles' butts.

The words spoken over Bowser's coffin—used for centuries by the Church of England to celebrate death and eternal life in "the living Church of Christ Jesus"—were as familiar to the sailors who heard them as they are foreign to most of us today:

> I am the resurrection and the life, saith the Lord: he that believeth in me, though he were dead, yet shall he live: and whosoever liveth and believeth in me, shall never die. . . .
> I know that my Redeemer liveth, and that he shall stand in the latter day upon the earth: and though this body be destroyed, yet shall I see God: whom I shall see for myself, mine eyes shall behold, and not as a stranger.

No doubt, for many of the eighteen-, nineteen- and twenty-year-old men, the words of the Book of Common Prayer had often been little more than rote sayings. Now, however, through these words and the prayer for the burial of the dead at sea—

> Unto Almighty God we commend the soul of our brother departed, and we commit his body to the deep; in sure and certain hope of the Resurrection unto eternal life, through our Lord Jesus Christ; at whose coming in glorious majesty to judge the world, the sea shall give up her dead; and the corruptible bodies of those who sleep in him shall be

changed, and made like unto his glorious body; according to the mighty working whereby he is able to subdue all things unto himself.

—young men mourned their captain and their shipmates who never got off the hull built at the very headwaters of the St. Lawrence, those whose bodies were blasted as they thrashed in her waters, and the thirty-eight men from *Raccoon*. None of these men would ever rest in a proper grave.

CHAPTER FIVE

WHAT CYRIL PERKIN SAW

SEPTEMBER 15 AND 16, 1942

SS *Saturnus, Inger Elizabeth* and *Joannis*

Shadow by shadow, stripped for fight
The lean black cruisers search the sea.
Night-long their level shafts of light
Revolve, and find no enemy.
Only they know each leaping wave
May hide the lightning, and their grave.

—ALFRED NOYES

The decision to close the St. Lawrence to transoceanic shipping had far-reaching logistical and economic implications for Canada's war effort. Most important, it meant severing Montreal, Canada's largest port, from the convoy system that had been carefully built up since the outbreak of war in 1939. The convoy system was much more than the thousands of ships that assembled by the score in Halifax's Bedford Basin before braving Dönitz's wolfpacks on the stormy North Atlantic. It began in the nickel mines of Sudbury, on the wheat fields of the Prairies and at the ends of aircraft and tank assembly lines in Ontario and Quebec. It included tens of thousands of rail cars choreographed to be unloaded and sent back across the country. Between the railroad cars and the ships, hundreds of shipping clerks and thousands of stevedores took the lead in this complicated dance. The clerks were responsible for making sure that the cargo was stowed so that cargo for the first port of call could be unloaded without unloading the entire ship. The stevedores did the loading; they were the men who packed tons of TNT into dark holds. They were the men who knew how to load a ship with ten thousand tons of iron ore so that during a storm the ore wouldn't shift and break the ship's back. Any disruption in this complicated system could cause logistical chaos.

Even though the U-boat offensive in the St. Lawrence had meant adding another thousand miles of convoying to Canada's responsibilities, Naval Control of Shipping considered the Port of Montreal an important logistical asset. The city's ready supply of skilled labour ensured that merchant ships could be repaired faster than in Halifax's congested yards and dry docks. Montreal may have been ice-bound for several months a year, but the time lost to Father Winter was less than the time lost because of Maritime labour patterns in Halifax, Sydney and Saint John. (Many stevedores returned to their farms and fishing boats for seven months of the year.) Accordingly, in 1940 and 1941, Montreal recorded an average turn-around time of less than four days as compared with up to two weeks in Halifax. Added to this efficiency was the fact that guns and mines, wood and iron ore and aircraft, trucks and tanks loaded in Montreal did not have to be hauled six hundred miles by rail to the Maritime ports.

Though ships assembled by the score in Halifax's Bedford Basin, most merchant ships were not loaded at this most famous eastern Canadian port, home to both the Western Local Escort Force and the Mid-Ocean Escort Force. The forces consisted of 115 Canadian and 23 British warships. The docks were so full that in 1941, when *Charlottetown* arrived in Halifax, it tied up on the water side of the Free French corvette *Alysse*. Halifax's repair yards were so busy that when the Canadian navy decided to upgrade the corvette fleet's asdic and radar, it took six months to do the work.

Second call on Halifax's dockside facilities went to the "troopers." The largest piers, 21 and 22, were all but reserved for *Queen Mary* and *Queen Elizabeth*, each of which sailed time and again with more than 15,000 troops aboard. Third call went to small refrigerated ships, whose cargoes of meat were hauled by rail to dockside, and to small tankers that could be turned around fast enough to be assigned to the next convoy heading out.

In 1940, the first full year of the war, Montreal, Quebec City and other St. Lawrence River ports loaded 596 ships; a year later the number had jumped to 704. In 1942 the number dropped to 278. In 1943 it fell by another 100 to 178, a number that includes scores of naval ships built along the St. Lawrence.[1]

Canada's maritime ports were not, however, capable of absorbing "even half the customary trade of Montreal"; they became, according to naval historian Gordon N. Tucker, "congested and inefficient." Trade was diverted from the traditional east–west corridor, established by Sir John A. Macdonald's National Policy and the CPR, to a north–south axis. By 1943, Canadian arms, food and other supplies were being shipped from New York, New Orleans, Savannah and even Galveston, Texas.

The economic dislocation caused by the drop in shipping can be measured by the decline in tonnage of foreign-going cargo being loaded at St. Lawrence River ports. In 1941 Montreal's stevedores loaded 4,078,070 tons of foreign-going cargo; in 1942 the tonnage had dropped to 1,600,935 tons before falling further to 1,089,447 tons in 1943. Quebec City dropped from about 320,000 in 1941 to 142,308 in 1942. The economic fallout of this new north–south axis created a political headache for King's wartime government.

Quebec's premier, Adélard Godbout, complained that Quebec was being shortchanged by the federal government. On March 4, 1943, Onésime Gagnon, member of the Quebec legislative assembly for Matane, charged that Montreal and Quebec City had been harmed by the closure of the St. Lawrence in 1942 and would "suffer enormous prejudice" if the river remained closed in 1943. Five days later, his Union Nationale colleague from the riding of Îles-de-la-Madeleine, Hormidas Langlais, protested against the continued closure of the St. Lawrence: "This decision caused considerable misery among the population, it would further harm the value of the ports [of Montreal and Quebec City] and benefit those of St. John and Halifax," which he went on to point out were in Minister Macdonald's part of the country (Macdonald represented a Halifax riding). A few days later, in Parliament in Ottawa, Sasseville Roy claimed that shifting the shipping of war material to rail traffic cost the Canadian taxpayer an extra $1 million a year. Even after the river was reopened in 1945 and traffic in Montreal and Quebec City rebounded (to 4,904,744 and 544,280 tons, respectively), the issue did not go away. Maurice Duplessis, who had defeated Godbout a year earlier, reiterated Gagnon's and Langlais's 1943 charges. On March 7, 1945, Duplessis petitioned the federal government to declare the Port of Quebec City a "free port."

But in the days that followed the September 9, 1942, decision to close the St. Lawrence, establishing secure coastal convoys was the more immediate concern to the Naval Control of Shipping office in Quebec City. Shepherding those ships that could not be loaded at other ports to Montreal or Quebec City and then leading them safely out of the gulf was the first priority. In order to provide better air coverage, albeit from training aircraft based on Prince Edward Island, convoys were routed south of the Îles de la Madeleine. To replace the seventeen corvettes that were being sent to take part in Operation Torch, the invasion of North Africa, Admiral Murray attached two older British destroyers, HMS *Salisbury* and *Witherington*, to the Gulf Escort Force. As well, on September 15, the Commanding Officer Atlantic Coast (COAC) received the recommendation that fixed convoy routes be abandoned because they were too predictable. Evidence for this accumulated even as the COAC was receiving the recommendation. Within hours of this signal having been sent, Hartwig torpedoed the USS *Laramie* and SS *Saturnus* and *Inger Elizabeth*; a day later Hoffmann destroyed SS *Joannis*.

SEPTEMBER 15, 1942

- Three thousand five hundred miles east in Bremen, workers lay the keel for U-863.
- Five thousand five hundred miles east in Russia, fighting rages in the main railway station in Stalingrad.

- Four thousand five hundred miles east in Ukraine, members of the Jewish community from Kalushare are deported to Belzec death camp; hundreds of Jews in Kamenka are murdered.

Three hundred and nine feet long with a beam of 30 feet and a displacement of 1,090 tons, HMS *Salisbury* was the largest warship in the Gulf of St. Lawrence on September 15, 1942. Its crew, including its commander, Lieutenant M. H. R. Crichton, RNR, were originally slated for HMS *Cameron* but had been transferred to *Salisbury* after Göring's Stuka dive-bombers destroyed *Cameron* in dry dock on December 15, 1940.

"We'd heard about the sinkings in the St. Lawrence," says Signalman

Cyril Perkin, then a twenty-one-year-old Cornishman whose two older brothers were also in the Royal Navy, "but after what we'd seen on the North Atlantic, the St. Lawrence, especially in the beautiful late autumn, sounded like a vacation. At the beginning of 1942 we twice escorted the USS *Wasp* as she delivered Hurricanes to Malta. We got lucky because we weren't attacked. But they were very tense trips—constant danger from U-boats and aircraft—and we knew from the destruction of the *Cameron* what dive-bombers could do to a ship."

Before those missions, Perkin's ship spent almost two years on the North Atlantic run. "We were based on the River Clyde in Scotland and would range far out into the Atlantic to pick up convoys. When we weren't firing depth charges, we were picking up ravaged convoys. You could always tell when there'd been a terrible battle because the hulls of the ships would still be black with oil and the escort ships would be filled with survivors and signal us that they were low on fuel."

"Our time in the St. Lawrence really did begin with a milk run," he recalls. "Before being sent on our first escort patrol, we were given liberty in Prince Edward Island. I remember us going into a store to buy some milk and then the lot of us sitting on the sidewalk drinking it straight from the bottle. By that point, we hadn't seen or tasted any milk for more than three years."

The immediate reason for assigning *Salisbury* to the Gulf Escort Force was Prime Minister King's decision to agree to Churchill's request for corvettes to take part in Operation Torch. As well, Admiral Murray hoped that, led by a warship equipped with up-to-date anti-submarine electronics and attack systems, the Gulf Escort Force might be able to reproduce the success other forces were beginning to have in the North Atlantic.[2]

On June 16, ONS-102's escorts, led by HMCS *Restigouche*, fought off an attack by five U-boats. Dönitz attributed the escort's success to both aggressive Allied patrolling and the inexperience of several of the U-boat captains. In St. John's, Murray attributed the success of the largely Canadian escort force to the fact that the larger escorts were equipped with shipborne HF/DF, which allowed them to plot the U-boats as they were radioing their positions to Lorient prior to the attack. In late August, though they could not prevent every U-boat attack, the escorts of ONS-122, led by HMS *Viscount*, used their 271 radar—which allowed the escorts to spot the U-boats while they were still beyond the convoy's escort screen—to break up thirteen attacks on the convoy.[3] No doubt Murray hoped that perhaps one or two 271-equipped escorts could turn the tide in the St. Lawrence.

Though *Salisbury* was decades older than *Arrowhead,* the lead escort of SQ-36 until *Salisbury* joined the convoy on the fifteenth, the British ship's asdic and radar were a generation ahead of its Canadian consort's. "Jock" Smith and his fellow asdic operators aboard *Arrowhead* had to manually rotate the ship's asdic transducer in what amounted to five-degree increments. To ensure complete coverage, they had to turn the wheel connected to the transducer in the dome behind the bow ten degrees forward toward the bow or stern, then five degrees backward to the original position, then ten degrees forward (or backward). *Salisbury*'s asdic rotated automatically. But the bathyscaphe effect twenty miles off the eastern tip of the Gaspé Peninsula nullified this advantage. Because *Salisbury*'s 271 radar broadcast in 10-centimetre waves, it was able to pick up much smaller objects than was *Arrowhead*'s 286 radar, which used wavelengths of 1.4 metres: the smaller a radar's wavelengths, the smaller the object it can pick up. Hartwig's tactics after spotting SQ-36 at noon local time vitiated *Salisbury*'s radar's advantage.

Hartwig followed the same procedure he'd used with such devastating efficiency a week earlier when he sank three of QS-33's ships in thirty seconds. Rather than attacking at once, he stayed submerged and ran ahead of the convoy, positioning himself so that it would run over him. Just before 2:30 p.m., the convoy commodore signalled a 3° change of course to 330° NW, which, Hartwig recorded in his war diary, put him "outside the [main body of the] convoy on its starboard [right] side." To Hartwig's port, 400 metres away, ran *Salisbury,* its radar operating and its lookouts, including Cyril Perkin on the bridge, scanning the water.

Had Hartwig attacked at night, as he had on July 3 when he destroyed SS *Donald Stewart* up in the Strait of Belle Isle, chances are U-517 would have been partially surfaced. Had he been partially surfaced, not only would Perkin have been likely to see him, but *Salisbury*'s radar would surely have caught him, even though a full sweep took almost two minutes. Had this attack occurred a year later, SQ-36's other escort ships would have been equipped with centimetric radar and at least one would likely have picked him up.[4]

But at 1:30 p.m. on September 15, 1942, Hartwig's periscope was hidden from *Salisbury*'s lookouts by the shadows and wash of the convoy's own ships. *Salisbury*'s radar was unable to distinguish an object as small as a periscope—especially one only a couple of hundred metres off her starboard bow—from among all the other readings and echoes generated by twenty-one merchant ships and seven escorts. What Hartwig called his "sixth sense, like a tiger in a jungle," served him well; he came to periscope depth "just as the OAS air patrol had flown out ahead of the convoy."[5] It returned forty minutes after he "fire[d] off a salvo of four torpedoes at 2 overlapping steamers in the second formation" on what Perkin remembers as a beautiful late summer day.

At 1:38 p.m., as *Salisbury* steamed one mile to the convoy's starboard, Perkin, who had been on watch for almost two and a half hours, had just completed another sweep toward the bow. "It was exhausting work, looking through the binoculars, sweeping forward methodically, pausing ever so slowly over a swell to see if behind it was a periscope or the churning water of a torpedo. As soon as the fo'c'sle came into my view," he recalls, "I slowed, allowing my sweep to pass just over the bow, where it intersected with the lookout's on the other side of the bridge. Then I started my sweep back."

A second or two before Perkin began to turn once again toward his starboard side, two torpedoes sped away from Hartwig's U-boat 120 metres away.

One might have broken surface and crashed into cliffs south of Cap-des-Rosiers. The other blasted a hole in the Norwegian freighter SS *Inger Elizabeth*, the lead ship of the sixth column.

"It happened in an instant," recalls Perkin. "I was sweeping toward the stern, and the merchant ship had just come into focus. It was only in my field of vision for just a moment. But in that moment, that exact moment, it was torpedoed. I saw the flash and a geyser, but what was even more amazing was that I saw the ship literally jump up."

Within seconds, *Salisbury*'s officer of the watch, Lieutenant Wilson, rang Action Stations and Captain Crichton was on the bridge. Two miles ahead of the convoy, aboard *Arrowhead*, Captain Skinner rang for Full Speed and turned back toward the convoy.

Before Skinner received instructions—remain in front of the convoy and continue carrying out an anti-submarine sweep—the lookouts aboard SS *Saturnus*, a 2,741-ton Dutch steamship, were yelling to their bridge. The portside lookout had seen a periscope, something for the DEMS gunners to aim at. The starboard lookout spotted torpedoes 400 yards away—and closing.

Captain Jacob William Korthagan ordered a hard turn to port and rang for Full Speed. It wasn't enough. At 1:30 p.m., torpedoes "hit the stern about propeller depth," Korthagan reported. P. Kool, a gunner manning the aft 4-inch gun, vanished as hundreds of almost half-inch steel plates, riveted to I-beams and ribs weighing as much as ten tons, disintegrated.

Kool was the third man to die in less time than it took Perkin to complete his lookout sweep. The first two had died as *Inger Elizabeth*'s engine room was turned into a fireball three minutes earlier. A fourth aboard *Inger Elizabeth* drowned during the otherwise orderly evacuation of the ship.

While survivors of both ships were running for their lifeboats,[6] for the first time in the Battle of the St. Lawrence DEMS gunners went into action. Lookouts aboard another Dutch ship, SS *Llangollen*, and aboard the two British ships SS *Cragpool* and *Janetta* spotted Hartwig's periscope. Immediately, the three ships' gun layers and trainers began aiming their 3- and 4-inch guns. Had they been on land and firing at a stationary target, wind and barometric pressure would have been the only major factors to take into account. A strong wind could push a large shell as much as fifteen yards off target; changes in barometric pressure could result in over- or undershooting a target by hundreds of yards. But naval gunners also had the relative courses and speed of their own ships and their targets to take into account.

Had their lookouts spotted a conning tower or trimmed-down submarine 1,000 to 4,000 yards away, the gun layers would have used their handheld Cotton rangefinders to determine the range of the gun. To aim at a periscope a couple of hundred yards away, they depressed their guns' barrels and judged by eye. As gun layers turned the cranks that depressed their guns so that they would be shooting as low as possible, gun trainers looked through small mounted telescopes and turned cranks that moved the gun from left to right. And while the gun layers and trainers were doing their

Survivors of the SS *Nicoya* coming ashore on May 12, 1942.

Sandy Beach at HMCS *Fort Ramsay*, Gaspé, Quebec.

HMCS *Drummondville*, the first RCN ship to engage the enemy
in the Battle of the St. Lawrence.

Lieutenant C. Ian Tate in the newly opened wardroom
of HMCS *Fort Ramsay* in the summer of 1942.

The corvette HMCS *Arrowhead*. In the eighteen hours beginning at 11 p.m. on September 6, 1942, it saw four merchantmen and HMCS *Raccoon* go down.

HMCS *Arrowhead*'s asdic operator Geoffrey Smith; note the size of the depth charge below his right arm.

SS *Donald Stewart* sunk by by U-517 on September 3, 1942.

HMCS *Raccoon*, formerly
the yacht *Holonia*.

U-165 (Eberhard Hoffman) cruising on
the surface of Canadian waters in the
late summer of 1942.

SS *Oakton*, Ted Read's ship.

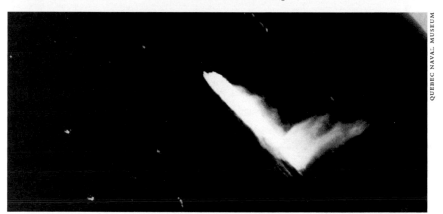

An unsuccessful Eastern Air Command attack on U-517 (Paul Hartwig).

The launching of the corvette HMCS *Charlottetown* on September 10, 1941.
This launch was watched by young Francis MacLaughlin.

The only Nazi torpedo to strike Canada, at St. Yvon, Quebec.

The aft section of the torpedo that ran aground at St. Yvon, Quebec; note the two propellers.

The ferry SS *Caribou*: on October 14, 1942, 136 men, women and children drowned when U-69 torpedoed her.

The crew of HMCS *Magog*.

The frigate HMCS *Magog* in dry dock after being torpedoed; note that the aft bulkhead survived the blast.

The corvette HMCS *Shawinigan*, the last of His Majesty's Royal Canadian Navy ships to be sunk in the Battle of the St. Lawrence, November 25, 1944.

"Kurt," the German automated weather station set up in Labrador.

The plotting room at Naval Service Headquarters in Ottawa.

jobs, the breech worker took off the safety and assured that the contact fire switch was set to "on." Then, after warning everyone to step back, the gun layer pulled the trigger. Nanoseconds later, 3- and 4-inch shells were hurtling toward the periscope.

None of the three DEMS crews expected their first shell to hit the periscope. Indeed, the periscope was not their real target—what they wanted to hit was the top of the conning tower beneath the water. Normally the first shell overshot. Then, as the gun layer rating made a few quick mental calculations and the gun trainer adjusted the gun for deflection, the breech worker opened the breech, expelling the spent casing. Barely was it out before he was ramming another shell, handed to him by the loading number (a merchant seaman who trained with the DEMS crews), into the breech.

"The whole procedure, from spotting to shooting, took a few seconds," says Max Reid, who served as a gun layer in Canadian and Norwegian merchant ships. "We were supposed to fire a spotting round and wait for the splash, make corrections and continuing firing, trying first to bracket the target. In reality, when faced with an enemy for the first time, you got as many rounds as possible into the air and made corrections after the first rounds landed. A good crew could get off twenty-five rounds a minute."

Though none of their shots hit the periscope, their aim was good enough to force Hartwig to reverse his course and, after a run of 2,800 yards, dive.

Five minutes later Captain Crichton had his contact: "Range 250 yards, inclination slight closing." His orders were textbook—one pattern of five charges set to 50 metres.

Before they could explode, Asdic Rating Smith, aboard *Arrowhead*, which was in position ahead of the convoy, called out: "Target 2,500 yds, no doppler, target steady." Thinking that Smith's asdic was pinging off a convoy vessel, his anti submarine officer, Crockette, told him to disregard.

"Even though I'd been told disregard," Smith recalls, "I was so certain that it was a viable contact, I kept after it as the contact moved toward the starboard side of the convoy. After explosions occurred in the centre of the convoy [the sounds of the shelling], Crockette came back into the asdic hut and told me to sweep to the starboard side of the convoy towards the stern of the convoy. Instead, I told him that I had the contact.

"We then raced in towards the contact. About five hundred yards from it, we lost it. Instead of 'pingwup,' I got just a mushy sound, which I later learned was caused by the U-boat's anti-asdic weapon, the *Pillenwerfer*."

Contact or not, Skinner continued the attack. Just seconds after the geysers formed by *Salisbury*'s depth charges collapsed, *Arrowhead* steamed over the same spot, firing another ten-charge pattern. Sixteen minutes later, *Arrowhead* dropped yet another ten-charge pattern over the same area.

The bloodless tone of Hartwig's war diary—"Because of depth-charge attack have to go down (A*+40) [120 meters]. At A+60 [180 meters] there is a sharp metallic sound, presumably a tube caved in"—hardly captures the moment. At least one of the explosions must have been terrifyingly close, for not only did the attack put the "after torpedo angling gear out of order," it damaged the torpedoes that were stored in the upper deck compartment between U-517's pressure and outer hulls. A little bit closer and the Canadian-produced pressure wave would have cracked the steel bubble that protected Hartwig and his forty-nine men.

More revealing of both the emotions of the moment (which included the Admiralty's growing unease at the state of the RCN's training) and the "fog of war"—and, as Geoffrey Smith suggests, the Admiralty's attempt to pass off one of its own failures to the RCN—is the "Analysis of Attacks by U-Boat on Convoy SQ-36 on 15th and 16th Sept. 1942." The part of the Remarks section that deals with the attack on the fifteenth minces few words: "The absence of any escort organization is clearly shown in this attack. 'Salisbury' left Sydney after the remaining escorts had sailed and was therefore not able to hold an escort conference. On joining the convoy at 2045/13 [and becoming the chief escort ship] 'Salisbury' was informed by 'Arrowhead' that, in his opinion, previous sinkings in the River were caused by mines and not torpedoes. However there would still appear to be no apparent reason to account for the absence of escort organization, especially as there was ample time in which to signal instructions."

"Captain Skinner could not have told *Salisbury* that 'in his opinion, previous sinkings in the River were caused by mines and not torpedoes,'" says Smith. "Even when we were told by the captain of the *Aeas* [on September 6] that he thought he'd struck a mine, Skinner ordered HMCS *Raccoon* to screen us as we picked up the *Aeas*'s survivors; you only screen if you think torpedoes are a possibility. A day later, when the SS *Oakton* and two other ships were sunk, Skinner knew that they were torpedoed because I reported to him that I had seen the torpedoes pass twelve yards behind our stern. He knew damn well on the fifteenth that those sinkings and *Charlottetown*'s were caused by torpedoes. It's hard not to think that the report isn't slanted towards her [*Salisbury*]."

Whether the report was purposely slanted is an open question. What isn't in doubt, however, is that it was written before HMCS *Vegreville* and *Chedabucto* and one Fairmile had filed their action reports, none of which provide support for the report's assertion that Skinner believed that the previous sinkings were caused by mines.

Smith's view of the report is mirrored by Perkin's, who believes that one claim — "After realizing that a ship had been torpedoed, 'Salisbury' failed to order 'Artichoke' or pass any instructions to the escort, and did not herself take any action until 12 minutes after the torpedoing, and 5 minutes after having sighted a periscope in the centre of the convoy. The periscope was under observation by 'Salisbury' for 7 minutes"—amounts to a calumny of his captain. "As soon as we saw the ship explode," says Perkin, "we were at Action Stations. It was only a matter of a few moments before the captain ordered a hard turn to take us around toward the position the U-boat had to have been in when it fired." *Arrowhead*'s logbook and, ironically, the report's own summation of *Arrowhead*'s actions disprove the report's claim that *Salisbury* "failed to pass any instructions to the escort."

Six months later, on March 15, 1943, Sasseville Roy, the MP for Gaspé, rose in the House and said that Canadian authorities had had a pretty good idea of where Hartwig was *before* he attacked on September 15, 1942. At "exactly eleven o'clock in the morning" on September 15, U-517 had been seen by the Cap-des-Rosiers lighthouse keeper, Joseph Ferguson, a member of the Air Detection Corps (ADC). Ferguson immediately telephoned Captain Côté, who was in charge of the ADC, and another ADC watcher, Walter Lequesne, in Fox River, some twenty five kilometres away. Roy's captivating story continued: "A few minutes later from the lighthouse a convoy could be seen coming up from the southeast, toward that very spot," the one Ferguson had indicated on a map. "It was evident something was going to happen to the convoy when it reached there."

It was so evident that Lesquesne's two daughters and Albert Morris's daughters "climbed up inside the church steeple to watch what was going to happen down there." But, according to Roy, nothing was done. "No aeroplane showed around there to help the corvettes." Why, he asked, had there not been wireless messages from Gaspé, Halifax or Quebec ordering the convoy to change course? "They had plenty of time to do it. The civilian population knew what was about to happen. They were watching the events. It was the navy and airforce which did not seem to be aware of those facts."

Macdonald's response—"Does the honourable member think he is helping the river St. Lawrence traffic by making such a speech as he is making tonight?"—is pure parliamentary camouflage meant to conceal what the minister knew to be the true story: a major intelligence failure had occurred.

Ferguson did see U-517 at 11 a.m., but EAC did not receive word of his sighting until 3:10 p.m., five minutes before *Arrowhead* was ordered to break off its search for the attacking U-boat. The reason was twofold. First, according to Field Officer H. M. Boucher, an ADC officer who was sent to investigate what went wrong on the fifteenth, "army headquarters at Gaspé was only dimly aware of the ADC, and had been instructing civilians on the coast to pass submarine sighting reports through army intelligence." Second, and more important, Boucher reported to his superiors that the public telephone line controlled by Côté was not integrated into the ADC system: "Captain Côté is something of an eccentric. He could see no reasons why ADC calls should be given priority over calls from his 'regular customers.' He objected to the charges on these calls being made 'collect' to the Reporting Centre; i.e. Gaspé. He is a lighthouse keeper who is disposed for political partisanship. After considerable discussion and humouring, he finally 'saw the light.' His [commercial telephone] operators . . . had never heard of ADC before this date [September 15]." Boucher concluded that "Captain Côté intentionally withheld instructions from his operators re. ADC." This arrangement, which relied on commercial telephone operators, was an accident waiting to happen.

As Roy spoke and as Jean-François Poulliot, a Quebec member of parliament, yelled out that "he [Roy] was showing that the minister is incompetent," no doubt Minister Macdonald was chomping at the bit to tell the House that three days earlier (March 12, 1943), a committee formed under the chiefs of staff of the army, air force and navy, and including the Dominion and Quebec Civil Defence organizations, the RCMP and the Quebec Provincial Police, had agreed on a major reorganization of the ADC. Among changes were the establishment of new reporting centres at Chatham, Mont Joli and Sept-Îles, each to be staffed with bilingual personnel; the establishment of field parties to train volunteer observers; the establishment of a twenty-four-hour service using commercial telephone lines; and the distribution of wireless sets where telephone service did not exist.

SEPTEMBER 16, 1942

- Three thousand miles east in Hamburg, U-647 and U-648 are launched.
- Five thousand miles east in the Aleutians, Japanese troops evacuate Attu Island.
- Four thousand five hundred miles east, 6,000 Polish Jews are killed at the Treblinka death camp.
- Nine thousand miles southwest, US Marines continue to hold their position on Guadalcanal against the Japanese.

At 7 a.m., the Canso flying boat escorting SQ-36 was several miles ahead of the convoy. Airborne escorts relied on what sailors had relied on for millennia: the well-trained eyes of their crew. Later in the war, such planes would be equipped with airborne radar that could pick up periscopes. On September 16, 1942, however, the best the Canso's radar could have picked up would have been the shoreline and the presence of the largest ships in the twenty-seven-ship convoy. A few miles off BA 3833, some seven miles off Cap-Chat, flying over waters that a week earlier had seen Hoffmann torpedo SS *Aeas* and HMCS *Raccoon*, blips on oscilloscopes had not yet replaced the sighting of wakes, bubbles and torpedo tracks.

Behind the Canso steamed the twenty merchant ships, arranged in five columns of four, with seven escorts, led by *Salisbury*, positioned two miles ahead of the convoy's centre column. *Vegreville*, *Summerside* and Q-063 covered the port side, while *Chedabucto*, *Arrowhead* and Q-082 covered the starboard side. The Admiralty would later criticize *Arrowhead* for positioning the Fairmiles in the rear, noting that the assumption that the previous day's attack was made by a U-boat that had penetrated from the rear was "unsupportable" because submerged U-boats were unable to travel fast enough to enter a convoy from the rear. However, the deployment decided by *Salisbury* provided asdic coverage of the entire convoy.

CONVOY SQ-36 FROM 7:00–7:15 A.M. ON SEPTEMBER 16, 1942

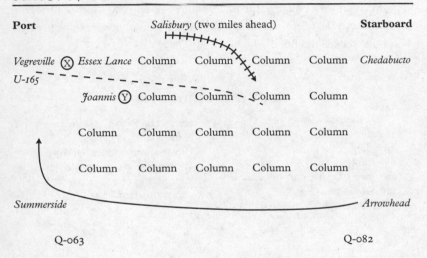

Q-063   Q-082

- - -   Approximate course of U-165.

ⓧ   SS *Essex Lance* torpedoed on port side.

ⓎY   SS *Joannis* torpedoed on starboard side.

⸻   HMCS *Arrowhead*'s course immediately following the torpedoings.

┠┼┼┼   HMS *Salisbury*'s course following receipt of signal that a periscope had been sighted between columns three and four.

At 7:09 a.m., the lookout aboard the British ship SS *Essex Lance* spotted a torpedo track some 4,200 feet off the ship's starboard bow.

Once again, Action Stations was called.

Once again, the black flag (signifying enemy action) was run up the yardarm.

Once again, a ship's telegraph rang for Full Speed as the ship tried to go to starboard.

Once again, men waited as the relentless laws of geometry and mathematics played themselves out.

Once again, a white-hot fireball blasted through tons of steel.

SS *Essex Lance* and her crew were luckier than most of the other ships attacked in the St. Lawrence: the evasive action worked. Instead of hitting amidship, Hoffmann's eel hit between the propeller and the rudder. Though tons of water poured into the stern, the ship's bulkheads held and it was soon taken into tow by *Vegreville* to Quebec City, where it was repaired.[7]

This time Skinner didn't wait for instructions. The convoy's lead ship, *Salisbury*, was over two miles ahead of the main body of the convoy. Skinner was closer and rang immediately for 175 revolutions of his propeller per minute. Within seconds, the three-bladed propeller some 150 feet behind the bridge was biting into the water 515 times a minute. *Arrowhead* was steaming at 16 knots and ordered a course behind the stern of the convoy and then up its port side.

Three miles away, *Summerside*, commanded by Lieutenant F. O. Gerity, immediately altered its course to do a sweep outward. A quick check by radio telephone with *Vegreville*, the ship closest to *Essex Lance*, confirmed what Gerity's lookouts had told him: the torpedo had come from the port side.

Two miles ahead, *Salisbury* was steaming at flank speed back toward the convoy, on a course that would take it between the third and fourth columns—where, it already knew from flagged signals, one of the merchantmen had seen a periscope.

But before Skinner could join *Summerside*, before *Salisbury* could bear down on the reported periscope, before the Canso could return, Hoffmann fired again, at what his war diary calls a 6,000-tonner: SS *Joannis*, laden with 4,800 tons of anthracite coal and travelling at 10 knots.

Again, a lookout saw tracks, this time 7 cables (4,256 feet) off the ship's starboard beam.

Again, a ship's telegraph rang for Full Speed.

Again, a helmsman turned the polished wheel, following the order Hard to Port.

Again, the relentless logic of geometry.

Again the blast, this time in the after peak (just behind the starboard bow).

Again, tons of water poured into a hull, this one built in 1909 by Richardson and Duck Co. in Stockton, England.

Again, the order to abandon ship, this time given by Captain George Mandraka.

Thirty-two men scrambled into lifeboats and rowed for their lives through debris-choked waters. From their lifeboats they watched, a scant ten minutes after the torpedo struck, as the stern of their ship lifted out of the gulf and tons of water flooded in through the hole blasted in her hull.

Hoffmann's war diary doesn't mention the five 400-lb. Mark VII depth charges fired by *Salisbury* or the two that Skinner dropped on a contact Smith picked up at 8:04 a.m.

The signal sent on September 17 by Group Captain M. Costello, senior staff officer of EAC—"convoy patrols have very little chance of sighting and attacking submarines, but are useful in forcing the enemy to submerge and preventing him from carrying out attacks"—was overly defeatist. A day earlier, Pilot Officer R. S. Keetley had attacked Hartwig's U-517, an attack that showed that EAC had begun to learn its trade. "1503 Aircraft. Crash-Dive. 4 aerial bombs, Grid 1449," was all of Hartwig's sparse report on the aerial attack on the sixteenth.

Keetley's offensive owed more to electronic intelligence than it did to "luck," the word Keetley used to describe it. Finding even a surfaced U-boat in the great expanse of the St. Lawrence was never easy, but Keetley's patrol path was anything but chance. After taking off from Chatham, he set his Hudson on a course that would take him close to the U-boat; huff-duff reports had allowed EAC to triangulate Hartwig's position when he radioed Lorient at 0126 (01:46 GMT). Three and a half hours later, Keetley spotted Hartwig, fully surfaced three miles away, north of Cap-de-la-Madeleine.

Keetley's cruising altitude was over 800 feet, and his bombing altitude was 40 to 50 feet. He knew U-517 was in his sights, but he quickly realized, even as he pulled up on the plane's controls and changed the fuel mixture so that his twin engines slowed down, that he could not dive fast enough to successfully bomb Hartwig. Nevertheless, as Keetley flew over the U-boat at 800 feet and then banked, which slowed the Hudson enough so that the second overpass was at the correct attack altitude, his gunners opened fire. "I could see the traces splashing all about the conning tower," Flying

Officer P. G. Hughes told the *Halifax Herald*. "It was like the 24th of May"—Victoria Day fireworks.

Less than half a minute later, Keetley's plane was in an even better position. "I knew we couldn't miss that baby," recalled Hughes. "He stood out like a white corvette with this camouflage." As the sixty five-foot Hudson passed over the U-boat, Keetley fired his machine guns and four depth charges, spaced at sixty-foot intervals.

Hartwig escaped, though the presence of a small oil slick indicated that he had received some damage.

Over the next few days, as EAC added nine planes to its patrol force, Hartwig became the hunted. Between the sixteenth and the nineteenth, he was attacked twice more—attacks that did more than simply keep him under. His report to Lorient on September 22 indicates that, while he'd not been mortally wounded, the cumulative attacks were beginning to tell; his starboard inner exhaust flap could not be moved at all, and the port flap could be moved "only with great difficulty."

On the twenty-fourth, Hartwig was "surprised by [an] aircraft" piloted by Maurice Jean Bélanger. Under bright moonlight, Bélanger's bombs were dropped from a height of only forty feet and were accompanied by streams of machine-gun fire that raked the conning tower.

Hartwig's war diary—"2 powerful explosions astern. 3 bombs dropped; 3rd bomb right next to ship's side so that the stern gets flooded over by impact. Presumably a dud"—is as bloodless as ever. But the scene aboard U-517 must have been more chaotic. Over the next eleven hours, U-517 crash-dived four more times.

Bélanger bombed Hartwig again the same day. Accuracy when bombing a diving submarine was not easy. Shortly after 2 p.m., Bélanger got everything right, coming over Hartwig while his decks were still awash. The pattern of dropping one bomb every forty feet was designed to catch the moving object. One depth charge exploded within five to ten feet of U-517's pressure hull but did not breach it.[8]

Five days later (on September 29), at 2:23 p.m., Bélanger again pulled on the controls, causing his Hudson 624 to bank sharply. Seconds later, levelling off at fifty to sixty feet, machine guns firing, he dropped another four bombs on U-517 as it crash-dived. Bélanger's report—"The depth charges were seen to explode all around the hull slightly ahead of the conning tower. One large explosion occurred around the hull of the U-boat. The U-boat's bow came up out of the water and all forward motion stopped. It then appeared to settle straight down"—cannot be squared with Hartwig's, which says only, "crashed dived to evade aircraft. 3 well-placed depth charges." But the backhanded compliment makes clear the margin by which Hartwig escaped.

On the twenty-ninth, EAC almost got its kill. Several hours after what Hartwig called a skilful bomb and machine-gun attack, he surfaced to find that a bomb had lodged in his hull forward of the 10.5-cm gun's ammunition locker. Had U-517 descended much farther during its escape dive, the bomb that Hartwig, his chief engineer and two other crew members pried off their boat's hull and pitched into the sea would have exploded, destroying the plating and sinking the sub.

Over and over again in the weeks that followed the sinking of *Joannis*, Hartwig closed in for the kill. Again and again, close work by the RCN and air escorts frustrated his ambitions. At 4 p.m. on September 24, for example, Hartwig had surfaced and was maintaining contact with a fifteen-ship convoy. "Unfortunately on the port side [of the convoy at] bearing 50°," recorded Hartwig in his war diary, "there is a single steamship moving fast to catch up to the convoy. I am between the steamship and the convoy, can't get ahead of him or go around the lone vessel." Two hours and sixteen minutes later, another crash-dive and another depth charge. A day later, and he wrote this in his war diary:

> 0133 hrs. [Berlin Time] surface. Bright moonlight, clear night. Tried to catch up [with the same convoy] at three-quarters speed.
>
> 0352 hrs. Grid BB 146 surprised by aircraft. 2 powerful explosions astern. 3 bombs dropped; 3rd bomb right next to ship's side so that the stern gets flooded over by impact. Presumably a dud.
>
> 0353 hrs. Crash-dive.

0559 hrs. Surfaced, back to pursuit.

1145 hrs. Convoy at bearing 192°, bow right 100 Grid BB 1853. Turned sharply away as too close in half-light.

1205 hrs. Crash-dive to evade 2 aircraft.

1247 hrs. Surfaced.

1316 hrs. Crash-dive to evade one aircraft.

1428 hrs. Surfaced.

1445 hrs. Crash-dive to evade one aircraft.

1559 hrs. Surfaced.

2030–2045 hrs. 3 aircraft in sight. So far have kept contact with aircraft. Should be ahead of convoy by 2100 hrs after coupling. Make for convoy at 300°; at 2203 hrs. in Grid BB 4325 am surprised by a fast land-plane. 3 aerial bombs which are well placed. Until 0139 hrs. travel at periscope depth; nothing seen and nothing heard. Presume convoy has put to sea via BB 46, 49 or 50.

Finally, on October 5 at 8 p.m., one day before he left the gulf, Hartwig was in position to attack a convoy when suddenly an aircraft with a searchlight overflew him. Twenty-three minutes later, he fired, using his day-attack periscope because "nothing [could] be seen through the night-target periscope as it [had] been completely shattered." The torpedoes missed. Twenty minutes later, at 8:45 p.m., just before he tried again, "the fire-control calculator [broke] down." The four eels sailed harmlessly into the night.

When he left the St. Lawrence, Hartwig's damage-control report listed,

- Water-distilling plant (reduced from 50 to 10 gallons);
- Torpedo angling gear;

- Upper-deck torpedo storage compartment;
- Torpedoes stored in upper-deck storage compartment;
- Two caved-in torpedo tubes;
- Night target periscope;
- Fire-control calculator.

For destroying 52,000 tons of shipping, Hartwig was awarded an Iron Cross. But during his final twenty-one days in Canada's home waters, he sank nothing.

On December 17, 1942, Prime Minister Churchill wrote to his Canadian counterpart, "I appreciate the grand contribution of the Royal Canadian Navy to the Battle of the Atlantic, but the expansion of the RCN has created a training problem which must take some time to solve." Five days earlier, in *Analysis of Attacks by U-Boat on Convoy SQ 36 on 15th and 16th Sept. 1942*, the UK's director of anti-submarine warfare called attention to "a very grave lack of efficiency on the part of the Canadian escort force." Although he does not name Rear-Admiral Jones, the director clearly lays the blame on the manning policy Jones authored: "Much of this [the inefficiency of the RCN] is undoubtedly due to the difficulties that have prevented Canadians from forming permanent groups, that can be trained to act together as teams." Even during the height of the Atlantic war, one-third of RN ships were routinely detached from escort duty to train with a live submarine at Tobermory, Scotland; by contrast, 90 per cent of the RCN's ships were at sea. Murray's plans for Canadian training with a live submarine were derailed when, after Pearl Harbor, the bulk of the US Atlantic Fleet sailed for the Pacific and the RCN took over responsibility for escorting convoys across the North Atlantic.

Called "piratical" by Rear-Admiral Murray in Halifax, Jones's manning policy was designed to spread the talent around the rapidly expanding Canadian fleet. Jones feared that had Canada followed normal practice and kept crews together on a ship and ships together in groups that could be trained as a unit, the ships would have been largely unmanned.[9] The fleet had expanded exponentially—from 13 ships and 3,600 officers and ratings

in 1939, to more than 43,000 officers and ratings and more than 200 warships in 1942. (In 1945 the numbers would be 93,000 officers and men, 373
warships, including 2 aircraft carriers, and 563 other types of ships.) The
only way to crew the hundreds of new ships—and thereby provide escorts
to the convoys—was, Jones believed, to take what few trained men the RCN
had and put them on the ships as they came down the slipways. These men
then formed the nucleus around which the untrained crew was formed.
Training often occurred on station at sea.[10]

However defensible from a manning point of view, Jones's policy damaged
the RCN's convoy-escort role because it militated against the concerted training of groups of ships to work together in convoy protection. In a report that
examined the effectiveness of the largely Canadian escort force of SC-52—
which, on November 1, 1941, became the only convoy driven back to port—
the Admiralty wrote, "RCN corvettes . . . have been given so little chance to
become efficient that they are almost more of a liability than an asset to the
escort group." According to historian Marc Milner, Murray protested vigor-
ously against Jones's policy: "One of the more damnable effects of this policy," Murray wrote in a memo to NSHQ, "was that it worked the few good
people who were available to near exhaustion." Lieutenant Brigg's *Orillia*, for
example, had recently been ravaged by Halifax manning personnel, and
Murray warned that she "may be unfit for further duty at sea for some considerable time period" following the completion of its later passage. Briggs
was now the only qualified watch keeper aboard *Orillia*, and the corvette had
spent twenty-eight days at sea during the month of October.

Almost a year before the attack on SQ-36, Murray had called for a manning policy that assigned new crews to new ships—and then kept them
together for training. In December 1941, Naval Service Headquarters in
Ottawa turned down the plan. According to Milner, "The RCN was quite
prepared to accept a 'temporary' reduction in efficiency for long-term benefits of producing a larger cadre of experienced personnel" and the ability
to man the navy's existing ships. The lives of the merchant sailors, their ships
and their cargoes were the coin that paid the price of both Jones's manning
policy and the years of neglecting the RCN's staff list prior to the war.

In his December 21 memo, the director of the Trade Division was even
more blunt: "Should they [U-boats] return" to the area between New York

and 49° W (the mid-Atlantic)—the area of Canadian responsibility—"the result may well be disastrous unless some way can be found of improving the standard of training of the Western Local groups." On the same page, though dated a few days later (December 24), he continues, "It was understood that training facilities would be made available at St. John's and Argentia but complaints have been made that in the case of Canadian ships this training was much interfered with by the continual changing of crews." Interestingly, given the criticisms the report makes of *Salisbury* itself, it goes on to say, "This should not affect British manned vessels, such as the SALISBURY and the remainder of the ships in the support groups"—perhaps, as Smith suggests, another example of the Admiralty's desire to put the best gloss on things directly under its control.

The final part of the director's analysis is also important. First, it illuminates an important difference between the RN and the RCN—indeed, between the Canadian and British armed forces in general. Before rehearsing the usual criticisms about the changing of crews and the reluctance of the Canadians to form attack groups, the director of anti-submarine warfare notes that "the individuality of the officers . . . makes them reluctant to accept instructions in official publications and to obey them, or to accept the lessons learnt by others." No doubt part of what the Admiralty was getting at here was the exuberance of youth. Because of the huge expansion of the RCN, its officers were on the whole much younger than the RN's. But another part of what the Admiralty was saying no doubt stems from the social differences between the RN and the RCN. The RN was England's senior service, its officers products of long-established naval colleges and of a navy stretching back hundreds of years.

Lieutenant Desmond Piers, commander of the destroyed HMCS *Restigouche*, had passed through these schools. So had Lieutenant R. J. Pickford, commander of the corvette HMCS *Rimouski*, who had been trained first at HMS King Alfred and then at HMS Auspry and who held an RN watch keeper's certificate. But few other Canadians had such qualifications.

Bonner was a merchant seaman—from the Admiralty point of view, a notoriously individualistic lot. Skinner was a rum-runner, Lade a yachtsman.

The report's penultimate paragraph stung especially hard: "It has been estimated that 80% of all ships torpedoed in transatlantic convoys during

the last 2 months were hit while being escorted by Canadian groups."
Though correct, Milner has shown that the raw numbers conceal almost as
much as they reveal. The vast majority of convoys Canadians escorted were
slow convoys, and slow convoys were much easier targets both because they
spent as much as 30 per cent more time at sea and because their lack of
speed made them less able to respond to tactical situations.

From a Canadian point of view, the Admiralty's remarks are incomplete.
The first gap is the failure of ADC on September 15 to warn of the U-boat's
presence. The second is the failure of *Salisbury*'s 271 radar to pick up the
presence of U-517 within the convoy. Both contributed mightily to the tactical disaster of SQ-36.

CHAPTER SIX

OCTOBER WAS THE CRUELLEST MONTH

OCTOBER 9, 11 AND 14, 1942
SS *Carolus*, *Waterton* and *Caribou*

Unnumbered ghosts that haunt the wave
Where you have murdered, cry you down;
And seamen whom you would not save,
Weave now in weed-grown depths a crown
Of shame for your imperious head,—
A dark memorial of the dead,—
Women and children whom you left to drown.

—HENRY VAN DYKE, 1917

The age-old tradition of sailors picking up survivors of ships that their munitions destroyed—what *Grossadmiral* Karl Dönitz called a "fine Freemasonry"—and the emotion-charged meetings of veterans who, generations after they fought each other, meet and reminisce about their all-too-human battle against steel, shell and the ever-present sea should not elide the differences between His Majesty's Royal Canadian Navy and the *Kriegsmarine*. Still less should the passage of time obscure the marked differences in training and in beliefs between the men who manned the U-boats that invaded Canada and the officers and ratings who served on the armed yachts, corvettes, Fairmiles and Bangor minesweepers that defended Canada.

The *U-Bootwaffe* had risen from a secret Weimar program to the most professional of Hitler's armed forces. Like the crews of the RCN, the RN and the USN, its crews were volunteers. U-boat commanders were products of a three-year training program that began with three months of basic infantry training on Dänholm, what U-553's captain, Karl Thurmann, called a "godforsaken island" in the Baltic. Then three months on a square rigger; next, a year as a midshipman aboard a cruiser. A nine-month course in navigation, tactics, naval architecture, marine engineering, oceanography and English (to study Nelson and Drake in the original) followed. Commissioning came after still another cruise—with an experienced commander. The expansion of the U-boat Arm from 40 submarines in 1939 to 265 in the beginning of 1943 (and the need to replace crews lost in action) meant that as the war continued, training was speeded up. Still, an engineering officer cadet of 1940 underwent over two years of training. As late as 1944, U-boat crews trained for up to nine months before undertaking operational cruises.

Men like Lieutenant Desmond "Debbie" Piers, RCN, captain of the destroyer HMCS *Restigouche*, spent years earning their command qualifications, most of it with the British navy and staff colleges. But the initials RCNR (Royal Canadian Naval Reserve) after the names of the men who commanded most of the small ships—captains Skinner, Bonner, Lade and Cuthbert—and RCNVR (Royal Canadian Navy Volunteer Reserve) after those of captains Denny (Fairmile 074), Simpson (Fairmile 063) and Strange (Fairmile 084), as well as of most of the ratings who served in the St. Lawrence, indicate that the vast majority of the men who matched wits with Dönitz's marksmen belonged to the maritime equivalent of the militia.[1]

With twenty years at sea, Bonner may have had almost a decade's more experience than did Hartwig, but prior to the outbreak of the war Bonner's military training consisted only of a course every year or two. The men of the RCNVR trained one or two nights a week at local drill halls and two weeks a year at Halifax or Esquimalt. Upon being activated, these men received another two months of training. Of course, both naval lore and training experts agree that while it may take two years to build a ship, it takes five years to train a sailor.

By 1942, the navy's need for men to crew its more than two hundred ships meant that training could be measured in weeks. Between 1939 and the end of 1942, the navy grew from 131 officers and 1,634 ratings (backed up by another 181 reserve officers and 1,649 reserve ratings) to more than 1,514 officers—the vast majority of whom were "wavy navy" (RCNVR) men—and some 45,000 ratings.[2] By 1945 the total number of men serving in the navy was over 95,000. Gavin Clark became executive officer on Fairmile 085 straight from a four-month training program at Royal Roads in Victoria, British Columbia; less than a year later, at twenty years, five months and seventeen days old, he took command of the Fairmile. Like thousands of others, Léon-Paul Fortin had never been aboard a ship before *Charlottetown*'s commissioning; most of the crew were so green that they were seasick in the first storm.

Depending on the experience of a U-boat's captain, the time allotted for working up a crew varied. In 1942, six months was the norm—six months that included torpedo-firing drills, diving drills, emergency-escape drills. Six months that included navigation and more English study. Six months that included wolfpack tactics. *Charlottetown* worked up for eighty-five days—less than three months—most of which included more chipping paint than gunnery practice. Its regimen did not include training with a Dutch submarine that had been seconded to Halifax.

The U-boat captain—the lone wolf, wearing a worn leather jacket, looking through a periscope, finding his prey—and his "band of brothers" fearfully trusting that the pressure hull of their 160-foot trench will hold are powerful and romantic images that, especially as the decades have passed, have come to obscure the essential difference between the men who sailed under the swastika and those who sailed under the White Ensign.

Even on such useful Web sites as uboat.net, debates rage about whether Dönitz was a Nazi. Both he and his deputy were card-carrying members of the Nazi party, as was U-boat ace Eric Topp (U-552). Participants on uboat.net endlessly point out that the tens of thousands of officers and ratings who made up the *U-Bootwaffe* were not Nazis and that, in fact, the service itself was officially apolitical. If so, the reason is because it could afford to be—the men who crewed Hitler's U-boats had had years of National Socialist indoctrination.

By 1942, nineteen-, twenty-, twenty-one-year-old midshipmen had all been part of Nazi-run organizations for almost a decade. They had seen their primary schools "cleansed" of Jewish teachers. Their school readers likened Jews to animals and disease: "The Poisonous Serpent" ended with the words, "If we do not kill the Jewish poisonous serpent, it will kill us!" *Deutschland: Sechster Teil*, a middle-school geography textbook, inveighed against the *Versailles Diktat* and called for the return of Germany's African colonies. Even math textbooks were Nazified. Algebraic word problems asked how much a bomber weighs when empty if "on takeoff [it] carries twelve dozen bombs, each weighing ten kilos. The aircraft takes off for Warsaw, international centre of Jews. It bombs the town."

Outside of school, the Hitler Youth taught obedience to Hitler. German rearmament would secure them their living space and their place in the sun. Hartwig's twenty-one-year-old *Leutnant zur See* (second lieutenant) was, according to the *Report of the Interrogation of Survivors from U 517*, "a typical Hitler Youth movement product, entirely lacking in manners and making a very poor impression." The twenty-five-year-old Hartwig himself was "filled with ideals of false heroism and unyielding devotion to his Fuhrer." *Kapitänleutnant* Rolf Schauenburg, who took U-536 into the Baie des Chaleurs in 1943, was described in a similar report as a "fanatical and idealistic Nazi."

Older officers, such as Helmut Martin, Hartwig's engineering officer, born in 1913, might have been out of school by 1933 when Hitler took power, but they were no less influenced by the currents that Hitler melded into National Socialism. Even during the Weimar Republic, Germany's schools denounced Versailles as a *Diktat* and pressed for its removal. Naval histories—not to mention wardroom chatter—blamed Germany's loss in the First World War on politicians who temporized before authorizing "unrestricted submarine warfare" until it was too late; a mere seventeen U-boats almost brought England to its knees.

As historian Michael Hadley has shown, popular culture hardly depicted the navy as being free of anti-Semitism. *U-boots-Maschinist Fritz Kasten* (*Fritz Kasten: U-boat Engineer*), published in 1933—the year Hitler consolidated power—underlined the "breakthrough of the racial ideal" embodied by National Socialism and tellingly ended with a scene of German sailors marching in columns with Nazi "brown shirts who were ready to sacrifice their lives for this hour." A year after the war began, U-boat ace Joachim Schepke wrote in *Submarines of Today: Narrated by a U-boat Commander* that while the youngest member of a U-boat crew might be called Moses, no one should think that he was a Jew, for no "seaman would . . . share their space with such an aberration of nature."³

The men who saluted the White Ensign grew up singing "God Save the King" and believing that the swath of pink that girdled the map on the wall was as immutable as the white cliffs of Dover. Their history was of expansion across an all-but-empty continent, of stopping the Americans at Lundy's Lane in Niagara and at Crysler's Farm and, more recently, of defeating the kaiser's army at Vimy Ridge. But though Canadians had shed blood in South Africa, their imperialism was more imaginative than real. Fed by the writings of Rudyard Kipling and the now-forgotten George A. Henty, Canadian boys grew up wanting to be like *Clive in India*—while at the same time learning that the real end of empire was self-government, something even discussed for India.

Canadian school readers contained stories about dogs stealing food from unsuspecting country folk. Longfellow's "The Village Blacksmith" is typical of the fare in the 1927 edition of *The Atlantic Readers*. The 1935 edition of *A Reader in Canadian Civics* surveyed the municipal, provincial and federal governments, explained how taxes are collected and pointed out the "curious fact that the Dominion cabinet has no base in law, and is not even mentioned in any statute, but is what is called a 'convention' of the constitution." Published the same year Hitler pulled Germany out of the League of Nations, the reader ended with a chapter explaining Canada's relationship to the League. History textbooks in the thirties gave as much space to the conscription crisis as they did to Passchendaele, the Somme and, of course, Vimy Ridge.

For men such as Geoffrey Smith, Ian Tate and John Chance (Chance, as commander of Fairmile 058, would search for survivors of HMCS *Shawinigan* in November 1944), the words "for King and Country" were redolent of more than just George VI and the land north of the 49th parallel. At Upper Canada College, Smith learned of the Long Parliament and the English Civil War, and of Drake and Nelson, who were honoured for both their martial brilliance and the part they played in the story of protecting English liberties. Tate, whose father served in the Royal Navy (and who received an OBE for his work on hydrophones), learned the same at

Trinity College School in Port Hope, Ontario, and Chance studied the same Whig interpretation of history at Lisgar Collegiate in Ottawa. "When King George VI spoke on the radio at Christmas," he remembers, "the three Chance boys stood up in the living room."

For others—perhaps for most of the lower decks—political theory and even Nelson and Drake meant less than did the rough-hewn democracy of local elections and family allegiance to the Grits or the Tories. Theirs was the same democracy that made it difficult for Canadian servicemen to salute when the officer was the fellow who lived in the same town and used to deliver the mail, the same democracy that shocked the British officer corps when Canadian troops booed Prime Minister Mackenzie King when he visited them in England.

Frank Curry, who ended the war as a leading seaman of HMCS *Caraquet*, remembers growing up in Winnipeg. "My father and older brother didn't believe war would come, but I knew from listening to Hitler's rantings and ravings through the 1930s that war was coming. When I joined the navy in 1940, I left a good clerking job in Ottawa, one that I'd just gotten after taking a nationwide test; it paid $90 a month, which was fantastic money after the long, dark years of the Depression.

"I joined a day after another guy from the office joined. I remember he told me he was going to join, and then I realized that I had a duty to my country. And the men who joined with me, we all felt that Canada had taken on this war and that we had to stand up with Britain and against Hitler and all he represented. There was no rah-rah enthusiasm, but we knew what we were fighting against and why."

OCTOBER 9, 1942

- Nine thousand miles southwest in the Solomon Islands, American marines wipe out a Japanese battalion west of the Matanikau River.
- Eight thousand five hundred miles southeast in Madagascar, British troops occupying the capital, Tananarive, move south to link with the troops that had landed there at the end of September.

> • Four thousand five hundred miles east in Miedzyrzec, Poland, thousands of Jews are deported to the Treblinka death camp.
>
> • Four thousand five hundred miles east in Moscow, Joseph Stalin decides to remove political commissars from Red Army units, a move that strengthens the control of military commanders.

At 11:48 p.m. on October 5, 1942, the day after NL-9, a convoy of four merchant ships escorted by HMCS *Arrowhead* and *Hepatica*, sailed from Collinghams Cove, Labrador, for Rigolet, Quebec, Wrens (members of the Women's Royal Canadian Naval Service) manning secret listening posts at East Baccaro, Nova Scotia, heard a "whurrp" and reached for their pencils and blue message pads. Over the next few seconds, they copied down dots, dashes and call letters, which were then sent by secure land line to Halifax. A year earlier, the code would have been sent on to Bletchley Park, England, where Alan Turing's "bomb," the electronic marvel that unbuttoned the German Enigma code, would have been able to decode the message. Within an hour or two, it would have told the Admiralty precisely what *Kapitänleutnant* Ulrich Gräf on U-69 was telling Lorient.

As early as 1941, "Ultra" intelligence had allowed the Admiralty to route some convoys away from wolfpack concentrations. During the Battle of El Alamein, fought in early 1942, General Bernard Montgomery read Erwin Rommel's orders sometimes before the field marshal himself. In 1943, the speed of code breaking was similar; the Allies knew the Italian order of battle prior to the invasion of Italy. In mid-1942, however, after Dönitz became concerned about the security of the *Kriegsmarine*'s ciphers, a fifth wheel was added to the Enigma machine (the code was produced by the turning of the machine's wheels), temporarily closing the window Ultra had opened.

The huff-duff unit was established by Commander J. M. D. E. "Jock" de Marbois, Deputy Director Signals Division (Y).[4] Largely staffed by women who joined the Women's Royal Canadian Naval Service, huff-duff may not have told what the transmission said, but simple geometry told Naval Intelligence what it needed to know. By triangulating among different listening posts that picked up the message, Canadian authorities knew that another U-boat had entered the St. Lawrence and that, at twelve minutes to midnight on the fifth, it was in the area of 49° 30° N, 65° 30° W, what the navigational officer aboard U-69 thought of as grid square BA 3669, a few miles off Cap-de-la-Madeleine on the north shore of the Gaspé—a day or so ahead of convoy NL-9.

Thirty-six hours later, it was the turn of German radio technology to play a pivotal role.

Although two years older than Hartwig's U-517 and Thurmann's U-553, Gräf's U-69 was equipped with an up-to-date FuMB 1 Metox 600A radar detector. Developed after the Germans recovered an ASV MkI radar from a Wellington bomber shot down in 1941, Metox picked up 1.5-metre radar waves, the size generated by *Arrowhead*'s and *Hepatica*'s ASW radar. Metox registered radar waves at a distance of 30 miles, the distance and bearings being estimatable by the pitch and loudness of the tone. A month before entering the St. Lawrence, Gräf used Metox to great effect as he sneaked through the US defences off the Maryland coast on his mission to plant twelve mines in Chesapeake Bay.

The Metox alarm that sounded at 9:38 p.m. on October 8 did more than drive U-69 beneath the rain squalls sweeping across the St. Lawrence. Its character—"moderate length, grows louder, does not fluctuate"—told Gräf that his prey was near. Five minutes later and thirty metres below the surface, the six propellers of NL-9 were picked up by hydrophone microphones on the forward deck casing in front of the conning tower. Twenty-five minutes later, at 10:20 p.m., the sound waves rolling over U-69 were strong enough to give Gräf the numbers he needed: he surfaced, set a course of 250° and called for half speed in the hope that the convoy's own noise would mask his 426-kilogram propeller revolving at 165 revolutions per minute.

Then, at 10:40, helped by the "slight northern lights" and the "strong phosphorescence" caused by the "mirror-calm" waters, Gräf spotted "several silhouettes bearing 220[°]."

Unaware of what was happening out beyond the shores of Métis Beach, David Gendron sat writing a love letter at the family's rolltop writing desk in the large living room, the far windows of which looked out on the St. Lawrence. His family slept on.

At seven minutes to midnight, on both *Arrowhead* and *Hepatica*, the first watch (2000–2400 hrs.) was coming to an end.

"Watch keeping was both routine and extremely intense," recalls Frank Curry, who began his life in the navy as an able seaman on the corvette HMCS *Kamsack*. "At the beginning of each watch, a lookout was briefed by the lookout he was replacing and by the officer of the watch as to anything to watch out for: Is the second ship in column 3 making too much smoke? Is a ship beginning to drop out of the convoy?

"For the next four hours, a lookout's world was reduced to the elements— sun, darkness, rain, wind, fog (and, on the North Atlantic run in the winter, ice)—and 90° from the bow to the beam or the beam to the stern."

"Sweep after endless sweep," Curry recalls. "Each was a slow scan, and always you were looking out into the middle distance where the convoy's ships were or where an enemy periscope might appear. The time passed interminably slowly."

"Even towards the end of the watch," he remembers, "the tension did not let up. You always knew that your watch keeping might be coming to an end but that at any time all hell could break loose. At the end you expected your replacement—and if he was late, you had a few choice words for him. Then you could head to the mess deck and get a cup of coffee, or, if yours was an 8-to-4 duty watch, you had four hours of seaman's duties to do."

Aboard SS *Carolus* and *New York News*, which sailed ahead of *Arrowhead*, other men kept watch, as a third of their crews slept in their bunks.

Eight hundred metres away in U-69, no one slept. The control-room crew was on a knife's edge as the Metox indicated that the U-boat was well within a radar field. Gräf read out the numbers—"Speed 9, bows right 90, range = 2,000"—that aimed the torpedoes in tubes I and IV at "3 overlapping freighters." At 11:57 p.m., Gräf's *Oberleutnant* Johannes Hagemann pushed two buttons.

Immediately after firing from tubes I and IV, while being blanketed by full-strength radar waves, Gräf ordered his helmsman to turn U-69 180° to starboard so he could fire again. Within seconds the huge piston behind the torpedo in Tube V was released and tons of air vented into the U-boat as the piston sped down the tube, pushing the torpedo out at 30 knots.

As soon as the "clank" signalling the closing of the torpedo tube was heard, Gräf "opened out [proceeded] at slow speed"—some 9 knots—on course 50.

Three miles away, the huge light above David Gendron revolved four times per minute.

At three minutes to midnight, after one of *Arrowhead*'s lookouts spotted one of Gräf's torpedoes passing ten feet behind the ship's stern, Action Stations rang out. Skinner's helmsman swung his helm hard to starboard as *Arrowhead* once again started down the track of a Nazi torpedo.

Within seconds, an explosion ripped through the night. Less than a minute later, as Gendron, his family and other residents of Métis Beach were rushing to their windows, a second, much louder blast shook the Quebec night. Another eleven men died in the St. Lawrence.

Beneath the "tall dark explosive plume" and by the light of the "substantial flames" that Gräf reported back to Dönitz, the men on *Carolus* were running—as hundred of others had since the beginning of the Battle of the St. Lawrence.

Carolus's chief officer, who had just come off duty and must have been walking on the boat deck, told the Canadian Press, "The shock of the impact knocked me out on my feet for two or three seconds. When I came to, I tried to release the aft boats, but the ship was listing too sharply. I tried to get to a boat but couldn't make it." His ship was sinking quickly. He jumped into the water and swam for it.

Naval Gunner Henry Harley from London, England, and a few other men with him in the saloon boy's cabin fought their way through the ever-mounting rushing water that poured through the ship's passageways. By the time they got to the boat deck, *Carolus* was listing 20° to port. "When we got out on the deck I shouted to the second officer, Anderson, 'What's happened?' 'We're hit! Make off the boats!' he ordered," Harley told the Canadian Press.

But the boats Harley and his mates ran to were smashed. All around the ship, men were jumping into the water. They could feel the steel—thousands of tons of it, shaped by shipwrights in Sunderland in 1919—bending. Amid the cacophony of burst steam lines, the roar of flames and the rush of water, they could hear the scream of the steel being wrenched by hundreds of tons of force, wrecking the finely calibrated distribution that had been outlined by pencils on clean drawing desks during the Great War.

Just moments after Harley, Anderson and the ship's third officer, Barrett, jumped into the water, the ship broke in two. The part they'd just jumped off sank immediately.

Each man now fought not just to stay afloat but to rise to the surface of the water itself, for, recalled Harley, they "were pulled under by the suction as the ship went down."

Miraculously, each managed to fight his way to the surface. "When we came up, I got hold of two empty gas drums and hung on until we got hold of a raft," Harley told the Canadian Press.

Alex Dawson, a DEMS gunner from Montreal, was below deck when the torpedo hit his ship like a "heavy sledgehammer." Just as he was about to step out on deck, the ship's back broke. Immediately, the vertical hatchway Dawson was climbing through became horizontal. Though disoriented, he realized that "she was going over." Beneath him, as the stern, unable to displace its own weight in water, pushed into the river, the air trapped like a bubble inside pushed outward, bursting the hatches. The drums stored on the ship's deck, stowed to withstand the six-foot waves that St. Lawrence storms can dish out without being turned over 90°, broke loose from their moorings. Drums stored in the hold tumbled out of the blasted wreck. "One must have struck me, for I was unconscious when I popped out of the water," Dawson told James Essex. He had been saved, no doubt, by the lifebelt he had not even had time to put on properly before *Carolus*'s twenty-three-year-old keel disintegrated, killing two men instantly.

For a moment, both Octave Gendron and his father thought that the U-boat was firing its guns at the lighthouse, situated on a spit of land that pushes a quarter mile into the river. What they were hearing and seeing, however, was the boom and the arc of the star shells fired by *Arrowhead* and *Hepatica*.

The star shells, which turned night into bright, harsh day, were a gamble. If lookouts were to have any chance of spotting the U-boat and especially its periscope, they needed light. But that same light illuminated *Arrowhead*, *Hepatica* and the remaining merchant ships. If the U-boat was either far enough under or far enough into the shadows, both Skinner and Lade knew they were setting the stage for still another salvo and more dead men on the St. Lawrence. Skinner's men saw nothing. After a forty-five-minute search, Skinner ordered *Arrowhead* back to where *Carolus* had been. Once again Smith and his crewmates began the grim task of helping oil-soaked, shocked men aboard *Arrowhead*. Of the twenty-eight men who got off *Carolus*, nine drowned in the river.

Lade's men also saw nothing. At 1:53 a.m., however, after dismissing one asdic contact as doubtful, Lade heard the words "CONTACT, range 1,700 yards, inclination no doppler, target steady"—everything the textbook said was a U-boat lying still. He ordered a ten-depth-charge pattern, six to be rolled off the stern and two each to be fired from the port and starboard throwers, set varyingly for 100 and 225 feet. At 300 yards, the contact was lost, but he dropped the depth charges anyway before altering course to help with the recovery of *Carolus*'s survivors.

Hidden by the deep dark of the river, *Graf* saw the star shells, heard the depth charges and wondered why, since his Metox indicated that he was being blanketed by radar waves, the counterattack was so uncoordinated. His conclusion, that "the personnel operating the enemy radars were having an excellent sleep," may have played well in Lorient, but was unwarranted. The actual reason that neither corvette could "see" him was because their 286 radar sets were unable to pick up a trimmed-down U-boat.

OCTOBER 11, 1942

- Nine thousand miles southwest in the Battle of Cape Esperance (Guadalcanal), the Americans lose two destroyers and a cruiser; the Japanese lose a cruiser and one destroyer and manage to land artillery and tanks.
- Five thousand four hundred miles east in Russia, the battle for Stalingrad rages.
- Three thousand miles east, a Liberator bomber flying out of Coastal Command in the UK sinks U-597.
- Three thousand miles east in England, hundreds of assault ships and others—including seventeen Canadian corvettes—are readied for the launch of Operation Torch, the invasion of North Africa.

At 10:30 a.m. on October 11, 1942, SS *Waterton*, her holds filled with tons of wood sulphate and with huge rolls of newsprint lashed to her deck, rode low in the waters off St. Paul's Island in the Cabot Strait. Several hundred yards away, across the three- to four-foot swells caused by a 15-knot wind from the south, steamed the tanker SS *Omaha*, an American ship flying a Panamanian flag of convenience. Another few hundred yards to the starboard, their escort was the armed yacht HMCS *Vison*, commanded by Lieutenant W. E. Nicholson, RCNR. Despite the drizzle and the low cloud cover of between 900 and 1,000 feet, convoy BS-31 also enjoyed the protection of a Canso flying boat, which flew an inner submarine patrol a half mile ahead of the ships.

Three miles to *Waterton*'s port—much too far away for its lookouts or the Canso's to spot it—fourteen inches above the surface, U-106's periscope cut through the water.

Commanded by Hermann Rasch, U-106 had entered Canadian waters on October 10, 1942. Rasch's mission was to sink merchant ships and thereby disrupt enemy supply lines and force the Allies to devote precious men and ships to convoy defence. Thanks to the constant sounding of his Metox, U-106 would become something more akin to a real-time German version of USS *Nerka*, the submarine in *Run Silent, Run Deep* that endlessly practised emergency diving. "Operations in such coastal waters," referring to Canada's radar blanketed inland sea, had "become a continued up and down affair," he informed Lorient.

Rasch's war diary entry for 12:46 p.m. on October 10 indicates how effective EAC had become. After sighting a convoy at 12:24 p.m. and getting himself into a firing position ahead of it, "Emergency dive because of an aircraft which is escorting the convoy. When the steamers—4 of medium size and 1 escort—come into the sight in the periscope, they are at bows right, inclination 30, on course 090–100. Turned to attack course and closed at maximum speed. Despite this, I am unable to close to firing range, the convoy has turned away somewhat farther and when at inclination 90 the range is roughly 6–7000 m. Once again my attempt was unsuccessful."

Known only to Rasch, his coder and U-106's wireless operator, these last words betray a growing frustration. U-boat commanders, even Knight's

Cross winners (Rasch was awarded his on December 29, 1941), are not unlike elite athletes in that they are only as good as their last success. Some U-boat commanders, such as Peter Cremer, nicknamed "Ali" because of his habit of magically pulling out of a bad situation, were considered preternaturally lucky. Still others, such as Jost Metzler, U-69's original commander, were considered as having a fine touch. When Rasch broke off his attack on the tenth, it had been almost four months since his crew had been able to paint another sinking ship on their conning tower.

Between 10:30 and 10:57 a.m. on October 11, Rasch proved his crew's faith in him by closing from 3 miles away from the convoy to less than 300 metres from *Waterton*. Despite the fact that the seas that hid his periscope made his own view "very indistinct," Rasch no doubt enjoyed the moment when his attack crew realized he was splitting a very fine hair indeed—by aiming each torpedo slightly differently, "one forward, one aft below the funnel."

Then, with an audacity every bit as great as Hartwig's run into Fortuna Bay, Rasch pushed in to as close as 220 metres from his target. His Knight's Cross luck perhaps deserves the credit for two almost instantaneous decisions. Had he not fired when he did, his eels would have never exploded, for their run would have been 15 metres shy of the distance the propellers on their noses needed to revolve to arm their pistols. Had he not immediately after ordering "*Los!*" ordered a hard turn to starboard, U-106 would have "end[ed] up beneath" the "steamer [that] immediately settle[d] by the stern."

Once clear of the plunging *Waterton*, Rasch "went deep because of the flying boat" that was already circling back toward the stricken ship.

In the days to come, Captain William Lutjens and *Waterton*'s entire crew counted themselves lucky. Particularly grateful was F. Burton, who was blown overboard and saved by J. Paul, the ship's radio officer; in his report Lutjens wrote that Paul dived "from the starboard lifeboat and succeeded in dragging him [Burton] safely to the lifeboat." But in the minutes that followed the second torpedo explosion, not one of them would have taken a bet on their survival.

Rasch's first torpedo, which struck just forward of the stokehold bulkhead on the port side in No. 4 hold, doomed the ship. Lutjens reported, however, that it caused remarkably little apparent damage; nor did it produce a flash or throw up a column of water. The second torpedo, which struck the port side at No. 3 hold, forward of where the first torpedo hit, was louder than the first and threw up a "tremendous column of water." More important for the men who were now depending on their ability to run across a deck that had taken a 30° list to port, the second blast brought down the wireless aerial, blew off the hatch over No. 3 hold, scattered beams across the pitching deck and blew tons of newsprint into the water. The state of the deck can be judged from the fact that the Canso, which dived toward *Waterton* immediately after the first explosion, was "envelope[d] in a large cloud of smoke and debris, when it arrived 150 feet over the ship seconds after the second torpedo exploded."

For a few moments, Lutjens held out some hope that his ship might right itself. Then, after learning that the stokehold bulkhead was bulging and with the list increasing, he ordered his men to the boats. The last off his own ship, Lutjens was almost pulled under by the suction created by the sinking, but he managed to break free from the vortex and cling to some wreckage until he was picked up by the men in the portside lifeboat. The rest of his crew was picked up ten minutes later.

While the men aboard *Waterton* struggled to launch their boats and rafts and to save those in the water, Nicholson's asdic officer aboard HMCS *Vison* reported a firm contact. Within a few moments, the 422-ton yacht was over the U-boat, dropping one depth charge.

The setting was close. Rasch reported a "loud clear explosion at depth 30 m," which he incorrectly attributed to "aircraft bombs." Then, moments later, his crew, who a few minutes earlier had heard the "sinking of the steamer," were now shaken by another series of depth charges dropped by *Vison*. The first set especially must have been rather too close for comfort, for Rasch reported that they were "very well placed." As if to underline the tension in his boat, he reported that he was under attack by "2 destroyers," when just minutes before he'd not even mentioned the presence of the single small escort ship. Discretion being the better part of valour, Rasch stayed deep for the next eight hours as he headed out of the southwest.

* * *

The sinking of *Waterton* had the look and feel of another defeat, made all the more bitter by the fact that BS-31 had air cover. Indeed, the analysis written by Air Vice-Marshal N. R. Anderson comes close to questioning whether EAC would ever be able to counter the U-boat threat: "In spite of every effort not a sign of the U-boat could be located, not even the wake of the torpedo was visible. The high seas prevailing made it extremely difficult, if not impossible to see the periscope . . . . The high seas would also make it very difficult for the wake of the torpedo to be seen. The ASV [radar] was in constant operation, but failed to register a contact."

On October 14, defeatist words also came from two sources that did not yet know about the loss of *Waterton*: Gaspé's MP Sasseville Roy and the ultranationalist Quebec City newspaper *L'Action Catholique*. Roy told the *Ottawa Evening Journal* that he had sent the prime minister a letter demanding that he recall Parliament to debate the situation in the St. Lawrence, which, he said, was "even worse than when the House of Commons had held a secret session to discuss it last summer." Anyone familiar with parliamentary sparring could read between the lines when Roy stated, "My constituents want to be assured that the defences along the St. Lawrence are adequate and whether the air force's defences against the U-boat menace are directed along the most effective lines."

More potentially damaging to the King government—because it caught the attention of Quebec's Liberal premier, Adélard Godbout, who a few weeks earlier had criticized the decision to close the St. Lawrence to transoceanic shipping because of its effect on Montreal's economy—was a series of articles entitled, *"Ce qui se passe en Gaspésie"* ["What's Going on in the Gaspé"] that began running in *L'Action Catholique* on October 14. Written by Edouard Laurent, who had ties to former nationalist premier Maurice Duplessis, the articles are especially critical of both the navy and EAC. On July 19, the mayor of Les Méchins, Laurent wrote, reported to the EAC base at Mont Joli that a U-boat was offshore. According to Mayor Louis Keable, fully eight hours passed before a plane arrived over Les Méchins. Laurent charged that the delay was caused by *"Le RED-TAPE"*: RCMP agents had to travel the twenty-eight miles from Mont Joli to Les Méchins to confirm the sighting, and then permission had to be obtained from National Defence in Ottawa. Other charges included the claim that a corvette had been detached from regular escort duty to protect a fishing expedition of VIPs and that the government was not following its own blackout/dim-out regulations. It mattered little that Laurent's charges were easily disproved. What did matter was that he asserted that the Gaspé was gripped by *"l'atmosphère de malaise et d'angoisse."*

From the King government's point of view, Laurent's series was bad enough. It was made worse by the fact that within twenty-four hours of the first article appearing in *L'Action Catholique*, U-106 torpedoed the Newfoundland–Nova Scotia ferry SS *Caribou* in the Cabot Strait. Minister Macdonald announced the loss of *Caribou* on October 17, the day after the series ended and three days before the *Toronto Telegram* published one translated article under the title, "Charge Convoy Ships Sunk While Ottawa Guarded Sportsmen." That same day, a package containing Laurent's articles landed on King's desk along with a covering letter from Godbout, who said that they were "the most complete and objective articles I have yet seen on the subject."

Recognizing the political damage and the damage to national morale, King's government responded both publicly and through private channels. A measure of the government's concern, especially for the Liberal Party's traditional Quebec base (King held sixty-four of the province's sixty-five seats in Parliament as against fifty-seven of Ontario's eighty-two seats), was the decision to have Louis St. Laurent use a trip to Hamilton Steel on November 2 to rebut the *L'Action Catholique* charge that forty ships had been sunk in the St. Lawrence.

Beneath the leaden November skies, King's minister of justice and Quebec lieutenant addressed two different audiences. St. Laurent's presence in Hamilton, Ontario, spoke directly to the Steelworkers whose productive efforts were vital to the war effort. But the fact that St. Laurent, before becoming member for Quebec East, was a leader of the Quebec Bar meant that he was also making the announcement directly to Quebeckers. After assuring the public that the number of sinkings had been "exaggerated three-fold," St. Laurent said, "We are completing our effective forces and developing our navy to a point where we will be able to stop submarines from coming to hurt us as they did this year."

If anything, the private channels are even more telling of the government's unease. Defence Minister Charles Power signed a memorandum authorizing the release of classified information about the St. Lawrence sinkings—dates, names of ships and places—to Premier Godbout and to a Liberal Party organizer in Rimouski, who was then supposed to pass this information to both Laurent and the editors of *L'Action Catholique*. Given *L'Action Catholique*'s ties with pro-Vichy forces in Quebec and the Vichy government's puppet status, it is interesting to speculate whether the information Ottawa released to it following Laurent's articles contributed either to a November 4 article published in the Nazi party newspaper *Völkischer Beobachter* that trumpeted the U-boat attacks "from Capetown to Canada" or to a December 18 article (five weeks after the German army occupied Vichy) that accused Churchill of "flimflam" in denying that there had been "numerous sinkings in the Gulf of St. Lawrence" and that taunted Ottawa over the fact that its attempts to keep the sinkings secret had failed.[5]

Ironically, the perception of defeat, heightened by the sinking of *Caribou*, took hold just as EAC and the RCN had learned their trade. Not one of the four successful or twelve unsuccessful attacks in the St. Lawrence that followed Gräf's October 9 sinking of *Carolus* was carried out by a surfaced U-boat. As Gräf's and Rasch's war reports make clear, by mid-October 1942 there were few places in the St. Lawrence not blanketed by radar waves. The "screamingly loud detections" of Rasch's Metox and the resulting crash-dives so unnerved Rasch that he radioed to Dönitz that "we need a device that indicates distance as well as bearing."

In twenty days of patrolling after torpedoing *Waterton*, airplanes or Metox warnings forced Rasch under eleven times. On October 22, in his report of a failed attack, he told Lorient that air surveillance was not only "co-operating with surface search forces but also operating everywhere without surface forces." This is a tribute to EAC's coverage of the St. Lawrence: in response to the *Caribou* tragedy, twenty-four-hour coverage was being maintained only over the Cabot Strait.

Rasch's messages to Lorient on October 30 clearly indicate that EAC's patrols were not only disrupting his mission but also causing him to begin to question his own judgment. At 0400 he spotted a ten- to fifteen-ship convoy.

Two hours later he wrote, "Gave up pursuit as the continuous air cover that has been observed in this area means that a pursuit in daylight in this calm weather will be impossible." Forty-five minutes after that, after having dived and lost the convoy, he wrote in his war diary, "This decision was incorrect. I should have attempted to pursue after all." Later on the thirtieth, he reported to Lorient another price exacted by EAC's efforts: "Will have to depart [for home] in 8 days because potash cartridges will be expended." (Potash cartridges removed carbon dioxide from the air when it accumulated as a result of the inability to surface and fill the boat's air tanks.) The cost of having spent forty-two of ninety-seven days submerged, he confided to his war diary, was high: "Too much running under submerged ruins the fighting spirit."

Rasch's experience was shared by Gräf and by Hans-Joachim Schwandtke's U-43. In the five days between the sinkings of *Carolus* and *Caribou*, which Gräf came upon by accident while making his way out of the gulf, the Metox picked up radar signals at least nine times, while EAC and RCN patrols forced him to dive four times. On the sixteenth, he was "driven underwater by night aircraft" flying without the Leigh light system, which was still under development in England. Upon leaving the gulf, Gräf radioed Lorient that the patrols were "exactly like those in the [Bay of] Biscay," the approaches to Lorient and St. Nazaire above which the RAF had total air supremacy; this tactical advantage forced the U-boats to travel underwater, where they were much slower.

Kapitänleutnant Schwandtke entered Canadian waters early in the morning of October 19. He left on November 4, after a patrol that took him as far inland as Matane, bemoaning both the lack of river traffic and the "good co-operation between sea and air" that was "utterly disarming."

It would be an overstatement to say that the weeks that followed the sinking of *Waterton* presaged the defeat of the U-boats in May 1943, when hunter-killer groups, formed around such ships as the fleet aircraft carrier USS *Bogue*, destroyed forty-one U-boats and damaged thirty-seven others. Yet it is possible to see in those weeks the outlines of what has come to be called Black May.

Lacking the centimetric radar that would be available in 1943, EAC's planes were not always able to locate the U-boats in the St. Lawrence. Canadian escort ships were also hampered by the bathyscaphe effect that blinded asdic. Nor were Canadians equipped with "hedgehogs," which fired charges off the ship's bow, thus ending the problem of having to run over the submarine—a manoeuvre that meant that asdic contact was lost at the very moment the weapons were being fired. It was "hedgehogs" that helped turned the tide of the Battle of the Atlantic in 1943.

Nevertheless, by mid-October 1942, while they may not have registered any kills, EAC and the RCN had learned to work together well enough that they were routinely breaking up attacks—attacks that, because they were foiled, were unknown to Roy, the editors of *L'Action Catholique* and even the staff at Naval Service Headquarters. Indeed, no less an authority than *Grossadmiral* Dönitz credited Canadian "air power" with making the St. Lawrence a less-than-felicitous place for his "grey wolves."

OCTOBER 14, 1942

- Three thousand five hundred miles east in Lubeck, Germany, workers at Flender-Werke lay down the keel of U-318.
- Three thousand five hundred miles east in Hamburg, workers at Blohm & Voss launch U-951 and U-952; U-530 is commissioned.
- Five thousand five hundred miles east in Stalingrad, German soldiers nearly break through Soviet defences in the tractor factory.

At 3:25 a.m., after a forty-three-second run, compressed between the hull of *Caribou* and the body of the Type G7e torpedo, the firing pin in the nose of torpedo No. 20236 touched its ground. Instantaneously, electricity generated by the spinning of the small five-bladed propeller on the tip of the nose cone surged from a coil to the primer in the detonator. Nanoseconds later, 260 kilograms of *Schieswolle 36* underwent what chemical engineers call a "change-of-state reaction," which released enough energy to ignite the main charge. Within a second, the steel plates that divided *Caribou*'s engine room from the icy waters of the Cabot Strait were shattered by a white-hot bubble expanding at thousands of metres per second.

Before the geyser caused by the blast that ripped through *Caribou*'s hull collapsed, thousands of tons of water were already pouring into the ship's engine room. The combined effect of the explosion and the cold water washing over the ship's boilers ensured that within a minute or two they blew apart. As the water spread through her shredded bulkheads—as hundreds of men, women and children on the ferry began to run for their lives—the ionosphere above the St. Lawrence carried the message to Sydney: "*Caribou* torpedoed."

By morning, 137 men, women and children would be dead, including 31 of *Caribou*'s 46 crew. The small town of Port aux Basques, Newfoundland, lost 16 men and 1 woman, including three Taverners—Captain Ben Taverner, First Mate Stanley Taverner, Third Mate Harold Taverner—Fireman Garf Strickland and his brother Albert, an able seaman; Bosun Elias Coffin and his able-seaman son Bert; Assistant Steward Jerome Gale and Oiler George Gale; and Chief Steward Harry Hann and his donkeyman brother Clarence. On October 19, an unnamed, unclaimed baby boy found floating in a white nightdress was buried in Sydney, Nova Scotia.

The attack on *Caribou* did not come as a complete surprise. Long before people died in the Cabot Strait, tensions ran high on the main link between Newfoundland and Canada. "A year or two before she was hit," recalls Ruth Fullerton, who travelled to Newfoundland often to visit her parents, "there had just been a spate of sinkings off St. John's, so it was too dangerous to take a ship directly to St. John's. I took the *Caribou* to Port aux Basques (and then had to take the Newfie Bullet, the train to St. John's). We were very apprehensive on that trip; we had the sense something was going to happen. We stayed dressed and up all night. Mercifully, we arrived safely."

Even as EAC and the RCN were disrupting Gräf's, Rasch's and Schwandtke's war cruises, tensions mounted. Why, people in both Sydney and Port aux Basques asked, did *Caribou* keep to her published schedule? Why did the navy insist on her travelling blacked-out, at night and with an escort—all signals that she was a military ship and thus a legitimate target? Though, according to the Geneva Convention, since she carried military personnel and equipment, she was. Wouldn't her passengers and crew have a better chance of survival if she travelled during the day? Seven months after Gräf's torpedo struck *Caribou*, Onésime Gagnon, the unofficial deputy leader of the Union Nationale, told the Quebec legislature that federal air minister Power had been told of the planned attack fifteen days before it occurred.

On October 11, at her brother's urging, Fullerton abruptly changed her plans to travel from Sydney. "I had gone down to Sydney to see my brother, Lieutenant David M. Howrich, and wanted to go on to see Father, who was in Newfoundland," recalls Fullerton. "But David told me, 'Don't go. Lord Haw Haw has been saying they are going to take her [the *Caribou*] out.' I remember thinking that they'd never waste a torpedo on the poor old *Caribou*; three days later she was sunk."

The hours before and after *Caribou*'s sailing (right on schedule at 8 p.m. on October 13) were filled with prophetic warnings. After looking at his sailing orders, Captain Taverner told wireless operator Tommy Fleming, "They put us in a queer lane; this is the night we are going to get it."[6] William Lundrigan, who just a week earlier had crossed from Newfoundland without a moment's hesitation, was inexplicably uneasy. Nervous, both Vivian Swinamer and Gladys Shiers (who was travelling with her eighteen-month-old son, Leonard) decided to sleep with their clothes on. Hours before he found himself running for his life, William Metcalf told his cabin mate he had "a funny feeling that something is going to happened to this ship tonight."

By contrast, Royal Canadian Navy nursing sisters Agnes Wilkie and Margaret Brooke, who were returning to Newfoundland after a short visit home, were unconcerned. "We were not apprehensive at all," recalled Brooke, "when we boarded the *Caribou*. Usually you sleep with your clothes on, but for some reason, we just popped into our pyjamas."

Lieutenant J. Cuthbert, RCNVR, commander of the Bangor minesweeper HMCS *Grandmère*, began this mission with concern. Standard operation procedures laid down by Western Approaches headquarters in Liverpool dictated that when escorting a single ship, the escort should sweep behind the ship being escorted. Whether Cuthbert pointed out to his superiors that all RN escorts were equipped with radar that could sweep *ahead* of the ship being escorted is unknown, but there is no doubt that he knew *Grandmère* could not sweep ahead of a ship she was following. Worse, he told the commander of the Sydney naval base, if the *Caribou* was in front, the "noise of her engines would make it impossible for *Grandmère*'s Asdic operator to pick up the sounds of a U-boat's propeller." Cuthbert's commander rejected his suggestion that *Grandmère* zigzag ahead of the ferry or circle it. Hours later, while keeping his assigned escort station behind *Caribou*, Cuthbert's practised hand wrote, "very dark, no moon, funnel visible 2,500 yards. Very poor smoke discipline"—words pregnant with meaning. For they tell us that despite *Caribou*'s being blacked-out, the phosphorescence of the sea made the ship visible from at least a mile away.

At 12:30 a.m., as *Caribou* steamed into quadrant BB 5456, approximately forty miles off Port aux Basques, nursing sisters Wilkie and Brooke lay sleeping in their cabin. Lundrigan, who had given up his cabin to a couple with children, found that, unlike for his lounge mate Paddy Walsh of Corner Brook, Newfoundland, who went to sleep early, sleep would not come. Before he finally dozed off around 3 a.m., Lundrigan got up four times to trace his way to his lifeboat station. In the Mail Assorting Office, the domain of the Newfoundland Post Office, Ship Mail Clerk Howard Cutler tended to cancelling the stamps on the letters and cards in the 1,145 bags of mail that had been loaded in Sydney. On the bridge, Captain Taverner, perhaps having pushed his forebodings aside, no doubt savoured the feeling of command, for soon he'd relinquish the captaincy of *Caribou* to his eldest son, First Mate Stanley Taverner. Third Mate Harold Taverner's presence on board was equally serendipitous; he was substituting for a friend who had taken a few days off to get married.

A thousand yards away, its conning tower not more than twenty feet above the water, rode U-69, which after days of evading EAC's planes had been sent to the area to intercept three grain ships—SS *Eros*, *Formosa* and *Camelia*—only to find them to be Swedish ships and therefore neutral. In the darkened interior of the fetid submarine, clocks read 0530 Berlin time, and one-third of the crew clung to the last few minutes of sleep.

Four minutes later, Gräf spotted off his starboard bow "1 silhouette . . . with another, small one beyond." Helped by the "weak northern lights," across a sea with two-foot swells, he identified it, more or less as *Jane's Ships* for 1942 did: a "passenger cargo freighter of roughly 6,500 GRT [gross registered tonnes]." Like Cuthbert, he couldn't help adding that it was "belching black smoke." Had his identification of its escort off its starboard quarter as a "2-funnel destroyer" been correct, the 131 men, women and children who died before 5 a.m. local time might have made it to Port aux Basques alive—such an escort would have been a River-class destroyer, equipped with up-to-date radar and asdic that just might have caught U-69 sometime over the next three hours, time Gräf used to manoeuvre himself into firing position.

At 3:21 a.m.—while in Berlin commuters were thankful that the night of the thirteenth had passed without a heavy bombing—torpedo No. 20236 exploded, three feet below the waterline of a ferry in the St. Lawrence.

As Cuthbert's radio man tapped out the words *"Caribou* torpedoed," Cuthbert called Action Stations, rang for full speed and ordered a course toward the stricken ship. Engine artificers turned valves that let hundreds of pounds more of steam into the engines, which instantaneously started the reciprocating cranks—and thus the propeller—turning faster.

Several hundred yards away, another set of unyielding physical laws was at work. Thousands of tons of 54°F (12°C) water poured into the blasted hull, washing over the hot steel of *Caribou*'s already damaged boilers. The first few thousand gallons turned immediately to steam. Then, as the outside of the boiler's steel plates cooled toward the water temperature and the temperature inside the boiler remained above 300°F (150°C), *Caribou*'s boilers experienced thermal shock and, like a cold ceramic pot placed on a red-hot stove element, blew apart, further rending the ship.

The human drama in the ship's tilted, blasted passageways was compounded by other forces. The pressure of the water surging into the passages and hatchways nearest the shredded hull approached that in a firehose—enough to bowl over all but the strongest or those lucky enough to grab a fitting securely enough joined to the ship's bulkheads.

Laden with 235 souls, 450 tons of cargo, 4 railroad cars of PEI potatoes and 50 lowing cattle destined to feed Newfoundland, Taverner's ship was already sailing at the height of its Plimsoll lines.[7] Before Cuthbert's propeller was turning at full speed, those lines were irrelevant. *Caribou* had listed "down to her [port] railings," according to Gräf.

The blast, which destroyed two of the starboard lifeboats, knocked Harry

Jones, the ship's chief cook, from his bunk on the ship's port side, some ten feet behind the farthest reach of the wreckage caused by the torpedo's blast. Despite a fractured hip and shoulder, he managed to open his cabin door and then fought his way through the rushing water and tilting passageways to his lifeboat station.

Lundrigan was blown off the chaise longue upon which he'd finally fallen asleep. At first, he and the other men in the cabin were stunned. Then they realized they'd been torpedoed. People ran in all directions. The lights went out. They could hear the steam escaping from the blasted boilers—and the water rushing into the ship. Lundrigan ran to his lifeboat station, losing on the way a shoe that he'd carefully tied in the dark.

Asleep in the lounge when the torpedo hit, A. R. Fielding was just yards away from his lifeboat station. But because his wife was asleep in their cabin, as the ship began to tilt he ran into the darkened interior. Each step was a fight against the human tide of passengers who were struggling through the topsy-turvy passageways and hatchways. Somehow he found her, and together they joined the human tide rushing toward the main deck. When they got there, he put a lifebelt on her and, thinking it was her only chance, threw her overboard.

Before Fielding could dive in, a woman ran by and handed him her child, saying she was running back to her cabin for another. "I passed it on to someone on a raft . . . . She never reappeared." He never saw the baby again.

Captain Taverner could see none of this. He was in his cabin when the torpedo hit, and by the time he ran to the bridge, the deck was totally obscured by steam escaping from the blasted pipes and boilers. He then ran to the boat deck, where he discovered two horrible truths that Lundrigan and almost two hundred others were discovering: there were too few lifeboats and rafts left and too few crew left alive to properly launch them. The last sight anyone had of Taverner was of his returning to the bridge after trying and failing to launch a raft.

At Lundrigan's lifeboat station, a disaster unfolded. The lifeboat's lines were twisted, and, to make matters worse, men and women had boarded it before the lines were straightened. Still, Lundrigan and some other men tried to launch *Caribou*'s No. 2 boat. "We couldn't get the boats out. The ropes were twisted and they wouldn't slide down." Then apparent success, followed by more tragedy: "After a long time working at it, we got it down, [but] she wouldn't go down in a proper fashion . . . . And when she went down, she went down suddenly. When the twist came out of the ropes there was not a single soul in her when she went down into the water," he later told an interviewer.

As *Caribou*'s deck slid even farther into the sea, Lundrigan saw another boat, lifeboat No. 4, being piloted by Jack Dominie, one of Taverner's seamen. Though the lifeboat was crowded with people, Dominie brought it close enough to the wrecked hull so that Lundrigan and a few others could jump into it as it bobbed up and down, and toward and away from the sinking ship. Those who missed drowned. Within moments, however, Dominie, Lundrigan and others aboard the lifeboat realized that *Caribou* was about to go under and that, to save themselves, they had to pull away. By the time they were seventy yards away, the 2,222-ton ship, built in 1925 and refitted just two months earlier, had plunged to the bottom of the Cabot Strait, the twentieth ship sunk in the St. Lawrence.

Four minutes had elapsed.

In the moments before *Caribou*'s final plunge, as water rushed over the main deck, Swinamer and Shiers, carrying her son, ran for the bridge, almost a fatal decision. As they climbed the steps to the only part of the ship still above water, an explosion showered them with debris. Another moment later the rushing sea wrenched Leonard from his mother's arms and catapulted the two women into the sea.

Nursing sisters Brooke and Wilkie never made it to their lifeboat station. The precious seconds it took them to force their way out of their cabin (the blast bent the hatchway) could be measured only in feet. When they got on deck, it was already awash. Seconds later, a wave took them and they were struggling to survive in the sea.

For four minutes, the screams of men, women and children, the screech of steel being rent out of shape, the breaking of bulkheads and the awful lowing of drowning cattle filled the night, only to be followed by the sound of a whirlpool that formed as the ship plunged, fire and smoke pouring out of its shredded side. Then, before the whirlpool closed, the last of *Caribou*'s boilers exploded and a pillar of fire rose out of the water, illuminating for a moment the dead, the dying and those barely hanging on to life.

Just seconds after *Caribou*'s last light, the men and women in Dominie's boat realized that it was filling with water. Dominie realized that the seacock was out. "I tried the best I could to get the plug in, but I couldn't get it in . . . . She was loaded with people, the force of the water would blow it back every time . . . . Before I'd get a chance to drive it down with my foot, it would be back out," he recalled in an interview.

They tried bailing. It failed.

"She filled full of water and rolled, and the people all went into the water, the poor women and children, all of them. It was dark . . . . I don't know how many times she rolled over. When she was finished there were just a few of us left in her . . . . And when we were picked up there were only the four of us," including Lundrigan.

Metcalf remembered that terrible moment as the boat turned. After its first turn, a woman clung to him. "I tried to speak to her but she couldn't answer." The woman was ripped away from him a moment later as the boat again turned over in the unforgiving sea.

Cuthbert's orders were clear. At 3:39 a.m., his mission was to "ensure the safe and timely arrival of the convoy." A minute later it had changed. He ordered a course for the stricken ship. Then, as if on cue, before *Grandmère* was even close enough to throw lifebelts to *Caribou*'s survivors, one of Cuthbert's lookouts spotted a "U-boat on the surface ahead and to the starboard," 300 yards away. Immediately, his helmsman turned a course to ram it.

Gräf's war diary tells the story succinctly:

0821 At first, she [*Grandmère*, which Gräf called a "destroyer"] turns toward the steamer but then apparently sights me and alters course toward and comes foaming toward me.

0825 Opening out on the surface will not be possible because of the good visibility [Gräf did not know that the "destroyer's" flank speed was some 4 knots below his own]. Emergency dive! Went deep quickly. Turned in the vicinity of the sinking ship at full speed; the destroyer will not drop depth charges here. Loud noises of breaking bulkheads can be heard throughout the boat.

As Cuthbert ran over Gräf's swirl, he fired six depth charges "by eye." Gräf reported hearing only one explode, well above his pressure hull. For the next thirty minutes, Gräf and his crew heard the telltale ping of *Grandmère*'s asdic, but since no more depth charges hammered against his hull, he could guess that he "was not detected by the destroyer's asdic." His message at 2000 hrs. to BdU makes one mistake. He signalled Dönitz that "my decoy device," *Nebelbold*, which, like the *Pillenwerfer*, was designed to blind asdic by releasing tens of millions of bubbles into the water, "does not appear to have had any effect." In fact, *Grandmère* never picked up an asdic contact.

Years later, Cuthbert responded to criticism that he had erred in not searching for the U-boat in the waters directly beneath the survivors (where, in fact, it had hidden): "Oh my God, I felt the full complement of things you feel at a time like that. Things you have to live with. You are torn. Demoralized. Terribly alone . . . . I should have gone on looking for the submarine, but I couldn't. Not with women and children out there somewhere. I couldn't do it any more than I could have dropped depth charges among them. Judge me how you will," Cuthbert told Douglas How, author of *The Night of the Caribou*.

As Cuthbert searched for *Caribou*'s killer, the angel of death took the form of hypothermia and stalked the waters that glided over 47° 19′ N, 59° 29′ W. It found the wreckage of the lifeboat Fielding and eleven others clung to. "When we were picked up, there were only five of us left. Four of the women slid off the upturned shell and disappeared, as did several of the men, weakened with the cold water. We did everything we could to help them but it was futile," Fielding recalled.

Neither hymns nor prayers could keep the avenging angel from finding the capsized lifeboat to which nursing sisters Wilkie and Brooke clung. "The waves kept washing us off, one by one," recalled Brooke. "And eventually Agnes said she was getting cramped. She let go but I managed to catch hold of her with one hand. I held her as best I could until daybreak. Finally, a wave took her. When I called to her, she didn't answer. She must have been unconscious. The men tried to rescue her, but she floated away," Brooke told the *Halifax Herald*.[8]

Death claimed a woman here, a man there, a child. One shocked, cold and tired man was ripped from death's clutches—the other men on his raft slapped him back to reason after he stood up and tried to throw himself off the raft and into a cold death. But though Gladys Shiers wouldn't know it for hours, pity must have moved the angel of death, for it passed over Leonard Shiers and another infant, both of whom were kept afloat by air trapped in their rubber pants.

At 5:20 a.m., Cuthbert broke off his search and began the delicate task of picking up the survivors, now spread out over several miles. Only the few who were in lifeboats could easily be brought aside his ship. The rest—ninety-six exhausted, cold men, women and children—were floating on bits of wood, on capsized boats or by the grace of their lifebelts, their arms and legs all but numb and thus unable to grasp the scramble nets thrown from *Grandmère*'s side. Every advance into the human archipelago risked even more death. Even at its slowest speed, the movement of *Grandmère* through the water produced enough suction to bash rafts to pieces against her bow. Her engines may have moved safety toward the survivors, but they also threatened to pull them under. By 7:30 a.m., a Canso flying boat from North Sydney dropped smoke floats, telling Cuthbert that here, six miles away, were still more souls to save.

Half a continent away in Ottawa, Prime Minister Mackenzie King was waking out of what, no doubt, he later believed to be one of his prophetic dreams. As he recorded in his diary late on October 14, "Before waking this morning, I had a vision of standing, it seemed near a bookshelf in a library or church vestry where there were one or two books out. Suddenly, a bomb burst immediately outside." King's dream, however, differed greatly from the nightmare that had unfolded off Canada's eastern waters. For in his vision, there was "no panic" and no death.

By 9:30 a.m., after picking up 104 survivors, Cuthbert ordered a course for Sydney; two people died before they reached the quay from which they had departed sixteen hours earlier.

As *Grandmère* steamed to Sydney and U-69 prepared to leave the St. Lawrence, a small armada of skiffs, dories, fishing boats and, ultimately, two corvettes sent from Sydney converged on German grid square BB 5198 to pick up the dead.

As *Grandmère* steamed for Sydney, Norman Crane, an officer in the Newfoundland Rangers stationed in Tompkins, was already heading for Port aux Basques to help with the recovery duties. The town he reached on that clear October day was in shock.

"In 1942," he recalls, "Port aux Basques was not like small towns on the mainland. It was more like a nineteenth-century town. Yes, it was the terminus of the railway and the port, but the three towns around the harbour had maybe two thousand people. There was no electricity or running water. To take a bath you bought water for a quarter from a guy who sold it out of a wheelbarrow. There was one truck, one taxi, and if they encountered a horse-drawn cart, there was a traffic jam. They were a rough-cut bunch like most communities that relied on the sea were. But they were also very religious and respectful.

"The loss of the *Caribou* affected Port aux Basques more than you can imagine today. Ben Taverner wasn't just a well-liked captain of the *Caribou*, he was a respected man, known to have devoted his life to his boat and thus to their link to the outside world. His sons weren't just fun-loving fellows—although they were—they were Ben Taverner's sons, and that counted for a lot.

"Her second engineer, Tom Moist, was a friend of mine. He was old enough to be my grandfather and he had actually retired. His replacement's son was getting married, so he asked Tom to take the trip for him, so he could go to the wedding. Tom made the trip to help out a friend and never came back.

"When I got there, bodies had already started coming in."

Crane—who as a Newfoundland Ranger was responsible for everything from law and order through tourism, wildlife and nature preservation to school inspection—commandeered a shed and set up a temporary mortuary. "It was a long shed, lit with bare bulbs every twenty feet. The bodies came in one by one. By the end, we had twelve bodies laid out on bales of hay under the bare bulbs."

The macabre scene in the temporary morgue Crane helped set up was matched, he recalls, on the streets of the town. "The feeling was one of complete gloom. Eerie is probably the best way to describe it. The whole town felt like a mortuary—which in a real way it was."

Three hundred miles away in Sydney, word spread too. Leilo Pepper, the twenty-two-year-old wife of Howard Pepper, commander of Fairmile Q-062, found out about it at 2:15 a.m., when her husband returned to their small apartment for a brief rest before taking his crew to sea at first light. "At first it was hard to believe what Howard had told me," she recalls. "I knew that he'd just spoken to Captain Taverner a few days earlier and made plans to go fishing the next time the captain was ashore in Sydney. And now, here, in the middle of the night, Howard was telling me that the old ship we were so used to seeing was sunk."

Late in the afternoon, while walking her nine-month-old son on the esplanade that overlooked Sydney Harbour, Pepper saw *Grandmère* come in laden with its human cargo.

"They landed a couple of hundred yards away across the street," she recalls. "Some were able to walk. Many had to be helped. Others were carried on stretchers. The other women walking their children and I stood in a hushed group as the wind whispered over us.

"We'd all heard by then that the loss of life was heavy. And we knew enough to know that that meant that women like us and children like ours had died in the cold Atlantic waters."

Two days later, on October 17, naval minister Macdonald rose and told the House of Commons, "The sinking of the SS *Caribou* brings the war to Canada with tragic emphasis. We deplore the loss of officers and men of our fighting forces . . . . Yet those for whom our hearts bleed most are the . . . women and children . . . . if there were any Canadians who did not realize that we were up against a ruthless and remorseless enemy, there can be no such Canadians now. If anything were needed to prove the hideousness of Nazi warfare, surely this is it. Canada can never forget the SS *Caribou*."

CHAPTER SEVEN

1943: OPERATION KIEBITZ

And if it's sweeping mines (to which my fancy somewhat leans)
Or hanging out with booby-traps for the skulking submarines,
I'm here to do my blooming best and give the beggars beans

—C. FOX SMITH

The war that began washing up on the shores of the little villages of Cloridorme and L'Anse-à-Valleau on May 15, 1942, altered the lives of the men, women and children who lived in the scores of towns, villages and hamlets strung out along the north shore of the Gaspé Peninsula, at the end of which Jacques Cartier planted his cross in 1534. In 1939 Gaspesia, the name given to the region by the locals, counted just under 2,000 residents, 65 per cent of whom were English. By 1943 the population had increased to over 2,300, with another 650, mostly English-speaking soldiers, airmen and sailors stationed in the five military bases built around the town. Gaspesians, used to fishing and hunting where they wished, now found large tracts of land and the shoreline cut off by the fences of forts Prevel, Peninsula and Haldimand. Workers who had never built anything larger than a train barn or a small railroad bridge were hired to build structures they had perhaps imagined only as children playing with toy soldiers: an anti-submarine net to protect Gaspé's inner harbour and huge concrete emplacements that housed two 75-mm guns, two 4.7-inch guns and, after July 1941, two huge 10-inch guns.

Rimouski and the surrounding fields changed too, though not without debate. In 1939, Mont Joli was but a plateau twenty feet above the river, adjacent to the village of Sainte-Flavie, a mere point on the map ten miles east of Rimouski. On June 20, 1940, Senator Jules A. Brillant, who had extensive land holdings in Rimouski and on the Gaspé coast, called for the establishment of an air training school at Mont Joli. Built over the objections of Rimouski's archbishop, Monseigneur Georges Courchènes, by 1942 the base had almost six hundred pilot and bombardier trainees—the largest of the thirty British Commonwealth Air Training Plan air bases in Canada.

Monseigneur Courchènes's opposition to the base was of a piece with his opposition to Brillant's role in the Fusiliers du St-Laurent. According to Major François Dornier, historian of the Fusiliers, Courchènes saw Brillant as a rival moral authority who threatened the church's control of the Rimouski diocese. The benediction Courchènes delivered at Mont Joli's (long-delayed) official inauguration on August 15, 1942, refers obliquely to Sub-Lieutenant Jacques Chevrier's death the previous month but not to any of the naval officers, ratings or merchant sailors who had died in the Battle of the St. Lawrence in the preceding three months. Courchènes took time, however, to remind the airmen of their duty to uphold the "moral climate" of Rimouski. A year later, his attitude hadn't changed. After an episcopal visit to the parish of Mont Joli on September 12 and 13, 1943, Courchènes recorded that his "concern has grown because of the presence of strangers in the parish who are part of the neighbouring aviation base."[1]

The archbishop's prestige was immense, but it did not carry the day with the civilian authorities or, interestingly enough, with his own flock. A survey of the articles in Rimouski's *L'Echo du Bas Saint-Laurent* reveals public support for both the Fusiliers and the airbase—and for the money that building it would pump into the local economy. Perhaps even more telling is this February 1942 letter from Rimouski resident J. B. Côté to Claude Melançon, director of the federal Press, Information and Propaganda Service, occasioned by the visit of one of Vichy France's representatives to Courchènes's home in Rimouski:

At the very moment that I am writing to you, a certain Mr. Coursier is being hosted by Mgr. Courchènes, and do you know what they are debating? That the English propaganda is poisoning us, that the English are traitors to France, that the French are free under the German occupation and that their newspapers are not censored, that the Franco-mercenary

English are the cause of all of France's unhappiness, etc., etc. Everyone around the archbishop is converted to this beautiful doctrine which he spreads throughout the diocese while Mr. Coursier will go and implore another bishop to be well disposed to these colonialized ideas.[2]

Côté's anti-Vichy sentiment was not shared by Quebec's clerical and secular opinion leaders centred in Montreal; they continued to support Marshal Pétain's Vichy government through the end of 1942. *Le Devoir* routinely published transcripts of Radio Vichy's broadcasts, which were praised in Quebec for pointing out "the oppression exercised on French Canadians by Jews and the British."

The distance between *Le Devoir* and other Quebec nationalists' views and that of *L'Echo du Bas St-Laurent* could not have been greater. In 1940 the Rimouski paper editorialized against *"Les dupes de l'Allemagne,"* the French who thought that peace could be negotiated with the Nazis. *L'Echo* identified them with *"certaines tête chaudes* [hot-heads] *canadien-français"* who, like the Irish, "grasp with frenzy at a chimeric neutrality." On August 9, 1940, *L'Echo* declared outright, "We thank God that England's morale remains intact. Speaking honestly, England is at this moment alone capable of saving the world—and that includes Canada—from the darkness of barbarism and slavery."[3]

During August 1942, however—the same week in which Admiral Jones and Percy Nelles, chief of the Naval Staff, reiterated Prime Minister King's warning of a possible U-boat assault on the St. Lawrence—*L'Action Catholique* editorialized in support of the return of Pierre Laval to the Vichy cabinet. Laval, who had lived in Paris under the protection of the German army after Pétain sacked him in 1940, was one of the most Nazified of Vichy's politicians, notorious for seeing off French volunteers who served with German units that attacked Russia and, after his return to power, for agreeing to sending skilled French workers to Germany and giving the Gestapo permission to hunt down Jews in unoccupied France.[4] On April 16, in the run-up to the conscription plebiscite and one month before the sinking of SS *Nicoya*, *L'Union*, a small ultranationalist and anti-Semitic publication, called for a Vichy-like regime in Quebec. In September 1942—fully five months after men began dying off Quebec's shores—the Bishop of

Montreal, Monseigneur Joseph Charbonneau, speaking at the dedication of a new building of Collège Stanislas (to which the Vichy government had contributed funds), praised Pétain, claiming, "Despite the ordeals he has gone through, Marshal Pétain is a Good Samaritan and his blessed country always thinks of us. He dreams of France's traditional role. Here, like there, he says, 'I will maintain.'"

Despite the fact that the Bas St-Laurent was the part of Quebec that best received both Radio Vichy and the Nazi-controlled Radio Paris, Gaspesians were less interested in remaining faithful to *notre mère-patrie, la France* than were the intellectuals safely ensconced in Montreal. In 1940, despite Courchènes's public disapproval of the Fusiliers du St-Laurent and despite Radio Vichy imprecations to *les canadiens français* to refuse military service, 500 men volunteered for the Fusiliers. Two years later, No. 1 Battalion of the Fusiliers alone counted 773 men and 34 officers. A year later, the 2nd Battalion had more than 1,000 men and officers; by autumn the battalion's rolls had grown to 1,251 officers and men. Nor was the Gaspé's support for the Canadian military limited to enlistees; during the Christmas and New Year's holidays of 1941 and 1942, more than two hundred francophone families welcomed Australian, British, New Zealand, Canadian and American air trainees into their homes.

As the losses mounted in the St. Lawrence during 1942, more men enlisted in the Fusiliers. Between September and November 1942, 1,500 men enlisted, enough to create four new subdivisions.[5] In 1943, the 3rd Battalion alone had 49 officers and 1,877 men, 50 per cent of whom had had field battery training. Rimouski's 2nd Battalion counted 972 men. Along the north shore of the St. Lawrence, 737 men and 35 officers stood guard, in addition to 187 civilian ADC personnel. Across the Gaspé Peninsula, more than 1,000 ADC members watched the waters nervously.

In June 1943, six months after Vichy was occupied by Hitler's army and the last pretence that Pétain's government represented *la gloire de la France* vanished—and while Courchènes continued to worry about the moral effect of the airmen training at Mont Joli—Montreal papers, including *Le Devoir*, ran articles praising the Fusiliers, the home army under Brigadier-General Edmond Blais and Gaspesians' preparedness. "*Tout Gaspésien est devenu un soldat*," declared *La Presse* on June 17, 1943, in an article in which Roger Champeaux recounted the vulnerabilities of the Gaspé and then asserted that the army emplacements and ADC training he had seen on a tour of the Gaspé provided the necessary protection. *"Les Gaspésiens son aux aguets"* ("Gaspesians are on the lookout"), wrote *Le Devoir*'s Lucien Desbiens five days later while praising the training of ADC volunteers and Blais's soldiers, each of whom, Desbiens wrote, "is a specialist." A year later, journalists returned to the Gaspé and in their articles reported Blais's words. "The Gaspé has been, since the beginning of the conflict, the first zone of war in Canada. The Gaspé is the front line: its population has shown its bravery. This population, we have seen as nowhere else in the country, has been ready and able to combat the enemy."

MARCH 17, 1943

- One thousand two hundred miles east of the coast of Newfoundland, six U-boats sink nine ships in convoy HX-229; the loss of thirteen of thirty-nine ships over the course of the three-day battle almost convinces the Admiralty to abandon convoying.
- Three thousand miles east in London, the Royal Air Force establishes a secret bomber squadron whose mission is to destroy the dams in the Ruhr River.

- Four thousand five hundred miles east in Piaski, Poland, more than 1,200 Jews are killed in retribution for the killing of a much-feared SS trooper.
- Four thousand miles southeast in Tunisia, Field Marshal Bernard Montgomery's Eighth Army prepares for an offensive against German positions on the Mareth Line.

Hansard records the clash between Sasseville Roy and Naval Services Minister Macdonald as being part of the 1943 budget debate, which had begun a few days earlier. But every member of the House, every visitor in the gallery and the press knew that neither Roy nor Macdonald was speaking about either the budget in general or the Naval Estimates, which totalled

$3.6 billion. Rather, on March 15, 1943, with less than two months to go before the opening of the 1943 coastal shipping season, Roy had done nothing less than indicate his lack of confidence in the minister and, therefore, in the King government's handling of security on the St. Lawrence.

Shock at the loss of *Caribou*, the coming of the winter freeze-up of the St. Lawrence and Macdonald's statement on November 24, 1942, that there had been "20 sinkings in the whole river and gulf area" had, for a time, muted the kind of criticisms made by *L'Action Catholique*'s Laurent. On March 4, 1943, however, in a speech to the Quebec legislature, Onésime Gagnon, the Union Nationale member for the riding of Matane, returned to the rumour Justice Minister Louis St. Laurent had sought to squelch the previous November. According to Gagnon, whose provincial riding covered roughly the same territory as Roy's federal riding of Gaspé, "the federal Minister of Naval Affairs has not told the people of Quebec the truth—not 20 but upward of 30 ships were sunk in the Gulf of St. Lawrence last summer." Included in this number, he told the Quebec legislature, were "two United States destroyers that were torpedoed either in the St. Lawrence River or in the Gulf of St. Lawrence," a claim that was accepted by *Le Devoir* and *Le Droit*, and by other members of the Quebec legislature, even though the US had made no reference to the loss of a USN ship in the St. Lawrence.

Premier Godbout's response suggests that Macdonald's decision to share information with him in 1942 had quieted his fears. Godbout began by noting how Gagnon's attitude toward defence matters had changed since 1940. At that time, the premier reminded the Quebec legislature, Gagnon had complained that "the federal government buys cannons in place of giving bread to the people."

In Ottawa, Macdonald responded quickly. On March 7, the minister for naval services used a standing commitment to tour RCN ships in Halifax to challenge Gagnon: "If he gives me the date and the locality of each of the 30 sinkings, I will investigate each case." Judging well his crowd, the minister continued: "If Mr. Gagnon does not trust the Naval Service, we will appoint a committee to investigate." Macdonald's pledge that "this committee might include a representative appointed by the Quebec member and the navy," and an independent party agreeable to both the minister and

Gagnon, reveals as much about the perennial problem of Quebec–federal relations as does any other political statement during the war.

Two days later, on March 9, as Macdonald and Gagnon traded telegrams about the mandate of the proposed committee, Hormidas Langlais, the Union Nationale member of the Provincial Parliament for Îles-de-la-Madeleine, brought forward a motion demanding that the government of Quebec table "a copy of all correspondence" exchanged between it and the federal government pertaining to the St. Lawrence since 1937. After repeating Gagnon's claim that thirty, not twenty, ships had been sunk the previous year, Langlais protested the closing of the St. Lawrence to transoceanic shipping. "The weight of this decision," he thundered, "falls more heavily" on Quebec's population; the benefits "flow to Saint John and Halifax, where it has been necessary to expand in order to handle the increased traffic." Langlais then directly accused Macdonald, who represented a Halifax riding, of favouring ports in English provinces.

Langlais was answered by Godbout's attorney general, Léon Casgrain, who began by reminding his Quebec parliamentary colleagues that the questions are "posed to Mr. Angus Macdonald, naval minister. However, this man is in Ottawa." His next comment, "No one in this Legislative Assembly, none of us possesses the necessary lights, knows the facts or is qualified to discuss in detail questions of naval strategy," might, especially after some thirty years of constitutional wrangling with Quebec, sound strange to our ears, but was nevertheless true. Casgrain ended by saying that the government that stood before the opposition in the Quebec legislative assembly "will do its duty to work to administer our province and leave to the federal government their care of our defence."

In Ottawa the next day, March 10, Gordon Graydon, the leader of the opposition Conservative Party, asked Macdonald about the debates that had occurred in Quebec. Macdonald responded by explaining to the House his offer to Gagnon. The minister used his reply to Graydon's supplementary question, which again cited Gagnon's numbers, to begin to cut the ground out from under the Quebec legislator: "Mr. Gagnon says that he has a list of the names of the ships and the dates on which they were sunk. I asked Mr. Gagnon to produce this list for my investigation. I have asked him by telegram and he replied that surely my own department has the information. My department cannot have this information on ghost ships that have been sunk—flying Dutchmen or something of that sort."

After assuring the House that there were no bases in the St. Lawrence at which U-boats could refuel, Macdonald said, "I believe I am safe in saying that every possible precaution will be taken by the Canadian armed services—the navy, the army and the air force—to deal with every situation that can be expected to develop."

Maddeningly vague though the minister's words were, they were far from parliamentary bluster. During the winter, ADC had been reorganized and thousands more volunteers had been trained, bringing the total to 3,968 by the beginning of 1943, and rising to 9,943 by December 1943. EAC had been strengthened by the addition of 47 RCAF planes (for a total of 98) and more than 100 trainers (for a total of 386)—the largest group based at Mont Joli. RCN ships had been equipped with the more powerful Mark VIII depth charges. Further, the RCN had established "killer groups" designed to operate independently of the escort groups that provided "close protection of convoys." And, perhaps most important, at the National Research Council labs on Sussex Drive in Ottawa, work was proceeding apace on a microwave early warning radar, to be deployed early in the shipping season; this system used 10.7-centimetre waves capable of locating surfaced U-boats at greater distances than the equipment then being used.

King's naval minister then set about trying to drive a wedge between Gagnon and his constituents (and by implication, also between Roy and his constituents). "To cope adequately with a problem of this kind, however, involves co-operation of citizens in the area," Macdonald began, "and the co-operation of members of this House and of provincial legislatures. To disclose information which might be helpful to the enemy by asking questions in public or by making statements in public is not doing a service to this country or for the welfare of the parts of the country which are directly affected by this discussion or for the protection of the lives of those who must fight every threat that is made."

On March 15, after asking the House's leave to allow him to postpone his remarks on the budget, Roy repeated Langlais's and Gagnon's claim that thirty, not twenty, ships had been sunk in 1942 and made several new serious charges. The first touched on the RCN and the postal service. At the height of the battle the previous July, Roy said, a corvette had been detached to accompany *Jean Brillant* on a sport-fishing trip. The escort had been justified, Roy said, by a "request of the Postmaster General (Mr. Mulock) because it [*Jean Brillant*] was carrying mail to the north shore. However, the boat never dropped off mail on her way on but proceeded to the fishing trip for quite a few days."

Roy's second charge criticized the lack of co-operation between the RCN and the RCAF. He reported that in late July 1942, after witnessing a midafternoon "battle between two corvettes and a submarine," Laurent Giroux of Griffon Cove "rushed to a telephone and called the Gaspé operator, telling her to pass the word to the Gaspé military base, where we were supposed to have some bombers." Why, he asked, as the battle went on for more than an hour, did "no help ever come from Gaspé, though the distance to Griffon Cove as a bird would fly is only about six and a half miles?" To this example, Roy added the attacks of September 11, 1942, on HMCS *Charlottetown*, of September 16 on SS *Joannis* and of September 15 on SS *Saturnus* and *Inger Elizabeth*, including the story of lighthouse keeper Ferguson's efforts to alert EAC. He also reiterated Gagnon's claim that the RCAF could not do its job because it had to get approval from Ottawa before it could fly.

Roy's third charge concerned both the war economy as a whole and the economic health of Montreal and Quebec in particular. Though he did not produce any figures, closing the St. Lawrence to transoceanic shipping had, he claimed, done "much harm . . . to the harbours of Montreal and Quebec," an almost exact quotation of Gagnon's and Langlais's claim that closing the St. Lawrence prejudiced Quebec City and Montreal in favour of Atlantic Canadian ports. Roy then argued that the closing of the St. Lawrence had so overloaded the single-track railroad that connected Halifax with Montreal that the government was wasting millions of dollars of war material: "If some honourable members travelled between Montreal and Quebec, I am sure they must have seen tanks and other war materials [left] there to rot, through lack of means to send them to the places where they are so badly needed." Roy continued by citing an editorial from the *Chronicle Telegraph*, Quebec City's English newspaper: "The St. Lawrence is a strategic factor of first-rate importance in the battle of supplies. . . . It ought to be kept open and in use and there is no reason why it cannot be kept open and in use with reasonable safety—as much safety as can be claimed for any other Atlantic route."

On March 17, Macdonald moved quickly to end the debate about the number of ships that had been sunk in 1942. In contravention of his own censorship regulations and, he claimed, in a break from the practice followed by the US and the UK, he named eighteen merchant ships and two warships that had been sunk and indicated where they were sunk. Macdonald turned next to Roy's charge that a corvette had been sent to escort *Jean Brillant* on a fishing trip. Knowing that Roy would dismiss anything he said, the minister began with the extraordinary step of asking the House's leave to lay before it affidavits sworn out by *Jean Brillant*'s captain, the manager of the Lower St. Lawrence Navigation Company and Senator Jules-André Brillant, member of the legislative council of the province of Quebec (then the upper house of the Quebec provincial parliament), all of whom said that *Jean Brillant* "had had no escort." Not content with spiking Roy's story, Macdonald also took the occasion to directly attack Roy's credibility: "The point on which I criticize the Honourable Member for Gaspé in the *Jean Brillant* [affair] is this. He knows Mr. Brillant (the Legislative Councillor concerned), he knows some of the other gentleman who were on that trip, and he could have asked them, 'Were you accompanied by a corvette when going on the fishing trip?' He never took that trouble; he assumed the worst."

Macdonald next turned to Roy's claim that the RCN and RCAF were unable to co-ordinate their activities. Later in the speech, Macdonald would admit that communications problems had manifested themselves the previous September 15 (the day of the attacks on SS *Saturnus* and *Inger Elizabeth*). Seasoned debater that he was, however, Macdonald sought to cushion the blow of that admission by first undercutting Roy's credibility on tactical questions. Of the claim that in the "latter part of July . . . a battle was engaged between a submarine and two corvettes," Macdonald said, "I have had reports from the logs of the ships and I find that I must regretfully disappoint the Honourable Member for Gaspé. I must tell him that he has not had the privilege of witnessing a battle at all, and that all he heard was gun practice between two corvettes which were going up the river."[6]

Macdonald turned next to the necessity of closing the St. Lawrence. The river had to be closed to transoceanic shipping because, though the defences had become stronger, the RCN and the RCAF could not provide the kind of protection needed for transoceanic shipping to resume. Without getting into the details of what could be detected and what couldn't, Macdonald reminded the House of the problems inherent in detecting submerged and surfaced U-boats and of the immensity of the St. Lawrence area: "When some people speak of a river they think of a fairly small stream that can be bridged or that can be easily netted; they think of a river perhaps half a mile or a mile wide. Let them remember that the St. Lawrence river, at the point furthest inland where an attack was made least year, is thirty miles wide." This distance, he reminded the House, "is wider than the Straits of Dover between England and France." To drive home the point, he reached back a year to February 12, 1942, when the German battle cruisers *Scharnhorst* and *Gneisenau* humiliated the Royal Navy as they made their famous dash up the English Channel from the French port of Brest to the North Sea and finally to Germany: "If the great British Navy with all its experience and skill and strength and devotion to duty has not succeeded in making the Straits of Dover absolutely safe from submarines—indeed only a year ago it was unable to prevent certain great enemy ships from going through the straits—if that cannot be done there, is it to be wondered at that we cannot guarantee complete immunity for ships in the river St. Lawrence."

Despite the immense distances involved, the RCN and the RCAF had done well, Macdonald asserted. Yes, there had been deaths and losses, "but, I can say that of the total tonnage which used the river and the gulf last year, only three out of every thousand tons was sunk."

On June 9, the ever-present tension between English and French Canada briefly flared again when Roy rose on a point of privilege to take issue with a Montreal *Daily Star* editorial entitled "Opportunity for Service," directed squarely at Gaspesians. Roy dismissed the first part of the editorial as "stupid" for stating that "the population of that area are now being given an opportunity, which they will no doubt seize with alacrity, to share in their own defence." Given the number of civilians already in ADC and the number of enlistees in the Fusiliers, Roy's epithet surely was correct. He took further umbrage at the editorial's final paragraph, which went beyond chiding Gaspesians for a certain laxity in observing the dim-out: "The government plans a campaign to enforce "dim-out" regulations and to discourage *careless talk* and the circulation of sensational and inaccurate rumours many of which last year were repeated in the House of Commons itself by members of affected constituencies" (emphasis added).

The use of the term "careless talk" was more redolent than it is today. Especially in Maritime communities, this phrase was ubiquitous. The top half of thousands of posters showed a man being overheard telling another man in a bar, "She sails at midnight." The bottom half showed a ship going down after being torpedoed, above the words "CARELESS TALK COSTS LIVES." Thus the *Daily Star*, as Roy rightly noted, was doing more than underlining the importance of the dim-out. It was none-to-subtly impugning both his own and his constituents' patriotism.

Before ending his point of privilege, Roy tweaked the *Star*'s nose by saying, "I believe that every Canadian citizen would have been much more happy to learn that those reports of sinkings in the St. Lawrence were merely rumours, but unfortunately they were true." He then, rather deftly, took credit for having forced the government to acknowledge the sinkings "in this very House of Commons" and thus for the fact "that the government has decided to follow a new policy with respect to protection of the St. Lawrence."

By contrast with Parliament and the debate over the dim-out, after a flurry of activity between May 14 and May 16, triggered by a huff-duff report that correctly indicated that a U-boat had *left* the St. Lawrence, the river and gulf were quiet. U-262 entered the river on April 25 to pick up on PEI's south coast prisoners who planned to break out of POW Camp 70 in Ontario; it left Canadian waters on May 10, having failed in its mission and having sustained severe ice damage. Over the course of the year, scores of coastal convoys sailed safely—indeed, so safely that on September 4 the British Admiralty urged that British ships again be allowed to sail independently from Sydney to Montreal. Convoying was ended for all St. Lawrence ships nine days later, a decision that resulted in an increase in EAC flying time from 1,232 hours in August to 1,581 hours in September.

A report filed on January 20, 1943, by Thomas Lapointe and his son Lionel said that they had seen "signalling from shore one and one half miles due west of St. Godfrey [on the northern, Quebec, side of the Baie des Chaleurs, which divided the Gaspé from northeastern New Brunswick] in answer to flashing from seaward" and that "young Lapointe claims he read the letters EN RPT EK from seaward." After investigating, Sub-Lieutenant

Dick classified it as an "apparent exaggeration of many reports [from the area] and excitement of the natives." At the end of January 1943, there was no U-boat anywhere near Canada's inland waters.

Despite the improved training program used by ADC, civilian spotters remained an inexact source of information. On April 29, 1943, for example, Thomas Mill telephoned authorities to tell them that Germain Guité, Napoléon Cyr and Jean Cyr of Maria "stated that they saw lights from a submarine in Cascapedia Bay between Maria and Black Cape about midnight for last three nights." Signals intelligence, which included Ultra, clearly indicated that U-262, which on the twenty-ninth was all but trapped in ice near PEI, was the only U-boat in Canadian waters. Even trained observers, such as Sergeant Murphy of the Atlantic Command Special Investigation Section (ACSIS), were less than reliable. At 10:30 a.m. on April 5, Lieutenant Caissy and Sergeant Murphy reported "that at 23:00 on the 4th, May 1943, lights believed to be approaching shore at Pointe Luncotoe, New Richmond saw light ashore which appeared to be used as a guide. This report could not reach Headquarters any earlier because of a break in the telephone line." An investigation of the area where the lights were seen by Lieutenant Caissy of the Fusiliers, Sergeant Murphy and ACSIS found nothing. An RCMP investigation the following day "revealed a probability that some persons were using a boat for the Jacking of geese."

SEPTEMBER 26, 1943

- Four thousand miles east in Italy, the German rearguard withdraws before an advance of the British 10th Corps.
- Five thousand miles east in Russia, Waffen SS divisions are ordered transferred to Italy, but only the 1st SS Panzer Division is deployed; Canadian troops will later face this division in the battle for Normandy.

- Nine thousand miles southwest in New Guinea, the 5th US Air Force bombs a Japanese base at Wewak, destroying sixty-four planes and seven warships.
- Four thousand miles east on the island of Corsica, Free French forces occupy Ghisonaccia airfield.

The cryptic sentence "Only Aunt Kate is coming to dinner" told Lieutenant Commander Desmond ("Debbie") W. Piers, RCN, all he needed to know. Instead of four escapees heading his way, his men and the ships hiding behind the small islands that dot the south side of New Brunswick's Baie des Chaleurs had only one man and the U-boat sent to pick him up to hunt. "I didn't know it at the time," Piers recalls, "but the man turned out to be Wolfgang Heyda. Our plans were set to catch the really big fish, including U-boat ace Otto Kretschmer, who were planning to escape from a POW camp in Bowmanville, Ontario, and make their way to the shores of New Brunswick to be picked up.[7] But they never got out of the camp. Heyda did, and the plan worked. We caught him before he could make contact with the waiting submarine. Unfortunately, we were unable to coax the U-boat to the surface. Lieutenant Pickford's task force depth-charged it, but it escaped," recalls Piers, who stayed in the RCN after the war, rising to become a rear-admiral.

By the time Piers received that message, Operation Kiebitz, the planned breakout of Otto Kretschmer (U-99) and nineteen other men—including Horst Elfe (U-93), H. J. von Knebel-Döberitz (Kretschmer's executive officer) and Wolfgang Heyda (U-434)—had been underway for more than a year. The plan, developed by Kretschmer in the Bowmanville POW camp and approved by BdU, was audacious. The Lorient Espionage Group—the name Kretschmer gave to the 150 cell—set out to build a tunnel that would pass under Camp 30's fence. Since the camp's guards were constantly on the lookout for tunnelling, Kretschmer decided to hide the main tunnel by having his diggers build several 90-metre-long false tunnels that if found would throw the camp's authorities off the scent.

Called "a masterpiece in engineering" by Inspector Clifford W. Harvison, who later became Commissioner of the RCMP, the main tunnel was almost 300 metres long. Reinforced by beams and ventilated by air ducts made from cans placed end to end, it was lit by a string of lights that tapped into the camp's power supply. As well, secreted within it were five hundred boxes of food. Kretschmer's engineers even built a push-cart rail system that allowed the quick removal of soil, which was then put in sacks and carried to the barrack's attic. There the soil was packed behind the cork insulation.

Dönitz learned of the planned breakout in the first week of April 1943 when his receptionist, Mme. von Knebel-Döberitz, received a letter from her husband through the Red Cross. Using the Ireland code, memorized by all U-boatmen, Knebel-Döberitz informed BdU of the plan to break out of Bowmanville and make their way to Pointe Maisonette on the Baie des Chaleurs.[8] Hidden in Mme. Knebel-Döberitz's response to her husband was confirmation of the rendezvous planned for September 27 or 28. Later, using radio equipment either smuggled into the camp or constructed by an imprisoned aviator, Kretschmer was able to send and receive short Morse-code messages.

The Lorient Espionage Group was not, however, the only group active. In late July, Canadian Naval Intelligence summoned Harvison to a meeting where he was told that Naval Intelligence had cracked "certain codes" which indicated that the prisoners in Camp 30 were planning a mass breakout and that once escaped, the prisoners were to be picked up by a U-boat in the Baie des Chaleurs. To his surprise, as Harvison recorded in his memoir, *The Horsemen*, the navy did not want the RCMP to move into the camp, search it and put an end to Kretschmer's plans. The navy "added an almost equally incredible request. They had very compelling reasons for wanting to capture the German submarine, reasons that went far beyond the normal desire to make such a catch." Written in 1967 before the Ultra secret was declassified, this tortured circumlocution refers obliquely to the navy's desire to capture the submarine's Enigma machine.

The RCN wanted to use the escapees as bait to lure the U-boat to where it could be captured, but, according to Harvison, everyone at the meeting recognized that "'shadowing' escapees for some six hundred miles must be ruled out as totally impracticable." Instead, Harvison and Naval Intelligence decided on a two-phase operation. They would let the planned breakout occur, but they would station guards around the camp to immediately capture the escapees. To lure the submarine closer, as soon as the escaped prisoners were recaptured Naval Intelligence would broadcast information on radio frequencies monitored by German submarines off the Canadian coast—"news regarding the mass break, but nothing about the capture of the escapees."

To establish the perimeter, Harvison needed to know where the tunnel's exit would be. Along with Major Fairweather, a technician at Camp 30, Harvison spent a night "crawl[ing] along the lip of earth between the fence and the ditching working with a microphone attached to a long probe which we pushed into the ground every few yards." It did not take long for him to hear sounds of tunnelling. "Judging from the sounds that reached us over the microphone, the tunnel already extended a considerable distance from the main building toward the centre of the wooden fence" that ringed the camp. "We could clearly hear sounds of digging—long drawn-out scraping noises, as the receptacles containing loose earth were dragged back along the tunnel. At times, we could hear voices. The sounds were distant and muffled but unmistakable." Using this information, Harvison planned where he would place his men.

At the Crime Detection Laboratory in Regina, RCMP staff sergeant Stephen H. Lett examined a copy of a popular novel that had been sent to a POW in the camp. In his 1974 article, Lett reported finding that the cover binding "concealed a number of valuable escape documents in the form of a marine map of the eastern Canadian coast, a forged Canadian National Registration card and a quantity of Canadian and American currency." Lett's skill as an analyst was, if anything, equalled by his skill as a forger. For the navy's plan to work, the POWs in Bowmanville had to receive the intercepted information without knowing that it had been tampered with. Under Lett's direction, the Crime Detection Laboratory reconstructed the book—its poor-quality yellow cover was photostated—and secreted within its binding the intercepted information.

Three-quarters of a continent away from Regina, the RCN was putting together its own plans. "Admiral Murray sent for me," recalls Piers.[9] "When I entered the room I saw a submarine captain [Captain W. L. Puxley, a Royal Navy captain on loan to the RCN] and captain in charge of the destroyers [Captain J. D. Prentice, RCNVR], all of them senior to me. The admiral cut right to the point, saying, 'Gentlemen, I want you to know that this is absolutely super-secret. You are to tell nobody, not even your wife. Up in Bowmanville, there is a POW camp, and there are people like Kretschmer there who are planning to break out. Piers,' he said, turning to me, 'your job is to capture the submarine.' He told us that we had the date and the place, and indeed the challenge that the shore would make and the reply that would be expected from the U-boat."

Piers left Halifax immediately. His cover story, used even with his wife, was that he was going to New Brunswick to look for an area where the water conditions were better for anti-submarine training—believable enough, since Piers was then anti-submarine training commander.

When he came back, Piers presented his plan to Murray, who then sent it to the British Admiralty. Piers's plan called for the installation of two radar trucks, a mile on either side of the lighthouse at Miscou Point, in which he would set up his headquarters. To capture the U-boat, Piers commandeered a lobster boat, had it armed and trained a boarding party. "We trained them very thoroughly in the tactics for boarding the U-boat," he recalls. "Once they jumped from the lobster boat, which we chose because of its low keel, they'd throw a chain through the open conning tower. The party had grenades, revolvers, daggers and smoke grenades if necessary."

Several days after sending the plan to the UK, Murray received orders to shelve it, because, Piers said in a 1998 interview with Tony German, "the Admiralty was concerned that if they had successfully captured the U-boat, the Germans would have immediately realized that the Enigma cipher system [the Ultra secret] was compromised." Instead of trying to capture the U-boat, Piers was now ordered to set up a shore party to capture any POWs who might slip through Harvison's net and to have ships at the ready to sink the U-boat if it was seen or picked up by radar.

Piers's revised plan was divided into two parts, the second of which was only somewhat less audacious than his plan to board the U-boat. The first part of the revised plan retained the installation of the radar sets and the shore patrol centred on the lighthouse at Miscou Point. The second part involved one of Canada's most experimental ships, HMCS *Rimouski*.

During their 1943 refits, in addition to having their fo'c'sles lengthened and their bridges widened, *Rimouski* and HMCS *Edmundston*, original Flower-class corvettes, were equipped with an experimental system called "diffused lighting." "It may seem counterintuitive," says Marc Richard, a McGill University researcher who has studied Professor Edmund Godfrey Burr, the system's originator, "but what Burr discovered by accident—he had been watching a plane landing at night when suddenly it all but vanished as it passed over a field of newly fallen snow that reflected the light of the moon into the sky—was that diffused lighting reduced the brightness contrast between the ship and the background, which made the ship almost invisible from a distance."

Even on the darkest night, because of starlight, moonlight and even light reflecting off high-level atmospheric dust, the sky is not completely dark. The contrast between the sea and sky allows sailors to see the horizon. It also allowed U-boat captains to spot the distinctive silhouette of blacked-out ships.

"Diffused lighting," says Richard, "was achieved by the use of fifty-nine bluish-green floodlights—twenty-six aimed at *Rimouski*'s hull and thirty-three at its superstructure. The light did not make the ship completely disappear, but it did make it much more difficult to see. Depending on weather conditions and the range at which the ship was being observed, diffused lighting could reduce a ship's visibility by up to 70 per cent."

Captain John Pickford, who at twenty-two was the youngest commander of a major Allied warship in the Second World War, later recalled the effect as being "really weird. After years of being on a darkened ship, you could suddenly read messages on the bridge while knowing that you couldn't be seen."

Piers's plan was for *Rimouski* to lead a flotilla that included a British destroyer, three other Canadian corvettes and three Bangor minesweepers against the U-boat. We were "to steam slowly with navigational lights and diffused lighting on, pretending to be a small coastal vessel. Once in range, our orders were to open fire. If she dived, our orders were to fire depth charges," recalled Pickford, now a retired rear-admiral.

As Piers fine-tuned his plan, U-536, an IXC-40 U-boat commanded by *Kapitänleutnant* Rolf Schauenburg, left Lorient. No doubt the mission, code-named Operation Kiebitz in Schauenburg's sailing instructions, appealed to both his sense of adventure and his ideology. Schauenburg's war record gives ample proof that he was a committed, "fanatical and idealistic Nazi," as he was characterized by the British intelligence officers who interviewed him after he was captured. Interned after the scuttling of the pocket battleship *Graf Spee* on December 17, 1939, in the harbour of Montevideo, Uruguay, Schauenburg escaped and made his way across South America disguised as a merchant. Recaptured, he escaped and was captured again before returning to Germany through Chile in January 1941.

On September 12, 1943, U-536's radioman decoded the message "Execute Operation Kiebitz—No Amplification."[10] Soon after Schauenburg ordered his navigator to shape a course that would take them from the Azores to the Baie des Chaleurs. Two weeks later, U-536 was close enough to Maisonette Point for Schauenburg to "see [through his periscope] cars driving around, houses, even people."[11] His orders were to wait there for two weeks, surfacing for two hours each night.

But on September 14, two days after Schauenburg left the waters off the Azores and a week before the planned escape, Kretschmer's plans fell apart. In the middle of the night, the ceiling in the barracks collapsed under the weight of the earth secreted above it. Alerted by the noise of the collapse, the camp's guards rushed into the barracks and, realizing what had been going on, began searching for tunnels. Kretschmer and the Lorient Espionage Group did not, of course, know that the RCMP knew precisely where the main tunnel was, so they could not know that the search was carried out so that only the dummy tunnels were found.

Relieved that the main tunnel had apparently gone undetected, Kretschmer ordered the escape moved up to the following night. Then, during the afternoon of the fifteenth, after a heavy rainfall, a prisoner digging close to the camp's fence to fill a flower box pushed his shovel into the ground and the earth beneath the shovel gave way, exposing the main tunnel to the guards, who, rifles at the ready, reportedly said to the exposed subterranean diggers, "Well, well—where do you guys think you're going?"

The collapse of Kretschmer's escape plans did not, however, put an end to the operation of the Lorient Espionage Group. Elfe and Knebel-Döberitz immediately conceived of an even more daring plan. Using wires and wood taken from a window sash, they fashioned a bosun's chair that could slide along the power lines and thus out of the camp. Kretschmer's group chose twenty-nine-year-old Wolfgang Heyda, commander of U-434, for the breakout because he was only five foot six and slightly built.

Late in the afternoon of September 24, Heyda changed into civilian clothes that had been smuggled into the camp, and hid in the camp's sports shack. To cover his absence during the evening parade, his fellow inmates walked a mannequin in his place. After dark, to draw the guards' attention away from where Heyda was planning to scale a pole and then slide to freedom down the power line, the prisoners staged a fight on the far side of the camp. It took Heyda just a few moments to climb the pole, affix his bosun's chair to the power cable and slide to safety.[12]

Equipped with a false identity card for Fred Thomlinson of Toronto, a Northern Electric Company licence issued by the Royal Canadian Engineers and a document apparently signed by Admiral Murray authorizing geological research in the area of Pointe Maisonnette, New Brunswick, Heyda headed east. He stopped first in Montreal, where he hid for a day in a theatre, apparently watching a western. Then he caught a train to the Baie des Chaleurs.

As Heyda was making his way to the Baie des Chaleurs, Piers received the message "Only Aunt Kate is coming to dinner," telling him that an escape had occurred and that the attempted pickup operation was on. "We'd been there a couple of days before I got that signal," recalls Piers. "The radar units and shore patrols were set up, as was my headquarters in the lighthouse. And the ships were hidden a mile or two away. We played a lot of cards waiting."

Three or so miles away, another naval commander, U-boat captain Schauenburg, also waited. Early in the evening, he'd had a close call. "Just after going under," recalled his executive officer, Wolfgang Von Bartenwerffer, "we heard propeller noises, and this was surprising because everything had been so quiet." Von Bartenwerffer's commander summoned his officers to the mess and then asked each of them what he thought about the situation. "Something is wrong. We have a bad feeling, and it looks like a trap," they agreed. They then checked their map of the bay and found that there was only one spot with a depth of at least forty metres, deep enough for the U-boat to have a chance at surviving a depth-charge attack. Without risking raising his periscope again, Schauenburg ordered a course for the deepest water available to him.

"On the day we'd been told to expect something [September 26]," recalls Piers, "about 9 p.m., I got a call telling me that the radar had picked up the submarine. I decided to wait before calling the ships into action. Then I got another call, this one from the shore patrol. The message—'We have a guy here making his holiday. He's pretty mad. He says you are ruining his holiday. Should I let him go?'—was code. I immediately knew we had our man and replied, 'No, don't. Take the fellow and bring him up here. If he tries to get away, shoot him in the legs. Whatever you do, don't let him escape.'

"Twenty minutes later or so, they brought him up. I wasn't in uniform, so he did not know I was a naval officer. He began to harangue me about interfering with his holidays. He tried to make a strong case for himself. I asked if I could look in his briefcase. He produced a few papers that were in German. One of his papers was from Northern Electric. It thanked him for the work he'd done for the Battle of the Atlantic."

Piers then asked him, "What do you do for money?" The prisoner's wallet was full of ten-dollar bills, hundreds of dollars worth. "The only thing," recalls Piers, "was that they were all from 1911, honouring the coronation of George V. I knew they'd gone out of circulation years ago."

Piers reached into Heyda's briefcase and pulled out a circular typewriter-ribbon box. "I opened it and found in it a compass. 'That's what I use for orienteering,' he said."

Next Piers pulled out a small object wrapped in paper. He unwrapped it and found German chocolate issued by the Red Cross.

Finally, Piers pulled out a letter, apparently signed by Chief of Naval Staff Percy Nelles. "His other documents were rather finely done. His ID card, especially, looked just like a real one, even though it had been forged by hand. Nelles's signature was, however, nothing like the real one, which I knew quite well. After looking at it for a moment, I looked straight at him and said, 'I am Lieutenant Desmond Piers of the Royal Canadian Navy and you are Wolfgang Heyda, an escaped POW, and I will have to turn you over to the RCMP.'"

Just as Heyda was finishing giving his name, rank and serial number, Piers's radar operator called out, "Sir, we've got a contact." Piers alerted *Rimouski* to close in.

Had Schauenburg's Metox been working, he would have known he'd been picked up by Piers's radar, but since late on September 26, he had already suspected that the Canadians were waiting for him. According to his second lieutenant, just before leaving the Baie des Chaleurs on the twenty-sixth (so that he could surface and recharge his batteries), Schauenburg spotted Piers's task force. Instead of moving out of the bay, he stayed submerged, watching the disposition of the ships. At one point he saw "the corvette, lying off the point [where the pickup was to occur], move off" and be replaced by another, a manoeuvre that, in the words of the Allied intelligence officer who interviewed Schauenburg, made it "abundantly clear to him that the German plans were known."

Later, Schauenburg's suspicions were confirmed. Despite a dazzling display of the northern lights, he saw a light flashing "*Komm Komm*" ("Come closer, come closer") in plain Morse code instead of the pre-arranged signal. Scant moments later, "distant explosions of depth charges" were "heard." Taken on their own, they could have been "exercise bombs," but taken with the deployment of ships and the unexpected signal, Schauenburg recorded the explosions as either "scare bombs," designed to make him move and show himself, or real depth charges fired at a false target.

Schauenburg's assumption was wrong. The depth charges were real enough, but were not fired off as part of a carefully co-ordinated attack but, rather, as a defensive measure. "We cruised in," recalls Pickford, "feeling naked indeed. We had no defence against the Gnat torpedo. The tactics were to drop a depth charge from time to time "to distract the acoustic homing torpedo."[13]

Piers's radar bearings gave Pickford a general idea of where to attack, but, as had so often been the case in the Battle of the St. Lawrence, the RCN's plans were undone by the bathyscaphe effect. "The asdic conditions in the shallow Baie des Chaleurs were just hopeless," Pickford recalls. "We got no contact."

Schauenburg's next manoeuvre compounded the RCN's problems. Instead of making a run for it, he decided that the only way to save his ship was to do exactly what the attacking ships would never expect: to head for shallower waters, where the U-boat would be in greater danger if it were depth-charged but so would the attacking ships.

The ploy worked. *Rimouski* and its consorts and Piers's radar spent the rest of the day and the night searching the waters off Maisonette Point. "They couldn't find a bloody thing," recalls Piers. "The next morning, there was the sun sparkling on the water and nothing in sight, as if nothing had happened there."

Forty metres below the dappled water, however, the situation aboard U-536 was rapidly deteriorating. They'd been underwater for almost two full days. "We had no fresh air in the boat, and the crew needed to get out because without air we would start feeling sleepy and die."

With the Canadian ships still trawling for him, and with just a few metres of water above his conning tower and as little below his keel, Schauenburg used his silent electric motors to ease U-536 out of the Baie des Chaleurs. One officer recalled the nerve-racking experience during his interrogation: "We could hear with our own ears the propellers of the ships going over our boat, and we guessed that in the coming seconds depth charges would explode and sink or damage us, but nothing happened . . . . We said to each other, 'Our last hour has come.'"

But the gambit worked, though not before U-536 got caught in a fishing net. The fishing trawler was so close that Schauenburg's crew heard the sound of the boat's winches pulling in the net. Not until October 5, when he was within 180 miles of Cape St. Mary's, Newfoundland, did Schauenburg radio Lorient, *"Kiebitz verpfiffen"*: "Operation Magpie blown."

Six weeks later, on November 20, east of the Azores, U-536 became the only submarine that invaded the St. Lawrence to be sunk by a largely Canadian force. As Hadley writes,

The attack [by the corvettes HMCS *Snowberry* and *Calgary* and the frigate HMS *Nene*] was in fact devastating. The U-boat suddenly became stern heavy while lights failed, the fuse box burst into flames, and yellow smoke billowed. In short order, U-536 was thrust perilously into the perpendicular, balancing on its screws, and hurtling to a depth of 240m. Despite the violence of the movement, the resourceful chief engineer, Wilhelm Kujas, managed to stabilize the hopelessly damaged boat which he himself would not escape. As the U-boat rose to the surface and chlorine gas formed in the bilges [because of acid mixing with salt water], the crew gathered in the control room to abandon ship.

Most of the seventeen men who survived the depth-charging and the subsequent machine-gunning of those who made for U-536's deck gun were picked up by *Snowberry*. A story published on February 1, 1944, quoted *Snowberry*'s captain, Lieutenant J. A. Dunn, RCNVR, telling the Canadian people—who by then had endured four years of war, the disaster of Dieppe, the loss of nine warships including *Raccoon* and *Charlottetown* to enemy fire and the sinking of nineteen ships in Canada's inland waters, and who were now daily reading of their troops fighting in Italy—something they desperately wanted to hear: "There was no evidence to make us believe that these [men] were members of a 'Master Race.' They were a very docile and thankful collection of survivors."

CHAPTER EIGHT

1944

OCTOBER 14 AND NOVEMBER 24, 1944
HMCS *Magog* and *Shawinigan*

They that go down to the sea in ships;
and occupy their business in great waters;
These men see the works of the Lord;
and his wonders in the deep.

—BOOK OF COMMON PRAYER

On June 6, 1944, against almost 7,000 vessels (including 110 Canadian destroyers, frigates, corvettes and minesweepers) standing off the Normandy coast, the once powerful *U-Bootwaffe* could muster only 36 operational U-boats.[1] Over the course of D-Day, as the Allies disgorged more than 130,000 troops along a fifty-mile strip, famously divided into Gold, Sword, Juno, Utah and Omaha beaches, Dönitz's men sank a single ship, the Norwegian destroyer *Svenner*. Allied ships and planes sank nine U-boats before BdU ordered back to their bases the remnants of the fleet that had once terrorized the Atlantic and sailed as far up the St. Lawrence as Rimouski.

In the year since Black May, when 41 U-boats were sunk and another 37 badly damaged—numbers that prompted Dönitz to withdraw U-boats from the North Atlantic and to confide to his diary, "We have lost the Battle of the Atlantic"—thousands of Allied ships and planes had relentlessly pursued the U-boats. Deployed according to ever-more-accurate intelligence (Ultra decrypts were in Admiral Murray's hands in Halifax almost as fast as U-boat commanders had the original signals in theirs), Allied ships and planes with more accurate radar and sonar and more deadly munitions sank 286 U-boats. Allied shipping losses dropped from almost 525,000 tons in March 1942 to just under 165,000 tons in May 1943. A month later they had fallen to 18,000 tons. The average monthly losses in the six months leading up to D-Day were some 30,000 tons; in the month before D-Day, U-boats destroyed only 15,000 tons of shipping, the second-lowest monthly total since the war began.

Though overshadowed by the USN and the RN, which between May 1943 and D-Day sank fifty-six and eighty-five U-boats respectively, the RCN acquitted itself well. Between May 13, 1943, when HMCS *Drumheller* received partial credit for sinking U-753, and April 22, 1944, when HMCS *Matane* and *Swansea* combined to sink U-311, fourteen RCN ships had taken part in sinking another nine U-boats. By the end of 1944, another eleven RCN ships would sink eight more U-boats. On July 7, 1944, an attack group composed of HMS *Statice* and HMCS *Ottawa II* and *Kootenay* sank U-678. On August 18, 1944, an entirely Canadian attack group, EG-11 (HMCS *Ottawa II*, *Chaudiere* and *Kootenay*), sank U-621; it was U-984's turn two days later. Thus did the RCN demonstrate that it had overcome the manning and training difficulties that had caused its withdrawal from the North Atlantic in 1943.

But even as the *Freikorps Dönitz* lost thousands of men between May 1943 and October 1944, the U-boat force fought on. From the beginning of the war, *der Löwe* (the Lion), as his men called Dönitz, assiduously cultivated the *U-Bootwaffe*'s esprit de corps—by greeting returning boats at the dock, by arranging for special trains to transport crews on liberty to spas and other rest areas, by making allowances for misbehaviour on shore, by personally lending money, by ensuring that U-boat crews had special food and chocolate. He even allowed personal messages to be broadcast from Lorient, the most famous being the news to one expectant father that "a U-boat with a periscope arrived today."[2]

Morale held among the "grey wolves" despite devastating losses. During the first four months of 1944, 80 per cent of U-boats that put to sea were sunk. Still, Werner Hirschmann, chief engineer of U-190, recalls, "We were young and sure of ourselves; it was always the 'other guy' who wasn't going to make it back." *Kapitänleutnant* Helmut Schmoekel, commander of U-802, recalled in an interview, "We left Kiel in January 1944. I was so optimistic that I told my fiancée that when I get back in May we will be married."

As both Herbert Werner (U-415) and Peter Cremer (U-333) make clear in their memoirs, one of the reasons morale held was the *U-Bootwaffe*'s faith that Dönitz's long-delayed promise of new technologies would be fulfilled. In the middle of Black May, historian Peter Padfield notes in his biography of Dönitz, the *Grossadmiral* signalled all boats:

> In his efforts to rob U-boats of their most valuable characteristic, invisibility, the enemy is some lengths ahead of us with his radar location.
>
> I am fully aware of the difficult position in which this puts you in the fight with enemy escorts. Be assured that I have done and shall continue to do everything in my power as C-in-C [commander-in-chief of the German navy] to take all possible steps to change this situation as soon as possible.
>
> Research and development departments within and without the navy are working to improve your weapons and apparatus.

Four days later, in the signal that told that he was abandoning the North Atlantic, Dönitz again promised "new and sharper weapons" with which "you will be superior and will be able to triumph over your worst adversaries, the aircraft and destroyer."

The magic technologies—hulls covered with radar- and sonar-absorbing materials, the "Elektro boat" (a larger U-boat with huge electric motors that gave it an underwater speed of 17 knots, some 11 knots faster than either Type VII or Type X) and the "Walter boat" (which burned hydrogen peroxide, obviating the need for air for its engines)—either never arrived or arrived too late to affect the outcome of the war.[3] Two combat-design Walter boats were produced. On a shakedown cruise that began on November 15, 1944, U-2519, under the command of "Ali" Cremer, reached 17.5 knots underwater. On April 5, 1945, while it was in dock at Blohm & Voss in Hamburg, Allied bombers destroyed Cremer's boat. Walter boats undertook no operational cruises.

However, two technologies did arrive early enough to be deployed in the Battle of the St. Lawrence: the acoustic torpedo and the Schnorchel. The T-5 *Zaunkönig* acoustic torpedoes, nicknamed "Gnat" (for German navy acoustic torpedo) by the Allies, came into service in August 1943. Billed as "destroyer crackers," Gnats were equipped with acoustic sensors tuned to 24.5 kHz and attached to the torpedo's guidance mechanism. Instead of the mechanism executing a programmed course, it directed the torpedo toward the sound created by the target's propellers. Countermeasures such as altering a ship's speed, dropping depth charges (the explosion of which caused the Gnat's firing pistol to go off prematurely) and steaming noisemakers that attracted the torpedo away from the ship were routinely used by Allied ships after the middle of 1943 when U-boats were known to be near.

The *Schnorchel*, developed by the Royal Netherlands Navy in 1933, was a simple device that turned the U-boat from a submersible weapons platform into something approaching a true submarine. Prior to the introduction of the snorkel in 1944, U-boats spent on average only 10 per cent of their running time underwater because of limited air supply and battery power. The necessity of surfacing to recharge the ship's batteries and air supply meant that the Bay of Biscay, which was heavily patrolled by Allied ships and planes, became less a passageway to the Atlantic than a killing field. In 1943, twenty-seven U-boats were destroyed there; in 1944, another twenty-six were sunk.

A set of physically ungainly tubes attached to the conning tower, the *Schnorchel* was elegant in its simplicity. Each of the two 25-foot tubes extended no more than a foot above the surface of the water, making it invisible to lookouts and to all but the best Allied radar. One tube drew fresh air into the boat; the other served as an exhaust. Each was fitted with a valve (the most common was a ball-type float connected to a flap) that shut when water washed over the tubes. To keep the diesels running when waves washed over the *Schnorchel*, the float valve triggered another valve that allowed the combustion engine to suck air from the U-boat and to vent the diesel exhaust into it. Though fouling the boat's air was, of course, a concern, the immediate effect of this procedure was first a rapid decrease in air pressure and then an increase, which caused intense ear pain. Although Dönitz's engineers had originally thought that the snorkel would be used only for recharging a boat's batteries, tests revealed that U-boats could operate using a snorkel for long periods of time at speeds up to 13 knots.

Six weeks after D-Day, on July 17, 1944, as thousands of British and Canadian troops readied for the following day's attempt to break out of

Caen, some 15 kilometres from the Normandy coast, Dönitz again ordered U-boats into the St. Lawrence, in hopes of drawing Allied escorts off the North Atlantic. Over the next four months, four radio operators would hand their captains the following message from the *Führer der Unterseeboote*:

[This] operational area has not been occupied since 1942. Great surprise successes are possible as area has abundant traffic. Area was evacuated in view of appearance of a/c [aircraft] and location [anti-submarine radar], which impeded battery charge. But area is easily navigable with "*Schnorchel.*" . . .

4. Countermeasures: Situation in 1942
Medium to strong air with and without location [radar], especially after being observed. Sea [naval] countermeasures relatively slight and unpractised. Location [sonar] conditions very unfavourable to the enemy, as there is marked underwater density layering. Find out about this density layering, even for considerable depths, before a depth-charge hunt starts.

In General: Main defence by a/c. Sea defence little to be feared. Situation thought to have altered little since 1942.[4]

Between the beginning of July 1944 and the end of November 1944, U-802, U-541, U-1223, U-1228 and U-1231 invaded Canadian waters. Despite *Kapitänleutnant* Helmut Schmoeckel's claim that U-802 had sunk a "destroyer" on September 13 (the torpedo he fired at HMCS *Stettler* exploded prematurely), he had nothing to show for his patrol in Canadian waters. There were, however, frightening memories of being attacked by both the RCAF and USS *Bogue's* hunter-killer group. RCAF coverage so unnerved Schmoeckel that he credited Canadian land-based radar with being "able to pick up my *Schnorchel*," an ability it did not have.

Kapitänleutnant Kurt Peterson's bravado on U-541 led him to claim that the layering effect of the salt and fresh water in the gulf made him feel "as secure as in the bosom of Abraham."[5] His one attack in the gulf, however, was carried out on the surface. The attack was broken up by gunfire from the corvette HMCS *Norsyd*. Upon leaving Canadian waters, Peterson's war diary recorded the cost of having broken radio silence: "About two hours [after having broadcast] we heard weak signals on our radar warning devices . . . . Seconds after we had dived, bombs exploded in our vicinity. The boat was shaken and the periscope developed a leak. From my perspective the Canadian defences had reacted and operated magnificently. Swift detection of our radio transmission, good evaluation with precise position, good attack by aircraft with sparing and rational use of radar. If we had dived but a few seconds later, the bombs would possibly have hit us at the beginning of the diving manoeuvre."

All *Oberleutnant zur See* Paul Ackermann, commander of U-1221, had to show for his Canadian sojourn was the loss of Able Seaman Emil-Heinz Motyl, who apparently committed suicide by jumping overboard after having been disciplined for falling asleep on watch.

The two other U-boats drew Canadian blood. On October 14, 1944, two years to the day after the sinking of SS *Caribou*, a Gnat fired by U-1223, commanded by *Oberleutnant zur See* Albert Kneip, crippled the frigate HMCS *Magog*, killing three men. Six weeks later, on the night of November 25, *Oberleutnant zur See* Friedrich-Wilhelm Marienfeld (U-1228) destroyed the corvette HMCS *Shawinigan*, killing ninety-one officers and ratings of the Royal Canadian Navy.

OCTOBER 14, 1944

- Three thousand five hundred miles east, workers at Deutsche Werft AG lay the keel for U-2354; workers at AG Weser in Bremen lay the keel for U-3024.
- Three thousand five hundred miles east in Berlin, Field Marshal Erwin Rommel, who is suspected of complicity in the July 20 plot to assassinate Adolf Hitler, chooses suicide instead of a public trial for treason. Doing so protects his family from prosecution and he is given a state funeral.
- Four thousand miles east in Greece, British and Greek forces capture Athens.
- Seven thousand five hundred miles southwest in Burma, under heavy attack by the Japanese 33rd and 55th divisions, the British 123rd Indian Brigade is forced from its defensive positions at Rathedaung in Arakan.

At 10:25 a.m., some five miles off the Point-des-Monts lighthouse, the five-month-old River-class frigate *Magog* zigzagged off the starboard side of convoy ONS-33. *Magog* and two other 301-foot 6-inch, 1,440-ton frigates, HMCS *Stettler* and *Toronto*, were escorting a twelve-ship westbound convoy. Normally at this time in the morning, *Magog*'s captain, Lieutenant Commander Louis T. Quick, RCNR, would have been on the bridge. The crew would be mustered on the quarterdeck, where the officer of the watch, Sub-Lieutenant Herb Montgomery, would be leading a centuries-old duty: distributing the daily ration of grog.

At thirty-four minutes before eleven bells, however, Quick's first officer, Lieutenant Edgar T. Stanger, RCNVR, was officer in charge on the bridge. Quick, Montgomery and two other officers. First Lieutenant Verdun P. Gilbert, RCNVR, and Lieutenant (Engineering) Bertil F. Larson, were in the captain's cabin a short distance away.[6] Quick, whose career began when he joined the RN at the age of fourteen and who had quite a reputation for drinking when on shore, was "weighing off" Leading Seaman Ted Davis, known as "the Buffer," and several other ratings who had "raised hell in one of the pubs" on the thirteenth, the night before *Magog* departed Gaspé.[7]

"I was in the captain's cabin listening to him weighing off the sailors," recalls Montgomery, "when all of a sudden we felt a tremendous jolt and the ship took an immediate list."

The jolt was caused by the explosion of the first of two Gnats Kneip aimed at *Magog*. (The second exploded harmlessly fifty yards off *Magog*'s port quarter.) The blast that killed Petty Officer Ted E. Davis, Ordinary Seaman Gordon T. Elliot and Able Seaman Kenneth J. Kelly and badly injured three other ratings also blew off sixty feet of *Magog*'s stern. Half of the wreckage, thirty feet of hardened steel weighing at least one hundred tons, was literally peeled ten feet up over the remaining boat deck. Only the mass of one of the aft-deck guns, upon which part of the deck came to rest, saved the life of nineteen-year-old George G. Hunter, an engine-room artificer: "I was standing at the gun platform when the explosion occurred. Part of the [quarter]deck lifted up and folded over the top of my head . . . . The gun mounting took the shock of the weight . . . . I was knocked to my knees and dazed," he told the Canadian Press.

As *Magog* struggled to find buoyancy, settling finally at a 9° list, Kneip's *Leitender Ingenieur* ordered the closing of the compensation ballast tanks that he had opened in the seconds after the torpedo sped away from U-1223. Kneip's boat was back on an even keel before Montgomery, Gilbert, Ted Davis and Quick ran from the captain's cabin.

It took Quick about thirty seconds to get to his bridge. Stanger had arrived (from the chart room just off the bridge) seconds before, while debris was still falling from the sky.

Neither could see the ship's stern, which had been demolished.

Quick called Action Stations. Since he was not sure that the buzzer could be heard, he shouted it down from the bridge to ensure that the call was repeated throughout the stricken ship.

Deep in the ship, twenty-year-old electrical artificer Harold Robertson was stunned but alive. "I was just leaving the electrical stores," he told Canadians in an article not published until April 17, 1945. "I don't remember anything of what happened, but I do know that I came right through a steel bulkhead and landed in the water. There was a steel deck above me, below me and a steel wall around me, and even though I was injured, I figured I'm mighty lucky to be here." Robertson was one of three men picked out of the water by damage-control parties.

Gilbert ran first toward the wheelhouse. Then, after realizing the damage was to the stern, he ran aft. "As I reached the quarterdeck, I saw a man was stunned and walking toward the stern of the ship, so I grabbed him and two ratings took him forward. At the same time there was a man in the water and two ratings pulled him up," Gilbert wrote in his report.

Gilbert then headed for the engine room. By the time he got there, Chief Stoker Norman Howse was putting out a fire in one of the boiler rooms. Gilbert's report explains why Howse received special commendation for his actions: "Fire broke out in one of the boiler rooms. Howse put on a smoke mask and went down and saw that it was extinguished. That in itself may not have been remarkable, but at the time he went down [below the waterline] we were disabled and a pretty easy target."

After being told by an engine-room artificer that the "after bulkhead of the engine room was holding [and that there] was no water in the engine room," Gilbert ran back to the bridge and told Quick that he "thought she would float."

Gilbert wasn't the only one to bring Quick this hopeful news. Larson ran straight from Quick's cabin to the engine room. The artificers had already stopped the ship's 5,500-hp main engine, so he went straight to check the bilges for "signs of water." There were none, which told him that the aft bulkhead was holding. A few moments later, after examining the bulkhead itself and finding, despite the huge explosion that ripped one-fifth of the ship apart, that the aft "bulkhead had in no way been affected and was very sound," Larson sent a messenger to Quick to tell him that *Magog* was in no imminent danger of sinking.

Taking no risks, Larson ordered the engine-room staff to begin shoring up the aft bulkhead with two-by-fours. Using cloth-covered wooden wedges, he patched a small leak in the starboard side. Then he turned to correcting the ship's list. He ordered the pumping of fuel oil from the starboard and port tanks until *Magog* was once again on an even keel.

"Sub-lieutenants," recalls Montgomery, "didn't have a 'station' in the same way that the captain or the engineering officer did; we were responsible for the day-to-day running of the ship. I was officer of the watch, so when I ran from Captain Quick's cabin, I went first to my cabin to get my life jacket and then to the deck. Once there, I found myself being yelled to come here, come there."

Montgomery ran toward what was left of the stern. Men blackened with oil were crawling out of the wreckage. Some were covered with red, which Montgomery at first assumed to be blood. "It took me a moment to realize it, but the torpedo had blasted apart the ship's stores and almost everyone and everything was covered in tomato sauce."

Under the wreckage that covered the 12-lb. cannon on the boat deck, Montgomery saw legs sticking out. Together with some other men, he used two-by-fours to pry the wreckage up. As the wreckage lifted, "suddenly an arm popped out. And in the open hand, we saw a penny," recalls Montgomery. "We knew immediately that it was Ted E. Davis, who had a habit of flipping a penny and asking us to call it.

"Had I not been in the captain's cabin when the torpedo hit, the toll would have been much worse; I and a good part of the crew would have been on that quarterdeck."

*   *   *

At 16 knots, *Toronto* quickly bore down on the path cut by the torpedo through the water.

Kneip's hydrophones heard every turn of *Toronto*'s screw. They also heard what sounded to them like the squeal of a circular saw—the sound made by the anti-Gnat "CAT gear" streaming behind *Toronto*.[8] Soon they heard the explosions of depth charges and the firing of *Toronto*'s gun at what one lookout thought was a periscope.

Toronto's attack was undone by the devilish waters of the gulf. Neither *Toronto* nor *Magog*, whose asdic continued to work, ever heard the ping that would signal Kneip's boat.

Stettler too sprang into action, recalls Fred Linnington, then a twenty-two-year-old able seaman. "I was portside lookout on the bridge. Suddenly, I saw that instead of steaming along normally, *Magog* just slowed down and then began to list towards the stern. Lieutenant Commander D. G. King, our captain, immediately rang Action Stations. Our asdic operator got an echo, and soon we were running it down and dropping depth charges. After dropping a few, we kept searching but could not find another echo."

Just moments after the gruesome discovery of Davis's remains, Montgomery saw an even more ghastly sight. "There, just floating where the stern of the ship used to be, in amongst the wreckage, was a life jacket with just a torso in it. No head. No legs. Just a torso. We took note of the number on the jacket and realized it was Able Seaman Kelly, who'd been on lookout, who'd been killed there." The official report records that the remains of Kelly's body were lost while *Magog* was being towed to safety.

Shortly before 11:00 a.m., *Toronto* broke off its search and steamed back to Quick's ship. Before taking it in tow, Captain H. K. Hill sent his medical officer, Surgeon Lieutenant Léon Beicque, to *Magog*, which did not have a medical officer of its own. Beicque cared for the three injured sailors as *Magog* was towed to Godbout Bay by *Toronto*'s sister ship HMCS *Shawinigan*. "Just before dark," Montgomery remembers, "a twin-engined Catalina seaplane" appeared.

The transfer of men from *Magog* to the cutter and then to the Catalina was both difficult and dangerous. Decades later, Vancouver journalist Gordon Hunter recalled for Michael Hadley "the harrowing experience of lying strapped immobile in a Neil-Robertson stretcher and being lowered over the *Magog*'s ravaged side to the small boat surging and pitching below. One slip of the crew . . . would most certainly [have sent] him plummeting helplessly into the depths." Writing a day later, Surgeon Lieutenant Commander J. R. Smith, HMCS Fort Ramsay's medical officer, who was aboard the Catalina flying boat, still wondered that *Magog*'s men had been able to transfer the injured to the Catalina. Manoeuvring *Magog*'s cutter over to the aircraft, he wrote, seemed "physically impossible without jeopardizing both the craft and crew members."

In addition to the choppy seas, the cutter's crew also had to contend with the stream of the propellers, which were not turning (had they been stopped, it would have been impossible to line up the Catalina and the cutter). To keep the boat alongside the plane, the men in the boat had to reach out and grab hold of the plane. Smith made special mention of the farthest forward member of the boat's crew, who "crouched on the bow of the boat [and] was greatly endangered by the starboard propeller, wing and spars of the plane" as time after time he "tried to grasp the edge of the plane's starboard gun 'blister.'"

The torpedoing of *Magog* put an end to almost seven months of relative quiet for EAC's airmen. Between the beginning of the shipping season in April 1944 and that October, EAC's pilots had logged thousands of hours. With the exception of a relative handful of sweeps after the HF/DFing of U-802 in August (it was the appearance of U-802 that prompted Admiral Murray to reinstate the St. Lawrence convoys), they'd found nothing. Thousands of hours of uneventful flights led the diarist of one squadron based in Summerside, PEI, to write on July 1, 1944, "the crews returned with that monotonous rhyme on their lips, 'Nothing seen but miles and miles of waves and whales.'" A little over two weeks later he wrote, "Inclement weather overtook us and were I gifted with the philosophical wit of Plato, the rapier-like sarcasm of Voltaire or the analytical power of Tolstoy, I could not the more aptly pen a summary of the day than in the following words: 'Nothing further to report.'"

On the morning of October 14, a Canso flying boat escorting ONS-33, flying a search pattern fourteen miles ahead of *Magog*, immediately turned back and started to search for the U-boat. Shortly after it flew over the stricken ship, it dropped sonobuoys. For some eighteen minutes the buoys picked up what the Canso's anti-submarine officer reported to be the sound of the U-boat's propeller. However, according to historian Roger Sarty, "the sound was obliterated as the other frigates in the escort raced to counter attack." The Canso continued looking for the submarine for three hours before it was relieved by four other Cansos. Bad weather forced EAC to order all but one plane back to base at around 8 p.m.

As soon as the weather cleared on the fifteenth, EAC sprang into action again. Cansos from Gaspé and Sydney flew the "salmon" search pattern. This pattern called for the Cansos to patrol in three concentric squares around the suspected location of the submarine. One square was eight miles away from the contact point, one twenty-four and the third forty. The middle patrol group flew in a clockwise direction at one altitude; the other two flew counterclockwise at different altitudes. The patrol was flown for twenty-four hours, using the Leigh light during the night. After the cancellation of "salmon" on the afternoon of the sixteenth, other flights were made over the river and western gulf until the eighteenth.[9]

At 7:35 a.m. on October 17, the tug *Lord Strathcona* slipped its lines after having towed the shattered *Magog* to the jetty in the basin on the north side of Quebec's Lower Town. Later on the morning of the seventeenth, Francis MacLaughlin, who in 1941 had watched the men of Kingston Shipyards build HMCS *Charlottetown* and who was now an eighteen-year-old naval rating in training at HMCS Montcalm (a naval base in Quebec City), was part of a hastily trained honour guard that paraded through the streets of Quebec City's Upper Town. After the parade, MacLaughlin and some of his fellow ratings walked down from the heights of Quebec to the jetty.

"We had never seen anything like it before. We knew she'd been torpedoed and thought she'd have a hole in her. But what we saw was just as if a big hand had crumpled the aft part of the ship upward. The torpedo had folded her stern up onto the deck. The aft-peak bulkhead held, so she was still floating," recalls MacLaughlin, who after the war became a naval architect.

NOVEMBER 24, 1944

- Three thousand five hundred miles east, the US 3rd Army captures crossings over the Saar River, about twenty-five miles north of Saarbrucken, Germany.
- Three thousand miles east, the French 2nd Division (an element of the US 7th Army) takes Strasbourg, France.
- Six thousand five hundred miles west, the first B-29 Superfortress raid on Tokyo is conducted by 111 planes.
- Four thousand miles east, prisoners at Auschwitz are ordered by the SS to begin demolishing Crematorium II.

Few Canadian ships had seen more types of action than K136, a corvette built in Lauzon, Quebec, in 1941. Commonly known as HMCS *Shawinigan*, K136 was on the North Atlantic run in the early months of 1942, during the worst days of the "Second Happy Time," when German U-boats savaged shipping off the North American coast. In the last days of January, thirty-five miles or so southeast of St. John's, *Shawinigan* came across empty lifeboats from either SS *Williman Hanson* or SS *Belize*, both of which were sunk by U-754 on January 22. On September 7, 1942, *Shawinigan* was sent from Gaspé to search for HMCS *Raccoon*. It was part of the escort of NL-9, and it counterattacked after Ulrich Gräf sank SS *Carolus* within sight of Rimouski on October 9, 1942. Six months after its first refit, during which its fo'c'sle was extended and its bridge enlarged, *Shawinigan* was with HMCS *Rimouski* in the Baie des Chaleurs. A year later, on September 3, 1944, it picked up the fourteen survivors of SS *Livingston*, sunk by Kurt Peterson (U-541) after he left the St. Lawrence. On October 14, *Shawinigan* was sent to aid *Magog* and helped tow the stricken ship to Godbout Bay.

At 10:30 p.m. on November 24, 1944, *Shawinigan* was patrolling some thirty miles off Port aux Basques, Newfoundland, squarely within the sights of U-1228, which had entered Canadian waters eleven days earlier.

Of all the war diaries penned by the U-boat captains who invaded Canada's inland sea, *Oberleutnant* Friedrich-Wilhelm Marienfeld's is, perhaps, the most beguiling. As one reads of the recurring troubles Marienfeld had with his gyroscope, echo sounder and *Schnorchel*—the float valve caused him no end of difficulty—one is almost liable to feel a certain sympathy, if for nothing else than for the simple frustration that comes through even in translation. After Dr. Günther Spohn, who a lifetime earlier was Marienfeld's *Nummer Eins*, told me that following the war Marienfeld earned a PhD in philosophy, it became hard not to see a certain quality of mind in such entries as this: "Porpoises putting on a running show. A great deal of squealing, crackling and humming, sometimes to be heard with unaided ear," from November 14, 1944. Or in the entry for the morning of the twenty-fifth, "Coast shining beautifully in the moonlight, Table Mountain, Sugar Loaf, Cape Ray beacons showing up as gleams on the horizon."

But such reveries aside, Marienfeld's war diary makes clear (as Hartwig's war diaries do for him) that Marienfeld's was a finely tuned military mind. BdU criticized him for his rather longish reports and for excessive caution. His decision not to enter the river came in for special criticism: "Deductions about traffic wrong! First see whether traffic has really stopped after you have detected!" Still, BdU could also praise him for spotting the "destroyer" at 0210 Berlin time and for the "success" of the Gnat he launched twenty minutes later.

Spotting the "destroyer" was something of a fluke. Marienfeld was on the cusp of deciding to give in to his technical problems and leave the gulf when, at 0150 Berlin time (9:50 p.m. local time), his hydrophone officer reported picking up a bearing at 200° off U-1228's port quarter. Moments later, Marienfeld confirmed the sighting, the etchings on his attack periscope's prisms telling him that the "destroyer" in his sights was actually at 210°. Marienfeld could have fired then and counted on the Gnat's hydrophones and internal guidance mechanism to home in on the RCN ship's screws. But, perhaps because he had not yet had any successes, he chose to be more careful and ordered his helmsman to come around 140°.

Instantly, the 1,545-ton boat began to turn to the starboard. On paper the turn would make U-1228's course look like a P, with the U-boat ending up on a line that corresponds to the bottom part of the loop that joins the letter's stem. Then came the command "Open bow cap" and the reply "Bow cap open." From his position in the attack room above the bridge came the co-ordinates for the attack computer: "90, speed 10 knots, depth 4, steering WS, aiming point stern, estimated range, 25 hm." At 0230 Berlin time, the final order—"*Los!*"—the shudder as the "eel" was pushed into the sea, the clanking of the bow cap slamming closed.

Thirty miles away from U-1228's conning tower, at 10:30 p.m. on November 24, 1944, John L. Gullage, captain of SS *Burgeo*, the Newfoundland–Nova Scotia ferry that had replaced SS *Caribou*, lay in bed next to his wife. Gullage would be up early, for his ship was scheduled to rendezvous with *Shawinigan* before 8 a.m. for the return trip to Sydney. Suddenly, a "peculiar noise," a "sort of rumble," rolled through the deep quiet of the late fall Newfoundland night. Gullage and his wife disagreed about what they'd heard. He thought it was nothing but a car backfiring. She heard a deeper sound. The rumble, she told her husband, "made the house tremble."

At exactly the same moment, ten miles away in Grand Bay, Randall J. White and his wife were also in bed. There, the "explosion . . . sounded like a case of dynamite," a sound they knew well from the previous year, when the US Army Air Force had been blasting near their home. An ADC member, White reported that two minutes after the first explosion they heard a second, which he described as "a roar like thunder."

Through U-1228's hydrophones, twenty-four-year-old *Oberleutnant zur See* Friedrich-Wilhelm Marienfeld and the bridge crew of U-1228 heard things more clearly. First, just the sounds of the "destroyer's" screw. Then the swish of the torpedo as it exited Tube VI at 30 knots. A moment later, the "torpedo and screw noises merge[d]." After four minutes, the "screw noises disappear[ed]," replaced by the "great roaring and crackling sounds" of a hit, loud enough to be heard by Spohn, who wasn't on the bridge at the time. Less then two minutes later came six more explosions, which Marienfeld assumed were depth charges exploding as they sank.

Most of the ninety-one officers and ratings on *Shawinigan* likely never heard a thing before the torpedo destroyed their ship.

Like the loss of the *Caribou* two years earlier, the loss of *Shawinigan* involved more than the RCN and EAC. It also involved the Newfoundland Ferry and Railway Company. Only this time, the question wasn't why the RCN insisted on nighttime sailings. *Burgeo* sailed to Newfoundland during daylight on the twenty-fourth and was scheduled to meet *Shawinigan* the next morning for a return trip to Sydney. Nor was the question why the escort was abaft (behind) the ferry. *Burgeo* was in port, and *Shawinigan* was patrolling off Port aux Basques; the US Coast Guard's *Sassafras*, which had been part of *Burgeo*'s escort on the trip to Port aux Basques on the twenty-fourth, had departed about the time *Burgeo* tied up at the terminus of the Newfoundland Ferry and Railway Company dock.

Instead, the Board of Inquiry charged with the "Investigation of the Circumstances Surrounding the Loss of HMCS *Shawinigan*" focused on the Newfoundland Ferry and Railway Company ship's actions on the morning of the twenty-fifth. *Burgeo* left port on schedule at 7:45 a.m., expecting to rendezvous with its escort at Channel Head, some five miles from the quay that juts out from the Newfoundland Railway ferry terminus.

At first Gullage was not alarmed when he didn't find his escort waiting for him. According to his report, "It was not very light at 1015Z (7:45 a.m.) and the fishermen round about the mouth of the Harbour were still showing their lights . . . . We sailed without expecting to see HMCS SHAW-INIGAN until it got lighter."

Soon, though, Gullage became concerned. "I was about 11 miles off when I decided he was not around. The visibility was about 12 miles. I kept calling him on R/T [radio-telephone] but got no reply."

For this crossing, Naval Control of Shipping had given Gullage routing R. Convoy instructions, however, never varied. If for any reason the convoying vessel failed to meet the escort, it was "to return to Port aux Basques Harbour."

Gullage's decision to continue across the Cabot Strait unescorted earned him a stern rebuke from W. G. Mills, undersecretary of state for external relations (Newfoundland was a British colony in 1944). Mills dismissed Gullage's reasoning—that "there was every indication of a heavy northeasterly [storm] coming up and as my ship had not much stability due to lack of cargo, I decided to continue to Sydney"—curtly: "It is considered that the Master [of the *Burgeo*] took an unjustifiable risk" in "crossing the Straits unescorted."

Mills was equally blunt about Gullage's decision to maintain radio silence and not inform Sydney of *Shawinigan*'s absence. The time lag meant that naval authorities did not learn of *Shawinigan*'s absence until *Burgeo* arrived at the Sydney anti-submarine gate at 4:38 p.m. on October 25. "If any of 'SHAWINIGAN'S' crew survived the loss of their ship during the night of the 24th to 25th, they may have lived through most of the day but hardly through the following night."

Escorts were not always on their charge's tail. Accordingly, since the authorities in Sydney did not know that *Burgeo* had had no contact with *Shawinigan*, its absence at 4:38 p.m. when *Burgeo* arrived at the anti-submarine gate did not raise immediate alarm.

A little over a half hour later, however, concern began manifesting itself. "On the assumption that H.M.C.S. SHAWINIGAN had lost contact with S.S. BURGEO," Anti-Submarine Commander J. M. McConnell (who may or may not have known that *Burgeo* had had no contact with its escort ship) told the board of inquiry, "a signal was originated to H.M.C.S. SHAWINIGAN informing her that S.S. BURGEO had passed inward."

Standard operating procedure called for *Shawinigan* to respond. It did not. However, since atmospheric conditions, especially those associated with deteriorating weather (by the afternoon of the twenty-fifth a northeast gale had blown up), often resulted in difficulties in ships both receiving and broadcasting W/T (wireless telegraphy) messages, there was little surprise that *Shawinigan* did not answer the signal sent at 5:03 p.m.

Two hours later, at 6:54 p.m., McConnell began to assume the worst and notified Admiral Murray and the RCAF controller in Sydney of *Shawinigan*'s absence. He also ordered the first of twenty-three signals ordering *Shawinigan* to "signal position, course and speed."

Murray immediately tasked Escort Group 16, consisting of HMS *Anticosti* and HMCS *Springhill* and *Gananoque*, to search for survivors.[10] Poor weather grounded EAC until dawn of the twenty-sixth. The weather also hampered EG-16 and prevented it from being reinforced by Fairmiles. Nothing was found until well after daylight on the twenty-sixth, when *Anticosti* found an unmarked Carley float and a few pieces of wreckage that the wind and waves had pushed over forty miles southeast of where *Shawinigan* had been patrolling. At 1:24 p.m. on the twenty-seventh, *Springhill* rendezvoused with

HMCS *Truro* to transfer to it the bodies of Leading Stoker Gordon MacGregor, Telegraphist Howard Barlow and Able Seaman Dudley Garrett, as well as three unidentified bodies.

"Even before we got the message to put to sea to search for survivors, we knew from word of mouth that something had happened to *Shawinigan*," recalls John Chance, then commander of Fairmile 058. "The mood was very sombre. It was the first time for me or for my crew that we were involved in such an immediate action. We knew it had been the first run for *Shawinigan* since her refit. And now, she and all her crew were feared lost. We were out for a couple of days but didn't find anything."

The Board of Inquiry was unable to determine conclusively what had sunk Lieutenant William J. Jones's redoubtable corvette. Not until the interrogation of U-1228's crew after its surrender in Portsmouth, New Hampshire, on May 13, 1945, did naval authorities confirm that *Shawinigan* had been sunk by the last functioning torpedo to be fired in the Battle of the St. Lawrence.[11]

Since the torpedo was a homing torpedo, it's more than likely that it would have hit *Shawinigan* either squarely in the after peak or at the propeller. The similar attack on the frigate *Magog* destroyed sixty feet of its stern; *Magog* stayed afloat because its aft bulkhead held. Such an explosion on *Shawinigan* (a corvette like *Charlottetown* and thus built to maritime and not Admiralty standards of watertightness) would have demolished more than one-quarter of the ship, including the aft bulkhead.

In large measure, however, the last moments of this original Flower-class corvette had already been eerily foretold—indeed, twice foretold—by men who had miraculously survived the sinkings of two of *Shawinigan*'s sister ships. On August 8, 1944, HMCS *Regina* sank in twenty-eight seconds after U-667 torpedoed it off Cornwall, England. Thirteen days later in the English Channel, HMCS *Alberni* sank in twenty seconds, the victim of a Gnat fired by U-480.[12] The official report of *Alberni*'s sinking describes the scene:

The ship was hit on the port side towards the after end of the engine room . . . . The explosion blew all her aft bulkheads for in less than ten seconds her stern was awash up to the funnel and she was beginning to list to the port.

Not only had she sunk in 20 seconds, turning over on top of many of those who were trying to leave the ship by the port side, but those that managed to fight their way to the surface found no Carley Floats to help them. There had been no time to release one float or whaler . . . . Probably [the] very few [who] did escape from the mess decks must have dashed up without their life jackets on, since they were sitting down to lunch at the time and would have taken off their life jackets to eat . . . . In some cases, therefore, one lifebelt had to support two or three in the water.

Only one stoker escaped from the stoker's mess deck and he was the only man of his branch to survive from the engine room [which] was immediately flooded by the explosion . . . . None of the officers got up from the wardroom.

Could he speak, MacGregor surely would tell, as *Regina*'s Surgeon Lieutenant G. A. Gould did, of "an ear-splitting detonation"; of their ship being "blasted from under [them] and debris scattered for hundreds of yards"; of crewmen "mortally shattered by the tremendous blast [who] had already ceased to struggle"; of "others, trapped helplessly beneath the decks, [who] never had a chance." Perhaps Barlow would tell, as Gould did of himself, of being trapped under water by a "mass of tangled metal"; of "finally, after what seemed an eternity of suffocation," breaking the surface only to be blinded by a "film of oil." Had not Garrett's tongue been stilled, he too might have told of still more horror: "When the blinding film of oil cleared from my eyes, there, towering above me, were the last few feet of our funnel. It seemed certain to pin me beneath its massive form, but just as it was about to strike, it rolled away, then slithered beneath the surface."

Some minutes after 10:30 p.m. on November 25, 1944, the echo of the last Nazi torpedo to explode in the St. Lawrence rumbled over Port aux Basques. Within seconds, the sea once again opened to receive its dead before collapsing on itself like a "great shroud" that, as Herman Melville wrote at the end of *Moby Dick*, "rolled on as it rolled five thousand years ago."

EPILOGUE: 1945

A t the start of the 1945 shipping season, Canadian planners remained worried. True, in the eight months since D-Day the combined navies of Canada, the United Kingdom and the United States had destroyed 205 U-boats. Their armies had seized the ports of Saint Nazaire, Lorient and La Pallice, which since the fall of France in 1940 had given the "grey wolves" easy access to the Atlantic. Dönitz had been forced to pull his boats back to Bergen in occupied Norway and to Germany's Baltic ports. As shipping began that April, Allied armies had invaded Hitler's Germany from both the east and the west.

Still, the *U-Bootwaffe* remained a potent threat. On February 8, 1945, the *Times* of London carried a long article warning of a new U-boat offensive to be carried out by *Schnorchel*-equipped boats. Left unsaid were the Admiralty's worries about the Elektro boats and even the Walter boats, both of which were faster than most escort ships and all but immune to the existing munitions. Despite almost constant bombing, U-boat construction continued in secret underground factories staffed with slave labour, and even at the well-known Blohm & Voss shipyard in Hamburg.[1] On April 25, 1945, the day U-2552, the last of the more than 1,100 U-boats built for Hitler's Germany, went into service in Hamburg, the Allied armies were less than eighty miles away at the Elbe River. One hundred and fifty-four U-boats surrendered after the war.

In January 1945, four months before the opening of the shipping season, Canadian authorities already knew that in an effort to draw Allied naval forces away from Europe BdU planned on attacking shipping in the St. Lawrence. Indeed, as early as November 1944, the British Admiralty and the United States Navy believed that in 1945 Dönitz could send as many as seven U-boats back into these waters where the bathyscaphe effect would hide them from asdic searches. In January 1942, Operation Paukenschlag, the U-boat offensive against the United States, had been launched with a mere seven U-boats. On November 20, 1944, Air Vice-Marshal G. O. Johnson signalled C. G. Power, secretary of defence for air, "We must . . . expect and be prepared for a renewed submarine offensive in our area which may be very difficult to combat and will strain all available resources to the utmost."

Despite—or, rather, because of—the successes in Europe, keeping the St. Lawrence open to shipping was more important in 1945 than it had been in 1943. The armies that were liberating Europe consumed vast quantities of materiel. Diverting any appreciable proportion of the 705,000 tons planned to be shipped from Montreal alone to either Halifax or Saint John would have hopelessly overburdened those ports. Recognizing this, on March 7, the War Committee directed Minister Macdonald to "review and report on the anti-submarine measures to be taken in the Lower St. Lawrence." On April 16, the day the first transatlantic convoys entered the gulf, Naval Service Headquarters estimated that there were forty-five U-boats in the Canadian zone of the North Atlantic.

As they had in 1942, naval officials sought to prepare Canadians for attacks in the St. Lawrence. Citing Allied naval sources, the *Ottawa Journal* of March 31, 1945, warned of "Nazis Embarking on Last Minute U-boat Campaign." Four days later, in an article that announced that HMCS *Annan* had destroyed a U-boat, the *Halifax Herald* quoted Macdonald: "There is no reason to believe that Canadian coastal waters will be free of these underwater marauders."[2] And, as had happened six years earlier after the sinking of SS *Nicoya*, in the waning days of the war British underwriters raised the war risk premium on transoceanic shipping.

The RCN's plans for the defence of the gulf were ambitious. As in previous years, they were built around the redoubtable corvettes; five were to be recalled from mid-ocean groups. These ships were augmented by Bangor minesweepers (called back from the post-D-Day duty of sweeping the English Channel), trawlers and Fairmiles. Plans were put in place to quickly deploy two groups of frigates if the need arose. By mid-April, the RCAF "Plan for Air Defence of Canada 1945–46" was in operation. The Canso squadrons at Sydney and at inner gulf stations were augmented to eighteen aircraft. Even as Germany surrendered on May 7, a detachment of eleven Cansos, soon to be equipped with centimetric radar capable of picking up *Schnorchels*, took up station at Gaspé.

There was no final U-boat offensive in the St. Lawrence.

The war off Canadian shores ended with a ghastly coda—a coda that replayed not only the sinking of the minesweeper HMCS *Clayoquot* in the same waters four months earlier, on Christmas Eve 1944, but also the experience of the hundreds of men, women and children torpedoed in the St. Lawrence. At 6:35 a.m. on April 16, 1945, U-190, commanded by twenty-five-year-old *Oberleutnant zur See* Hans-Edwin Reith (her chief engineer being Weiner Hirschmann), torpedoed HMCS *Esquimalt*, then on patrol just out of sight of Halifax. Most of *Esquimalt*'s crew of seven officers and sixty-four ratings managed to get off the ship in the four minutes before it plunged to the bottom. But five officers and thirty-nine ratings died in the frigid waters off Halifax as they waited more than six hours for rescue.

Sixty years later, Terry Manuel, then a twenty-year-old ship's writer from New Brunswick (as ship's writer, Manuel was an administrator who reported directly to *Esquimalt*'s captain, Lieutenant Robert Macmillan, DSC, RCNVR), recalls this last torpedoing of one of His Majesty's Royal Canadian Ships in the Second World War and the last awful struggle of His Majesty's officers and ratings to survive in the cold waters off their own shore: "At around 6:10 a.m., I was released from my dark-hours watch at the starboard depth-charge thrower and went below to my quarters in the chief and petty officers' mess in the forward part of the ship, where there were three other officers. I figured I had an hour to catch a nap before I had to report for my regular duty post, so I stripped off my pants and socks and used my life jacket as a pillow.

"As soon as I laid down, I heard a loud thump that I thought was the minesweeping gear that we had loaded in Halifax shifting. Then I heard a large crash, and the ship shook and began to keel over toward the port side.

The lights glimmered and then went out. I jumped up from my bunk and ran to the emergency hatchway, which opened onto the deck. I found it in the darkness, but because the plates were buckled, it couldn't be opened.

"Then, as the ship continued to roll over on her side, I decided to try to go out through the communications mess. The hatchway to the companionway that led to that mess was now up above us. I climbed up the wall to get to the hatchway and then fell into the communications mess. Just as I got to the companionway that I hoped would take me to the deck, Carl Jacques, a petty officer from Nova Scotia, came charging up and vaulted over my shoulders and into the hatchway. But I couldn't hold on and fell back into the communications mess, which was now filling with water. Finally, I managed to get into the companionway. Just as I did, I saw on my right a huge wave of foaming water rushing towards me. The water pummelled me about and pushed me up the companionway.

"Below me I saw only darkness. Above me some faint grey light. Even though I could not swim, I began thrashing my way up. The ship rolled again and I was pushed out of the companionway onto the side of the ship. To my left I could see the ship's bow pointing upwards; she was on her way down. Within seconds I heard someone yell, 'Swim, damn it! She's going under!'

"I saw a life jacket and tried to get to it. As I did, another sailor also got to it. Each of us managed to get one arm into it. By then the ship was gone. Less than four minutes had passed.

"Soon the life jacket became too waterlogged to keep us both afloat. I saw a canvas kit bag floating in the water and grabbed hold if it. Then I realized that the sailor I was sharing the life jacket with was going under, so I grabbed him by the hair and held onto him.

"A few moments later, a Carley float appeared and I heard Carl Jacques yell, 'Hang on, scribe!' He jumped in the water and swam to us and then pulled us to the float. I hung on in front and he climbed back onto the cork ring of the float. Ten minutes later he was dead and we had to throw his body over.

"There were eighteen of us in and around the float in terribly cold water. It didn't take long for the water, chilled by the ice currents that came down from the Arctic, to take its toll. One by one, men around me died and floated off.

"Twice we thought we'd been spotted. Once by a plane about an hour after the sinking, but he later reported that he thought we were fishermen. Then, at 8 a.m., we saw what we called the four-o'clock navy, the minesweepers that patrolled off Halifax during the day. They were almost within shouting distance when they turned away and soon vanished over the horizon.

"And still more men died while we waited, until finally, after almost seven hours, another patrol plane, which I later learned had been sent to look for us because there had been nothing heard from us, spotted us, wiggled its wings and alerted the authorities in the light vessel, who alerted *Sarnia*.

"By the time *Sarnia* steamed into Halifax with the twenty-seven of us who survived and several bodies, we could see the streets were lined with people. Above the streets, standing on the roofs of their work sheds, stood silent workers with their hats off."

Fourteen days later, Canadian Wrens at a secret listening post in Coverdale, New Brunswick, recorded a signal sent by *Grossadmiral* Dönitz informing his U-boat commanders of Adolf Hitler's death and that, following Hitler's political testament, he, Karl Dönitz, was assuming the position of *Reichspräsident*. Seven days later, he signalled the fleet again, his rather grandiloquent words laying the foundation both for his defence at what he knew were the coming war trials and for the *U-Bootwaffe* mythology:

My U-boat men!

Six years of U-boat war is behind us. You have fought like lions. A crushing material superiority has forced us into a narrow area. A continuation of our fight from the remaining bases is no longer possible.

U-boat men! Undefeated and spotless you lay down your arms after a heroic battle without equal. We remember in deep respect our fallen comrades, who have sealed with death their loyalty to *Führer* and Fatherland.

Comrades! Preserve your U-boat spirit, with which you have fought courageously, stubbornly and imperturbably through the years for the good of the Fatherland.

Long Live Germany!
Your Grand Admiral[3]

Four of the U-boats that invaded the St. Lawrence surrendered. The first was Helmut Schmoekel's U-802, which surrendered on May 11 at Loch Eriboll in Scotland. The following day, Kurt Peterson's U-541 surrendered at Gibraltar. On the thirteenth, U-1228, commanded by Friedrich-Wilhelm Marienfeld, surrendered at Portsmouth, New Hampshire. A day later, Hermann Lessing turned U-1231 over to the British at Loch Foyle in Scotland. U-802, U-541 and U-1228 were scuttled. U-1231 was turned over to the Soviet Union, which rechristened it N-25; it served until the late 1950s and was broken up in 1960.

By September 1945, HMCS *Arrowhead* and *Vegreville* and all the Fairmiles that had served in the St. Lawrence had been turned over to the War Assets Corporation for disposal. HMCS *Rimouski* and *Trail* followed on August 30, 1946. HMCS *Truro* was paid off on September 17, 1946, seven years and sixteen days after the start of the Second World War.

IN MEMORIAM

SS *Nicoya* (May 11, 1942)

William John George
Henry Mills
James Stanley Newcomb
Douglas Phillips
Frank L. Smith
H. V. Woodthrope

SS *Leto* (May 12, 1942)

J. Breet
J. van Boven
M. A. de Keyzer
A. Eager
H. J. Holzhaeur
Frederick van Hoogdalem
J. Hoogenboom
Wilhelm Köning
G. J. Smit
A. J. Stanneveld
F. H. A. Thomas

**SS *Anastassios Pateras*
(July 6, 1942)**

Silvino Eugenio
John Howard
Ham Karamm

SS *Hainaut* (July 6, 1942)

Säid Nouman

SS *Dinaric* (July 6, 1942)

James Jameson
Henry Thomas
Herbert Walton
Slavko Ziganto

**SS *Frederika Lensen*
(July 20, 1942)**

Ali Edris
Ali Mossadden
Abudul Rajack
Robert James Spence

SS *Chatham* (August 27, 1942)

Emilio Blackstone-Pietranera
Francis S. Blake
Cornelius Clark
Abel De Souza
George T. Harrison
William Hurlston
Richard Scadding
7 known only to God

In Memoriam

USS *Laramie* (August 27, 1942)

Carmine Joseph Aloia
Dan Lynch
Erwin Wesley Parks
Gordon Leslie Spiering
James Curtis Voorhees

SS *Arlyn* (August 28, 1942)

John H. Bergeron
Roy W. Creighton
Charles J. Jeremias
Lawrence J. Lynch
Isidro S. Manzo
Mack Parks
Eladio A. Sanchez
John Taraza
Pedro Velez
Joseph L. Weeks
Jarvis S. Williams
George M. Willis

**SS *Donald Stewart*
(September 3, 1942)**

Romeo Gaudet
Harry Kaminsky
Harvey Sutherland

SS *Aeas* (September 6, 1942)

2 known only to God

**HMCS *Raccoon*
(September 7, 1942)**

George M. Adams
John M. Allen
James C. Anderson
Royden G. Ashmall
Roger Belanger

John J. Boudreau
Charles R. Champion
John E. Cherpeta
John F. Cook
Guy L. Dillabough
William Duncan
George Fowler
Owen W. Fralic
Frank J. Gallant
William C. Hamilton
Willam A. Harvie
Robert H. Henderson
Arthur G. Holmes
Ernst F. Howe
John J. Hughes
Joseph W. G. LaFlamme
Henry B. Lucas
Ralph O. Martindale
Russell H. McConnell
John H. McDonald
Harry F. Muller
John G. Parsons
Albert J. Payne
Louis H. Prowse
John E. Sheflin
John N. Smith
Beverly G. Stewart
Michael Sweeney
Glenwood L. Taylor
James E. Thomas
Percy J. Thomas

**SS *Mount Pindus*
(September 7, 1942)**

3 known only to God

**SS *Mount Taygetus*
(September 7, 1942)**

Georgeios Triantafyllarous[1]

3 known only to God

HMCS *Charlottetown* (September 11, 1942)

John Willard Bonner
Donald St. C. Bowser
Todd David
John C. Garland
John A. Grant
Peter K. Lovat
John Lundrigan
Thomas A. MacDonald
Edmond C. Robinson
Leonard A. Wharton

SS *Inger Elizabeth* (September 15, 1942)

P. Kool
3 known only to God

SS *Carolus* (October 9, 1942)

Knut Anderson
Verner Anderson
Pablo Cubbillas
Onni Heino
Niilo Helenius
Runar Karlsson
Eryitt Kukkonen
John Joseph MacDougall
R. F. McGraw
John Milmine
Sulo Aarne Seppala

SS *Caribou* (October 14, 1942)

Crew

Israel Barrett
Llewellyn Carter
Elias Coffin
James Hubert Coffin
Howard Cutler
Richard Feltham
Miss Bride Fitzpatrick
Charles Ford
Maxwell French
George Gale
Jerome Gale
Clarence Hann
Harry Hann
William Hogan
Charles Humphries
Victor Lomond
Thomas Moist
Charley Pearcey
James Pike
James L. Prosper
Joseph Richards
William Samms
Israel Sheaves
John Skeard
Albert Strickland
Garfield Strickland
Benjamin Taverner
Harold Taverner
Stanley Taverner
Arthur Thomas
George Thomas

Army Personnel

C. R. Abelson
C. G. Cochrane
T. A. Currie
P. Diamond

E. S. Francis
L. A. MacIntyre
J. C. B. McDonald
H. R. Mills
L. M. Sheppard
A. A. Sullivan
H. M. Tough

Royal Navy and Royal Canadian Navy Personnel

E. Barrett
Eli Maxwell Bishop
C. Creston
William A. Glasgow
A. Marshall
J. R. Masson
G. N. May
A. Nash
W. C. Poole
E. R. Quinlan
G. W. Randall
N. Rowe
R. J. Skinner
R. Smith
J. Tapper
W. J. Vey
E. Warren
R. White
Miss A. W. Wilkie
J. W. H. Windsor

Royal Air Force and Royal Canadian Air Force Personnel

J. H. Barrett
R. Chatson
F. G. Coulson
T. H. Cummings
H. H. Elkin
D. C. Glover

W. P. Howse
A. W. Jones
L. E. Legge
C. M. McCaroon
D. L. Mitchell
M. N. Oiring
G. W. Parker
E. A. Thistle
L. William Truesdale
E. G. Walker
R. Watson
W. B. Wilson

US Personnel

J. C. Abernathy
E. T. Bothsa
J. M. Burns
J. C. Elzer
E. Hand
R. M. Penfield
E. G. Shultz
J. Waldman

Civilians

Mrs. Ada Allan
Caroline Allan
Constance Allan
Claus Bang
Baby Girl Bernard
Mrs. Harriet Bernard
Charles Berry
Mrs. Pearl Beswick
Robert Butler
Harold Chislett
Albert Coombs
Preston Cowley
William Carteret Freeham
Louise Gagné

Mrs. Katherine Gardner
William H. Garth
Myrtle Gilbert
Hugh B. Gillis
Gerald Hammond
Wilfred Hathaway
Mrs. Maggie Hedd
Miss Myrtle Kettle
Edgar Martin
Harold McCarthy
Kevin McCarthy
George Penham
George Pike
Mrs. Elizabeth Randell
John Ronan
Margaret Rose
William Ryan
John Sheppard
Mrs. Blanche Short
Basil Skinner
Mrs. Kathleen Skinner
Nancy Skinner
Mrs. Gertie Strickland
Holly Strickland
Myrtle Strickland
Nora Strickland
Donald Tapper
Mrs. Hazel Tapper
John W. Tapper
Lillian Tapper
Catherine Walsh
Patrick Walsh
Mrs. Helen Wightman
Mary Young

HMCS *Magog*
(October 14, 1944)

Ted E. Davis
Gordon T. Elliot
Kenneth J. Kelly

HMCS *Shawinigan*
(November 25, 1944)

Stewart W. Anderson
William J. Anderson
Robert O. Armstrong
Haddow F. Baird
Howard C. Barlow
Joseph F. A. Beauchamp
Joseph B. A. Benoit
Ronald W. Bernst
Douglas J. Blaylock
Robert A. Brett
Joseph Y. P. Breux
Gordon O. Brown
Arthur H. Butler
William F. Callan
Alexander H. Campbell
James Campbell
George A. Chalmers
Eric M. Chisolm
Alfred E. J. Clayton
Harry C. B. Cole
Cyril W. Conners
Robert J. L. Cook
Ronald J. Dupuis
Alfred H. Duval
Ralph N. Earp
Clifford Eppler
David M. Evans
John J. Evans
Lewis B. Evans
Edgar L. Fiander
Leo H. Fougère

In Memoriam

Donald F. French
Dudley M. Garrett
Robert G. Grant
Arnold S. Hibbard
John W. Hodgson
William Hughes
Roy S. Hunter
Harold J. Hird
John L. James
Maurice W. Johnson
William J. Jones
Arthur E. Kemp
Robin D. H. Kendall
Wilmette R. Kennah
Joseph A. La Barre
Leslie B. Langfield
John C. Lawrence
Thomas E. Lawrence
Walter J. Lloyd
David A. MacArthur
William C. MacEachers
Gordon MacGregor
Vernon E. MacLanders
Jack MacWilliam
Donald T. C. McDougal
Donald B. McNeil
Patrick A. Mitchell
Ewan Morrison
David J. Morrow
Cecil R. Moss
Glenn S. Murray
Michael B. O'Gorman

John Ossachuk
Howard N. Parsons
James G. Phillips
Michael J. Piathowski
Robert F. Rayner
Clifford L. Rea
John J. Rigby
Edward E. Ritzer
Frank N. Roy
Alfred T. Savoy
Walter B. Sealey
Gerald J. Smith
William R. Smith
Stanley L. Smithson
Anthony Smrke
Arthur D. Snyder
George L. S. Stefiuk
Dirk C. Swart
Roger C. Thomas
Hugh L. Todd
Frank R. Trenholm
Eldon G. Vincent
Spencer Wallington
Wilfred Watson
Conway J. Watt
Clayton L. White
Arthur J. Whitehead
Milton E. Whymark
Harold G. Woods

Requiescat in pace

APPENDIX A

TWO SPIES AND A
WEATHER STATION

On May 14, 1942, two days after Karl Thurmann's U-553 sank SS *Leto*, U-213, commanded by *Oberleutnant zur See* Amelung von Varendorff, became the first of three U-boats to land on Canada's shores. Two, Varendorff's and *Kapitänleutnant* Friedrich-Wilhelm Wissmann's U-518, landed spies; the other, U-537, commanded by *Kapitänleutnant* Peter Schrewe, landed a weather station in Labrador. Neither of the two spies, *Leutnant* (M. A.) "Langbein" and Werner Janowski, operated in Canada as intended by their German handlers. And though set up without incident, the weather station, called Kurt, failed to supply BdU with weather information because a German radio station jammed the wavelength on which the weather station's radio broadcast.

"LANGBEIN"

After living in Canada between 1928 and 1932, working in both Alberta and Manitoba, the man known as Langbein returned to Germany prior to the outbreak of the war. After being mobilized, he was chosen for espionage training; his first mission was to Romania. Then, recognizing his ability to blend into Canadian society, *Abwehr*, Nazi Germany's military intelligence branch, sent him back to Canada on an intelligence-gathering mission.

Landed from U-213 at 3 a.m. on May 14, 1942, near the village of St.

Martin, New Brunswick, Langbein immediately buried his transmitter and some other equipment and assumed the identity prepared by German intelligence. His national registration card was prepared in the name of Alfred Haskins and gave his address as 183 Younge [*sic*] Street, Toronto. He was also supplied with some $7,000 in large US bills and either $12 or $13 in Canadian bills; surprisingly, none of St. Martin's shopkeepers noticed that the bills this stranger used were out-of-date dollars.

Given his prior knowledge of Canada, his ability to speak English and what one historian records as his "likeable character," Langbein should have been a valuable spy. What his handlers did not know, however, was that Langbein had become disenchanted with Nazi Germany and saw his mission to Canada as a chance to escape.

Langbein hitchhiked to Montreal, where he was able to cash his larger US bills in some of the city's less reputable establishments. Later, he was caught in a raid on a whorehouse. His identity was preserved, however, because, like the other patrons caught *in flagrante delicto* in such establishments, he was booked under an assumed name and then allowed to pay the fine.

A month after landing in Canada, Langbein settled in Ottawa, staying at the Grand Hotel, which stood at the corner of Sussex and George streets. The hotel's bar was, according to the *Ottawa Citizen* in a 1952 article on Langbein, "a favourite spot for the members of the armed forces and civil servants employed in the [now demolished] Daly Building across the street." Langbein did not, however, make use of this happy coincidence, preferring to live off his ever-diminishing bankroll. In 1943, probably to conserve funds, he moved from the Grand Hotel to a boarding house.

On November 1, 1944, Langbein walked into the Naval Intelligence Directorate on Sparks Street and informed an incredulous official that he was a German spy. The RCMP did not believe his story until, with Sergeant Cecil Bayfield watching, he dug up the transmitter and other equipment he had buried over two years earlier. The RCMP quickly established that "Haskins" had not engaged in espionage. He was interned until the end of the war, after which he was repatriated to Germany.

JANOWSKI

Werner Alfred Waldemar von Janowski had also lived in Canada prior to the war. He married an Ontario woman in 1932. Over the next six years, before he deserted his wife and went back to Germany, he toured the province to take pictures and paint waterfront scenes. He may have joined the French Foreign Legion and may have served with the German army at Dieppe. What is known for certain is that on November 9, 1942, U-518 landed him on the beach a few miles from New Carlisle, Quebec.

Unlike Langbein, Janowski buried only his naval uniform. He carried his two large suitcases (one containing a transmitter) into town. The suitcases, according to historian Michael Hadley, were "obviously of German manufacture." As it had done with Langbein, German intelligence supplied Janowski with a great deal of cash: $4,994 Canadian and $1,000 in US twenty-dollar gold pieces. His national registration card was issued in the name of William Branton of 323 Danforth Avenue, Toronto. As well, he carried a 1940 Quebec driver's licence. One of the two paperbacks he carried, likely to use as code books, was a 1939 edition of Mary Travers's *Mary Poppins*, published in Leipzig; imprinted on its cover were the words, "Not to be introduced into the British Empire or the USA."

Janowski attracted attention almost immediately upon presenting himself at a hotel in New Carlisle owned by Earle Annett and asking for a room in which he could bathe and shave before lunch. Annett's suspicions were aroused first by the strange man's "submarine smell" (the smell of musty clothes and diesel oil) and by the fact that the patron told him that he had just arrived in town by bus; the first bus would not arrive in town until noon.

While Janowski ate lunch in the hotel's dining room, Annett searched his room. He didn't find *Mary Poppins*. However, he did find several matches that he knew were manufactured in Belgium, with which, of course, Canada had had no trade for over three years. The bills Janowski used to pay for his room and meal, Annett recognized immediately, had been withdrawn from use several years before the war. Annett knew that Janowski planned to take the afternoon train to Montreal, so he sent his son to warn the Quebec Provincial Police.

The QPP acted quickly. Constable Alphonse Duchesneau, posing as a radio salesman from Toronto, took the train seat next to Janowski. After some conversation, during which Duchesneau noted to himself Janowski's German accent, he informed Janowski that he was a police officer and demanded that Janowski produce his identification. All but one of Janowski's papers were in order. His national registration card was printed in English on one side and French on the other, as they were in Quebec; Ontario cards were printed in English only.

Duchesneau demanded that Janowski open his luggage so he could search it. At that point Janowski declared, "I am a German naval officer. I landed from a submarine last night, and after landing, decided that I would desert. I therefore changed into civilian clothing and buried my naval uniform on the shore near the spot where I had landed. I insist on being allowed to recover my uniform and being given the treatment laid down for prisoners of war by the Geneva Convention."

Janowski led police to where he'd buried his uniform. Several days later, he demanded of RCMP Inspector C. W. Harvison, commissioner of the RCMP, who had come to interview him in a local jail, that he be "permitted to don his uniform and that he be treated as an officer and a gentleman." In 1967 Harvison recalled—with, no doubt, much understatement—that "my reply may not have been in the best military tradition, but as least it startled and served to deflate the prisoner," who had entered the room clicking his heels like a Nazi on parade. "Nuts," said Harvison. "I believe you are spy. Sit down and keep quiet until I speak to you."

Harvison then set out to "turn him around"—that is, to turn him into a double agent who would feed disinformation to German intelligence. The commissioner pointed out to Janowski that his handlers back in Berlin had not shown any great regard for his safety, the old-style bills and mistaken identity card being his evidence. "Those goddamn Gestapo," Janowski exclaimed after one of Harvison's men told him that some of the $20 bills had been poorly counterfeited. "The money was secured from them, and they have framed me. They wanted me caught and executed." Janowski then asked, "If I am executed, you think it will be by hanging?"—a question that told Harvison of Janowski's inner debate. Seizing the moment, the commissioner replied, "Most probably," after which his prisoner again fell silent for a moment before "sobbing and banging the desk while he repeated over and over again, "I will not be hanged, I will not be hanged."

Harvison waited and then told Janowski that he, Harvison, would be leaving the next morning and he would have to have Janowski's answer by then. Later that day, Harvison had Janowski brought back into the interrogation room, where the erstwhile German naval officer agreed to be a double agent.

Janowski's RCMP handlers kept watch on him for the remainder of the war. From December 1942 through November 1943, Janowski fed his handlers in Hamburg disinformation produced by special intelligence committees concerning the armed services units in and around Montreal and even Quebec City, the types of ships in port and anything he could learn about submarine nets. No record exists of Janowski's fate after the war; however, it is assumed that he was repatriated.

"KURT"

Named for its builder, Dr. Kurt Sommermeyer, the weather station called Kurt was the only German "base" established in North America during World War II. Similar automated weather stations, all manufactured by Siemens, were established in arctic or subarctic regions, including at Spitzbergen, in Greenland, and in the Barents Sea north of Norway.

The automated base consisted of twelve 1×1.5 metre cylinders, most weighing some 220 pounds, which had to be manhandled out of U-537's hold onto rubber dinghies, floated to shore and then carried 140 yards inland and up a 170-foot-high hill. Nine of the cylinders contained nickel-cadmium and dry-cell high-voltage batteries. One contained a sophisticated mechanism that recorded the temperature, wind speed and direction, humidity and barometric pressure, and then encoded this information in Morse code. The two other parts were the radio aerial and a tripod upon which were mounted temperature, pressure and wind sensors. Kurt broadcast at 3940 kHz with enough power to be picked up at stations in northern Europe. To throw off the suspicions of any hunter or fisherman who happened to find Kurt, each cylinder was stamped with the name of the official-sounding (but non-existent) Canadian Weather Service; the Germans also left Canadian cigarette butts and, for good measure, a few empty emergency-ration cans.

Twenty-eight hours after surfacing at 60° 5′ N 64° 24′ W in Martin Bay on the northeastern coast of Labrador on October 22, 1943, U-537's captain gave the order to weigh anchor. Kurt, or WFL-26 (*Wetterfukgerät-Land #26*) as it officially was known, broadcast its first weathergram three minutes later. For several days, every three hours Schrewe's radiomen picked up Kurt's broadcasts on schedule. Then they began noticing that the broadcasts were being jammed. One can only imagine their surprise when they discovered that the station jamming Kurt was in fact German.

Unlike "Langbein" and Janowski, who were known to Canadian authorities during the war and who disappeared after the war, Kurt remained unknown until the 1970s, when Franz Selinger, a retired Siemens engineer, wrote a history of the German Weather Service. Kurt's remains, which are on display in the Canadian War Museum in Ottawa, were discovered in 1981 by a team led by historian W. A. B. Douglas.

APPENDIX B

ANTI-SEMITISM AND
THE *KRIEGSMARINE*

The debate over the extent to which the *Kriegsmarine* or the *Wehrmacht*, as opposed to the *Einsatzgruppen*, shared Hitler's eliminationist anti-Semitism (to borrow Daniel Goldhagen's perfect phrase) continues. Even if we grant that Timothy Mulligan (author of *Neither Sharks nor Wolves: The Men of Nazi Germany's U-boat Arm, 1939–1945*) has a point when he argues that because the *U-Bootwaffe*'s bases were far from the death camps of Eastern Europe, it is going too far to say, as he does, that Dönitz's men were "isolated from the regime's true nature."

First, it is unclear that physical distance itself explains ignorance. Second, Mulligan himself cites U-boatmen who had heard of mass killings of Jews in Latvia. In his *Dönitz: The Last Führer*, historian Peter Padfield quotes Diesel Matt (U-333), who tells of having been presented with a wooden box containing watches after his 1943 return to base: "The watches were all second-hand, all in working order; a few were watches for the blind. Then we knew exactly. That was too macabre. Nobody should say that he knew nothing. We knew at that time where they came from."

The more stolid members of the *Wehrmacht* may have been shocked and even revolted by the wanton killings by the SS in Poland and the east and by the factories of death of Auschwitz, Treblinka and Birkenau. But, as many histories have made clear, the German army and General Staff stood by and did precisely nothing.

Perhaps more revealing than the statistics of deportations and killings is this 1942 report, quoted by Jonathan Steinberg in *All or Nothing: The Axis and the Holocaust, 1941–43* (a comparative study of Italian and German attitudes toward the Holocaust), from a German army counterintelligence officer in Libya who was complaining of the Italian army's scandalous attitude toward the Jews under its control: "It becomes clearer every day that the local Jews sit 'in an iron barrel' [that is, are protected], as the Italians appropriately put it . . . . A closer look reveals that the Italian administrative apparatus itself is 'the iron barrel,' which surrounds the Jews protectively and allows them to go on pursuing their dirty business. One frequently hears from Italian officials the astonishing opinion that the Jews of Libya are 'decent chaps.'. . . The police make no distinction between Jews and Italians." Steinberg goes on to comment: "The German intelligence officer, [was] not an SS fanatic but an army counter-intelligence specialist . . . . [He] simply cannot imagine how Italians could call Jews, any Jews, 'decent chaps.' He is amazed that the Italian police do not distinguish between Italian and Jew . . . . German anti-semitism was not the special preserve of a few fanatics in black uniforms but a pervasive, widespread and fundamental attitude found throughout the entire *Wehrmacht*. In many years of intensive research in German army archives, I have found fewer than five examples of German officers expressing anything other than the opinions quoted above."

APPENDIX C

SHIPS TORPEDOED IN THE ST. LAWRENCE RIVER AND THE GULF OF ST. LAWRENCE, 1942 AND 1944

Date	Ship (Flag)	Deaths	U-boat (Captain)
11 May 1942	SS *Nicoya* (UK)	6	U-553 (Thurmann)
12 May 1942	SS *Leto* (Netherlands)	11	U-553 (Thurmann)
6 July 1942	SS *Anastassios Pateras* (Greece)	3	U-132 (Vogelsang)
6 July 1942	SS *Hainaut* (Belgium)	1	U-132 (Vogelsang)
6 July 1942	SS *Dinaric* (UK)	4	U-132 (Vogelsang)
20 July 1942	SS *Frederika Lensen** (UK)	4	U-132 (Vogelsang)
27 August 1942	SS *Chatham* (US)	14	U-517 (Hartwig)
27 August 1942	USS *Laramie* (US)	5	U-165 (Hoffmann)
28 August 1942	SS *Arlyn* (US)	12	U-517 (Hartwig)
3 September 1942	SS *Donald Stewart* (Canada)	3	U-517 (Hartwig)
6 September 1942	SS *Aeas* (Greece)	2	U-165 (Hoffmann)
7 September 1942	HMCS *Raccoon* (Canada)	36	U-165 (Hoffmann)
7 September 1942	SS *Mount Pindus* (Greece)	3	U-517 (Hartwig)
7 September 1942	SS *Mount Taygetus* (Greece)	5	U-517 (Hartwig)
7 September 1942	SS *Oakton* (Canada)	–[a]	U-517 (Hartwig)
11 September 1942	HMCS *Charlottetown* (Canada)	10	U-517 (Hartwig)
15 September 1942	SS *Saturnus* (Netherlands)	–	U-517 (Hartwig)
15 September 1942	SS *Inger Elizabeth* (Norway)	4	U-517 (Hartwig)
16 September 1942	SS *Joannis* (Greece)	–	U-165 (Hoffmann)

Ships Torpedoed in the St. Lawrence River and the Gulf of St. Lawrence

Date	Ship (Flag)	Deaths	U-boat (Captain)
16 September 1942	SS *Essex Lance** (UK)	–	U-165 (Hoffmann)
16 September 1942	SS *Pan York** (UK)	–	U-165 (Hoffmann)
9 October 1942	SS *Carolus* (Finland)	11	U-69 (Gräf)
11 October 1942	SS *Waterton* (UK)	–	U-106 (Rasch)
14 October 1942	SS *Caribou* (UK)	136	U-69 (Gräf)
14 October 1944	HMCS *Magog* (Canada)	3	U-1223 (Kneip)
3 November 1944	SS *Fort Thompson* (Canada)	–	U-1223 (Kneip)
25 November 1944	HMCS *Shawinigan* (Canada)	91	U-1228 (Marienfeld)

* Denotes ships torpedoed but not sunk.

a Both E. H. Read and L. Marchand dispute the figure of three men lost given by the Department of Veterans Affairs publication *The Battle of the Gulf of St. Lawrence*.

APPENDIX D

U-BOAT PATROLS IN THE ST. LAWRENCE

U-Boat	Captain	Actions
U-553	Karl Thurmann	2 ships sunk
U-213	Amelung von Varendorff	Landed spy near St. Martin, New Brunswick
U-132	Ernst Vogelsang	4 ships sunk[a]
U-165	Eberhard Hoffmann	3 ships sunk
U-517	Paul Hartwig	9 ships sunk
U-69	Ulrich Gräf	2 ships sunk
U-106	Hermann Rasch	1 ship sunk
U-43	Hans-Joachim Schwandtke	–
U-518	Friedrich-Wilhelm Wissmann	Landed spy near New Carlisle, Quebec
U-262	Heinz Frank	Attempted to pick up POWs from Prince Edward Island
U-536	Rolf Schauenburg	Attempted to pick up POWs from Baie des Chaleurs
U-802	Helmut Schmoekel	–
U-541	Kurt Peterson	–
U-1223	Albert Kneip	2 ships torpedoed
U-1228	Friedrich-Wilhelm Marienfeld	1 ship sunk
U-1231	Hermann Lessing	–

[a] Since SS *Frederika Lensen* could not be salvaged, naval records record it as being sunk.

SOURCES

The two most important historians of the Battle of the St. Lawrence are Michael L. Hadley and Roger Sarty. The former's *U-boats against Canada: German Submarines in Canadian Waters* (McGill–Queen's University Press, 1985) was the first scholarly work to give shape to the battle. Sarty's contribution to the recently published *No Higher Purpose: The Official Operational History of the Royal Canadian Navy in the Second World War, 1939–1943*, edited by W. A. B. Douglas (Vanwell, 2002), "The Battle of the St. Lawrence, February 1942–December 1941," is required reading, especially for those interested in how the battle fits into the overall story of the Royal Canadian Navy in World War II. Equally important are Sarty's articles "Ultra, Air Power, and the Second Battle of the St. Lawrence, 1944," in *To Die Gallantly: The Battle of the Atlantic*, edited by T. J. Runyan and J. M. Copes (Westview, 1994), and "The Limits of Ultra: The Schnorkel U-boat Offensive against North America, November 1944–January 1945," *Intelligence and National Security*, vol. 12, no. 2 (April 1997), 44–68. Less accessible but of great use to me are Sarty's unpublished "Eastern Air Command Anti-Submarine Operations in the Gulf of St. Lawrence, 1942" and "Eastern Air Command Anti-Submarine Operations in the Gulf of St. Lawrence, 1942," both of which were prepared for the National Defence Directorate of History; I thank Roger for making copies of this work available to me. More accessible is W. A. B. Douglas's *Creation of a National Air Force: The Official History of the Royal Canadian Air Force* (University of

---

This essay gives the publication information for articles and books used while preparing this book. In the interest of space, it does not provide bibliographic information for either newspaper articles or operation reports referred to in the text.

Toronto Press, 1986), particularly the chapter "The Battle of the St. Lawrence." More popular presentations of the battle can be found in Sarty's *Canada and the Battle of the Atlantic* (Art Global, 1998) and Sarty and Brian Tennyson's *Guardian of the Gulf: Sydney, Cape Breton, and the Atlantic Wars* (University of Toronto Press, 2000). The most accessible history of the Battle of the St. Lawrence is the excellent Web site maintained by the Musée Naval du Québec (Quebec Naval Museum), http://www.mnq-nmq.org.

Brian and Terence McKenna's documentary *War at Sea: U-boats in the St. Lawrence* (NFB, 1995) must be treated very carefully, for while they correctly depict the RCN's equipment problems, they leave the impression that both the RCN's staff and their political masters happily sent men to their deaths.

In her *U-boat Adventures: Firsthand Accounts from World War II* (Naval Institute Press, 1999), Melanie Wiggins devotes a chapter to *Operation Kiebitz*, as does C. W. Harvison in his memoir of the Royal Canadian Mounted Police, *The Horsemen* (McClelland and Stewart, 1967); Harvison's book also contains a chapter on Werner Janowski. Daniel Hoffman's *Camp 30, "Ehrenwort": A German Prisoner-of-War Camp in Bowmanville, 1941–1945* (Bowmanville Museum, 1988) contains a great deal of information about the operations of the Lorient Espionage Group. Stephen B. Lett's "A Book and Its Cover," *RCMP Quarterly*, vol. 39, no 2 (April 1974), tells how the RCMP disassembled and then reassembled the book that contained the maps being send to the Lorient Espionage Group. *Operation Kiebitz*, by Jean-Guy Dugas (Ed. Franc-Jeu, 1992) is a French-language history of the breakout and recapture of Wolfgang Heyda. Jak P. Mallmann Showell's *U-boats at War: Landings on Hostile Shores* (Ian Allan, 2000) contains important information about and excellent pictures of all three U-boat landings on Canadian shores.

The earliest treatment of the battle is in *Canada's War at Sea*, by Stephen Leacock and Leslie Roberts (Alvah Beatty, 1944). The first post-war treatment of the battle was Jack McNaught's two-part *Maclean's* magazine article "The Battle of the St. Lawrence" (October 15 and 22, 1949). Joseph Schull's *Far Distant Ships: An Official Account of Canadian Operations in World War II* (1950; Stoddart, 1987) sketches the battle. *The Battle of the St. Lawrence*, produced by Brian and Terence McKenna for the National Film Board (1995), is interesting but excessive in its criticism of the Canadian navy. More useful is the NFB series *Seasoned Sailors*, which contains interviews with both Desmond Piers (rear-admiral, retired) and John Pickford (rear-admiral, retired). Henri-Paul Boudreau's *Cette mer cruelle* (Ed. Nord-Côtières, 2000) is a French-language history of the battle.

Both *Arms, Men and Governments: The War Policies of Canada 1939–1945*, by C. P. Stacey (National Defence, 1970), and *The Naval Service of Canada*, vol. 2, *Activities on Shore during the Second World War*, by Gilbert N. Tucker (National Defence, 1952), are essential reading for anyone interested in policy, budgets, bases, building schedules and ship specifications. The first three chapters of *Out of the Shadows: Canada and the Second World War*, revised ed., by W. A. B. Douglas and Brereton Greenhous (Dundurn, 1995), are especially useful in understanding how Canada geared up for war production. "Army Participation in Measures Taken by the Three Services for the Security of the Gulf of St. Lawrence and the Lower River during the Period of German Submarine Activity, 1942–5," *Report No. 3 prepared for the Historical Section (G.S.) Army Headquarters,* is an excellent source of information on the army's role in the Battle of the St. Lawrence. The first volume of Tucker's history *The Naval Service of Canada, Origins and Early Years*, is the basis of every other history of the Canadian navy's beginnings. A more up-to-date work on the Canadian navy's history is Roger Sarty's *The Maritime Defence of Canada* (Canadian Institute of Strategic Studies, 1996). Sarty and Michael Hadley's *Tin Pots and Pirate Ships: Canadian Naval Forces and German Sea Raiders: 1880–1918* (McGill–Queen's University Press, 1991) is useful for understanding the basis for Canadian naval defence thought. *Ready, Aye, Ready: An Illustrated History of the Royal Canadian Navy*, by Jack Macbeth (lt.-cdr., RCNR, retired) (Key Porter Books, 1989), is a good introduction to the history of the RCN during the war.

Though they cover much more than the Battle of the St. Lawrence, Marc Milner's *North Atlantic Run: The Royal Canadian Navy and the Battle for the Convoys* (University of Toronto Press, 1985), *The U-boat Hunters: The Royal Canadian Navy and the Offensive against Germany's Submarines* (University of Toronto Press, 1994) and *Battle of the Atlantic* (Vanwell, 2003) are extremely useful for understanding the tactics and limits of anti-submarine warfare during the Second World War. More popular histories of Canada's navy in the Battle of the Atlantic are Donald E. Graves's *In Peril on the Sea: The Royal Canadian Navy and the Battle of the Atlantic* (Canadian Naval Memorial Trust, 2003) and *Tin Hats, Oilskins and Seaboots: A Naval Journey, 1938–1945*

(Canadian Naval Memorial Trust, 2000). Robert C. Fisher's "'We'll Get Our Own': Canada and the Oil Shipping Crisis of 1942," *Red Duster* (1993), also available on the Web, is a good introduction to the oil crisis that followed the U-boat offensive off the US east coast. Max Reid's *D.E.M.S. and the Battle of the Atlantic 1939–1945* (Commoner's Publishing Society, 1990) is the only available history of Canada's defensively equipped merchant ships.

Of the twenty-three ships sunk in the St. Lawrence, only SS *Caribou* has had a book written about it: *The Night of the Caribou*, by Douglas How (Lancelot Press, 1988). My source for information on the Postal Assorting Office aboard *Caribou* is C. R. McGuire's "Remember the *S. S. Caribou*: A Memorial to a Great Steamship Ferry," a three-part article published in the *Postal Historical Society of Canada Journal*, no. 110 (October 2001), no. 113 (March 2003) and no. 114 (June 2003). A three-part interview with William Lundrigan, titled "The *Caribou* Disaster: William Lundrigan's Story as Told to *Newfoundland Woman*" was published in three installments in *Newfoundland Woman*, vol. 3, no. 3–5 (October–December 1964). John Dominie's story was published under the title "I Survived the Wreck of the S.S. *Caribou*: The Words of John (Jack) T. Dominie" in *Downhomer*, vol. 13, no. 1 (June 2000). Thomas Fleming's story was published under the title "The *Caribou* Disaster: Thomas Fleming's Story" in an article by Cassie Brown in *St. John's Woman* (October 1963). Commander Fraser McKee and Captain Robert Darlington devote chapters to the sinkings of HMCS *Raccoon*, *Charlottetown* and *Shawinigan* in their *The Canadian Naval Chronicle, 1939–1945* (Vanwell, 1996). In his 1947 book *Wandelaur-Sur L'Eau*, the Belgian historian Paul Scarceriaux devotes a chapter to the sinking of SS *Hainaut*.

The battle is memorialized by James W. Essex and James B. Lamb, both of whom served in the St. Lawrence during 1942. Essex's *Victory in the St. Lawrence: Canada's Unknown War* (Boston Mills Press, 1984) is valuable for giving a feel for the men and the times but should be handled carefully; in addition to repeating the canard that the battle was hidden from the public, Essex includes a picture he claims is the sighting of a ship in the St. Lawrence through a periscope, a claim that cannot be substantiated. The sections devoted to the sinking of HMCS *Charlottetown* and SS *Donald Stewart* in Lamb's *On the Triangle Run: The Fighting Spirit of Canada's Navy* (Stoddart, 1986) are especially affecting. Together with his *The Corvette Navy: True Stories from Canada's Atlantic War*

(Macmillan of Canada, 1977), Lamb's work presents a most complete picture of life on Canada's corvettes. Two other books essential for understanding Canada's corvettes are Mac Johnston's *Corvettes Canada: Convoy Veterans of WWII Tell Their True Stories* (McGraw-Hill Ryerson, 1994) and Frank Curry's memoir *War at Sea: A Canadian Seaman on the North Atlantic* (Lugus, 1990). *Fading Memories: Canadians and the Battle of the Atlantic*, edited by Thomas G. Lynch (Atlantic Chief and Petty Officers Association, 1993), contains several useful short memoirs of life in the Canadian navy during the war. Though not Canadian, *The Battle of the Atlantic: The Corvettes and Their Crews, an Oral History*, by Chris H. Bailey (Royal Naval Museum, 1994), contains useful information about life on board these redoubtable ships. Also worth reading is Nicholas Monsarrat's novel *Three Corvettes* (Granada, 1972).

There are three books that are indispensable to anyone interested in the history and structure of Canada's corvettes: *Canada's Flowers: History of the Corvettes of Canada*, by Thomas Lynch (Nimbus, 1981), *Corvettes of the Royal Canadian Navy 1939–1945*, by Ken MacPherson and Marc Milner (Vanwell, 1993), and *HMCS Sackville 1941–1985*, by Marc Milner (Canadian Memorial Naval Trust, 1998). N. Roger Cole's four-part article "Despite All Odds: Flower-Class Corvettes and Temptress-Class Gun Boats," *Nautical Research Journal*, vol. 43 (1998) and vol. 44 (1999), contains much useful information about the building of corvettes. Maurice D. Smith's "Kingston Shipyards—World War Two," *Fresh Water: A Journal of Great Lakes Marine History*, vol. 5, no. 1 (1995), presents an invaluable picture of the building of these important ships.

David Zimmerman's *The Great Naval Battle of Ottawa* (University of Toronto Press, 1989) explains the infighting that led Canada's asdic and radar to lag behind both the Americans' and the Royal Navy's. Derek Howse's *Radar at Sea: The Royal Navy in World War II* (Naval Institute Press, 1993) presents a complete story of the role Canadians played in winning England's naval radars. *Best Kept Secret: Canadian Secret Intelligence in the Second World War*, by John Bryden (Lester, 1993), is the best source for information on Canadian huff-duff. The most complete history of huff-duff is Kathleen Broome Williams's *Secret Weapon: U.S. High-Frequency Directional Finding in the Battle of the Atlantic* (Naval Institute Press, 1996).

Stephen Kimber's *Sailors, Slackers and Blind Pigs: Halifax at War* (Doubleday,

2002) contains useful information on censorship rules and the feud between admirals Murray and Jones. Less accessible (but well worth the trouble to get) is Douglas How's unpublished MA thesis, "The Career of Rear Admiral Leonard W. Murray, C.B., C.B.E., RCN, 1896–1971" (Dalhousie University, 1972), which details this rivalry and the damage Jones's manning policy did to the RCN's operability. Commander Frederick B. Watt's memoir, *In All Respects Ready: The Merchant Navy and the Battle of the Atlantic, 1940–1945* (Prentice Hall, 1985), is the best available history of the Naval Boarding Service.

There are two histories of Canada's merchant fleet during the Second World War: S. C. Heal's *A Great Fleet of Ships: The Canadian Forts and Parks* (Vanwell, 1999) and *The Unknown Navy: Canada's World War II Merchant Navy*, by Robert G. Halford (Vanwell, 1995). *Running the Gauntlet: An Oral History of Canadian Merchant Seamen in World War II*, by Mike Parker (Nimbus, 1994), does not contain any information about the Battle of the St. Lawrence; it is, however, useful for getting a sense of the lives of the merchant seamen who sailed from Canada. Though not Canadian in focus, *Survivors: British Merchant Seamen in the Second World War*, by G. H. and R. Bennett (Hambledon, 1999), contains extremely useful information about lifesaving equipment and procedures.

My source for information about British shipbuilding is Correlli Barnett's *The Audit of War: The Illusion and Reality of Britain as a Great Nation* (Macmillan, 1986). Barnett's *The Collapse of British Power* (Methuen, 1972) is an invaluable source for understanding how the British Empire deluded itself about Nazi Germany's naval policy.

There are few books that deal with Quebec during World War II. The most important is Eric Amyot's *Le Québec entre Pétain et De Gaulle: Vichy, la France libre et les Canadiens français 1940–1945* (Fides, 1999). The history of the Fusiliers du St-Laurent can be found in *Soldats de la Côté: Les Fusiliers du St-Laurent d'hier à aujourd'hui* (Les Fusiliers du St-Laurent, 1992), by Major François Dornier and Marie-Claude Joubert. The history of the EAC base at Mont-Joli can be found in Major Dornier's *Des bombardiers au-dessus du Fleuve: Histoire de la 9e école de bombardement et de tir de Mont-Joli*.

General histories of the Battle of the Atlantic abound. Perhaps the single best is Martin Middlebrook's *Convoy* (Penguin, 1976). Three of the most recent are Spencer Dunmore's *In Great Waters: The Epic Story of the Battle of the Atlantic*,

1939–1945 (McClelland & Stewart, 1999), Dan Van Der Vat's *Standard of Power: The Royal Navy in the Twentieth Century* (Pimlico, 2001) and *At War at Sea*, by Ronald Spector (Penguin, 2001). Dunmore's book underlines the importance of the RCN's and Royal Canadian Air Force's contributions to winning the Battle of the Atlantic. Van Der Vat and Spector's histories are especially interesting because, though neither is written by a Canadian, both stress Canada's role and point out that for decades historians have underappreciated the fact that in the darkest days of 1941 and 1942, the RCN provided the margin that prevented the U-boats from cutting the supply lines to North America. Michael Gannon's *Operation Drumbeat: The Dramatic True Story of Germany's First U-boat Attacks along the American Coast in World War II* (Harper & Row, 1990) and his *Black May: The Epic Story of the Allies' Defeat of the German U-boats in May 1943* (Random House, 1999) are also essential reading. My source for information about the force of torpedo explosions in Robert H. Cole's *Underwater Explosions* (Dover, 1948). Perhaps the most accessible source of information on the Battle of the Atlantic is uboat.net; let me take the opportunity to thank the many correspondents on the site who steered me away from error.

The literature from the "U-boat side" is also quite large. A good place to begin is with Peter Padfield's biography *Dönitz: The Last Führer* (Cassell, 1984) or either of Bernard Edwards's books, *Dönitz and the Wolf Packs: The U-boats at War* (Cassell, 1996) and *Attack and Sink: The Battle for Convoy SC42* (New Guild, 1995). David O'Brien's *HX 72: The First Convoy to Die: The Wolfpack Attack That Woke Up the Admiralty* (Nimbus, 1999) is an especially good introduction to the Canadian role in fighting U-boats. Equally important is *Deadly Seas: The Duel between St. Croix and U305 in the Battle of the Atlantic*, by David Bercuson and Holger Herwig (Random House Canada, 1997). Bercuson and Herwig's *The Destruction of the Bismarck* (Stoddart, 2001) is my source for the quote from Herbert Wohlfarth (U-556) on page 17.

Though none of these memoirs should be taken at face value, Herbert A. Werner's *Iron Coffins: A Personal Account of the German U-boat Battles of World War II* (Da Capo, 1998), Peter Cramer's *U-boat Commander: A Periscope View of the Battle of the Atlantic* (Bodley Head, 1984) and Jost Metzler's *The Laughing Cow: A U-boat Captain's Story of the Terrors and Excitement of Undersea Warfare* (William Kimber, 1955) are important works for understanding the world the U-boatmen lived in. Graf's U-69 sank both SS *Carolus* and *Caribou*. A good short introduction to the U-boatmen is *Grey Wolf: U-boat Crewman of World War II*, by Gordon Williamson (Osprey, 2001). The two best English-language studies of U-boatmen (including their politics) are *Wolf: U-boat Commanders in World War II*, by Jordan Vause (Naval Institute Press, 1997), and Timothy P. Mulligan's *Neither Sharks nor Wolves: The Men of Nazi Germany's U-boat Arm, 1939–1945* (Naval Institute Press, 1999). Also useful is Erich Topp's "Manning and Training the U-boat Fleet," in *The Battle of the Atlantic, 1939–1945*, edited by Stephen Howarth and Derek Law (Oxford University Press, 1993); this book also contains important articles by William Glover, "Manning and Training in the Allied Navies," and Axel Niestle, "German Technical and Electronic Development." Mullmann Showell's *U-boat Commanders and Crews 1935–1945* (Crowood Press, 1998) is also exceedingly useful. Michael Hadley's *Count Not the Dead: The Popular Image of the German Submarine* (McGill–Queen's University Press, 1995) contains important information on the U-boatmen's view of themselves. A good introduction to the technical side of U-boat operations and torpedoes is Robert C. Stern's *Type VII U-Boats* (Brockhampton Press, 1991).

Histories of the Nazis and of German anti-Semitism abound. Among the most useful are Daniel J. Goldhagen's *Hitler's Willing Executioners: Ordinary Germans and the Holocaust* (Random House, 1996), Richard Bessel's *Life in the Third Reich* (Oxford University Press, 1987) and William L. Shirer's *The Nightmare Years: 1930–1940* (Little, Brown, 1984). My source for the difference between the Italian and the German attitudes toward Jews is Jonathan Steinberg's *All or Nothing: The Axis and the Holocaust, 1941–1943* (Routledge, 1990). Richard Grunberger's *The 12-Year Reich: A Social History of Nazi Germany, 1933–1945* (Holt, Rinehart and Winston, 1971) contains important information about youth and schooling in Hitler's Germany. Also useful is Paul L. Rose's *Heisenberg and the Nazi Atom Bomb Project: A Study in German Culture* (California University Press, 1998). My sources for Nazification of school texts is "Life in Nazi Germany" at the German Propaganda Archive maintained by Calvin College in Grand Rapids, Michigan. A short history of illegal rearmament during the Weimar Republic can be found in *Inspection for Disarmament*, edited by Seymour Melman (Columbia University Press, 1958). Uboat.net also contains a history of the illegal creation of the U-boat Arm, as well as links to other Web sites that detail this history.

NOTES

PREFACE

[1] Between 1939 and 1945, the Royal Canadian Navy lost twenty-four warships and more than two thousand officers and ratings; Canada's merchant navy lost seventy ships and almost two thousand crew members.

[2] See Appendix C for a list of ships torpedoed. Because the torpedoing of SS *Essex Lance*, *Pan York*, *Meadcliffe Hall* and *Fort Thompson* resulted in neither deaths nor destruction of these ships, I have relegated reference to them to endnotes.

[3] The first recorded use of the phrase "*la bataille du Saint-Laurent*" was by *L'Action Catholique* on May 18, 1942. The first English use of "The Battle of the Gulf of St. Lawrence" was in the May 1943 edition of the *Royal Canadian Monthly Review*.

[4] In his 1985 *U-Boats against Canada: German Submarines in Canadian Waters*, which more than any other work has given shape to the battle, Michael Hadley agrees with Schull's assessment. Unlike the historians to whom Sarty refers, however, Hadley makes extensive use of newspapers and of Hansard, thus demonstrating that the Battle of the St. Lawrence was not hidden from the Canadian public, even if on many occasions the articles were liberally sprinkled with fare that would go down well on the home front.

[5] Gerald F. Linderman, *Embattled Courage: The Experience of Combat in the American Civil War*, The Free Press, 1987.

[6] An earlier version of this preface appeared in the summer 2003 issue of *Gaspésie* (vol. 40, no. 1), which was published to coincide with the May 2003 opening of an exhibit on the Battle of the St. Lawrence at the Musée de la Gaspésie.

INTRODUCTION

[1] The US and UK were each granted the five capital ships in recognition of the US's two coasts and the UK's worldwide imperial responsibilities.

[2] During the First World War, this first generation of U-boats sank 5,700 Allied ships totalling over 11 million tons of shipping. During the Second World War, 830 U-boats sank 2,759 Allied and neutral ships, totalling 13 million tons of shipping.

[3] Nothing better illustrates the British Admiralty's "staggering lack of imagination," to borrow historian Peter Padfield's words, than its view of Germany's opening bargaining position:

> In this case Germany would have some 50 to 60 submarines, a situation which must give rise to some misgivings, but it is quite apparent from the attitude of the German representatives that it is quite a question of "*Gleichberechtigung*" [equal rights] which is really exercising their mind and not the desire to acquire a large submarine fleet.

In the present mood of Germany it seems probable that the surest way to persuade them to be moderate in their actual performance is to grant them every consideration in theory. In fact they are more likely to build up to submarine parity if we object to their theoretical right to do so, than if we agree that they have a moral justification.

4   Fo'c'sle: short for "forecastle," the forward part of a ship behind the bow in front of the "castle," the old Spanish term for "bridge."

5   Also, unlike their Canadian opponents, Dönitz's men had been thoroughly militarized by both school and the Hitler Youth. Within two years of Hitler's rise to power, the British cabinet received a report on Nazi education: "The German schoolboy of today is being methodically educated, mentally, and physically, to defend his country . . . . But, I fear," added Foreign Secretary Sir Eric Phipps, "that, if this or a later German Government ever requires it of him, he will be found equally well fitted and ready to march or die on foreign soil." The contrast with Canadian schooling is considered in chapter 6.

6   In addition to the Battle of the St. Lawrence, there were two other direct attacks on the North American mainland during the Second World War, both carried out by Japan. On the evening of June 20, 1942, I-26, a Japanese submarine, shelled the lighthouse at Estevan Point on the west coast of Vancouver Island. Twenty-five to thirty shells were fired; there were no injuries. Between November 1944 and April 1945, some 300 (of 9,300) bomb-carrying balloons launched from Japan reached North America. Bombs fell in Oregon, Washington, California, Alaska, British Columbia, Manitoba, the Northwest Territories and the Yukon. The bombs failed in their intended purpose—to start forest fires and thus divert resources from the war effort and to sow panic—however, there were casualties in Oregon, where a minister's wife and five children were killed by a balloon bomb. Both the United States and Canada maintained a complete news blackout about the Japanese balloon offensive.

CHAPTER ONE

1   Quoted and translated by David J. Bercuson and Holger H. Herwig in their *The Destruction of the Bismarck* (Stoddart, 2001), 88f.

2   All distances included in lists of historical events have been calculated from Gaspé, Quebec, and are rounded off to the nearest 100 miles.

3   The Finnish ship SS *Carolus*, sunk near Rimouski, Quebec, by U-69 on October 9, 1942, was also a prize of war seized by Canada after Finland allied itself with Hitler's Germany in 1939.

4   Gaspé's brush with fame came in 1940 during the height of the Blitz, when it was designated, under the so-called "spare bedroom" policy, as the port to which the British fleet would steam if England fell to the Nazis.

5   Vessel's weight in air = volume of hull immersed in water × water density.

6   This is exactly what happened to the 5,229-ton SS *Muneric*, its holds laden with heavy iron ore and hence more than half empty, after being torpedoed by U-432 on September 10, 1941. Two of *Muneric*'s convoy companions, SS *Joannis* and *Mount Taygetus*, were torpedoed in the St. Lawrence four months after *Nicoya*.

7   A 1948 study found that sailors immersed in 60°F (16°C) water could be expected to survive less than five hours; sailors in water of 40° to 41°F (4°C) had "minutes only." The average temperature of the waters where the *Nicoya* sank is 40°F (4°C); the average daytime air temperature is 44.5°F (7°C).

8   Nationwide, 80 per cent of voters voted to free the government from its "no conscription" pledge; in Quebec, 80 per cent voted to hold the government to its pledge.

9   Quoted and translated by Michael L. Hadley in his *U-Boats Against Canada: German Submarines in Canadian Waters* (McGill–Queens Press, 1985), 276.

10 Over the course of ten patrols, Thurmann sank thirteen ships, for a total of 64,612 tons; he damaged another two ships totalling 15,273 tons. Thurmann's U-553 was lost with all forty-seven hands in late January 1943; his last radio message was "*Sehrohr unklar*" ("Periscope not clear").

CHAPTER TWO

1   This tremendous industrial achievement is even more stunning when set in the context of North America's total wartime production and the difference between the two nations' populations. With 130 million people, the United States produced the above-mentioned ships and 297,000 aircraft, 193,000 artillery pieces, 86,000 tanks, 2,000,000 army trucks and some 87,000 landing craft; the United States Navy ended the war with more than 90 aircraft carriers. With a population of a little over 8 million, Canada produced the above-mentioned ships and 5,096 aircraft, 3,066 artillery pieces and anti-aircraft guns, and more than 7,400 tanks and heavy trucks.

2   One expert estimated that 166 million tons of cargo would fill eleven lines of railway box-cars stretching from Vancouver to Halifax.

3   Such public relations gimmicks were hardly needed. On March 6, 1942, just five days before the sinking of SS *Nicoya*, *L'Echo du Bas St-Laurent* crowed, "The Lower St. Lawrence and the Gaspésie buy more than $1,200,000.00" in Victory Bonds. The tiny village of Témiscouata subscribed for $59,950. For a full discussion of Canada's oil convoys, see Robert C. Fischer's "'We'll Get Our Own': Canada and the Oil Shipping Crisis of 1942" (*Red Duster*, 1993), and p. 407f of *No Higher Purpose* by W.A.B. Douglas et al.

4   The effort was one of Canada's great successes: 77 tankers in 14 convoys were escorted safely though the same U-boat-infested waters off the American coast in which more than 150 unescorted tankers under US control went to the bottom.

5   An improvised special convoy, QSS-1, sailed safely under escort on May 9, two days before the attack on *Nicoya* and *Leto*.

6   Had U-132 been perpendicular to the convoy Vogelsang would have said, "angle on bow = 0°"; had it been parallel, he would have said "angle on bow 90°."

7   In May 1943, a U-boat slipped through Halifax's outer defences and laid fifty-three mines. Port Defence Officer Geoffrey Smith, of whom we will hear much more later, suspected that a U-boat had crossed the asdic loop, and warned the harbour patrol boats; he recalls hearing the explosions of the mines being detonated by the Bangor minesweepers.

8   A measure of the power of the bathyscaphe effect is the fact that after the torpedoing of SS *British Freedom* on January 14, 1945, off Halifax, Allied ships were unable to get an asdic contact on the ship's stern—even though its bow was out of the water. US studies showed that in the Canadian zone of the Northwest Atlantic, asdic sweeps could not penetrate deeper than 200 feet, and in the St. Lawrence the effect would have been stronger because of the mixing not just of cold and warmer water but also of salt and

fresh water.

⁹ Godbout was, in fact, correct: U-213 had landed a spy, code-named "Langbein," on May 14. However, since "Langbein" immediately disappeared, neither Godbout nor any other Canadian authority knew about his presence until 1944. (See Appendix A.)

¹⁰ *Lensen*'s officer was mistaken about the number of lascars lost; the correct number is three.

¹¹ *Lensen* never left Grande-Vallée Bay. She broke up in early 1943, though pieces of it were still visible until late 1967, when they settled far enough into the bottom to be covered by the waters of the St. Lawrence. On June 19, 2003, Robert Spence's daughter, Maureen Hall, in a ceremony arranged by André Kirouac, Director of the Naval Museum of Quebec, dropped a wreath over the site where *Lensen* lies.

CHAPTER THREE

¹ Skinner's nickname, "Iff"—pronounced with the broad "eh" of a Newfoundland accent, "Ehh-ff"—came from his penchant for saying, "Eh-ff the Germans attack."

² Roberto was used to Canadian waters. In 1940, he was part of the crew that took USS *Crown Shelf* and *Wicks*, two of the four-stacker World War I–era destroyers that were part of the "destroyers for bases" deal, up to Halifax, where they were turned over to the RN. He was one of the first men drafted onto *Laramie*. "When we got to her, she'd been laid up for years. She was a real rustbucket. The engines and most of the equipment from the fire room had been taken topside and disassembled. We worked like buzzards putting her back together. We had to strip other ships in the yard to get pumps for her engines and fuel tanks," he recalls.

³ Three other crewmen were missing in action and presumed dead.

⁴ Boone and Mills, who had been asleep in the crew's forward quarters, abandoned ship after being "knocked down and washed half the length of the main deck by a wave of water and aviation gasoline which swept down the port side immediately after the explosion," wrote Executive Officer Keller, who recommended that they not be punished. After floating on rafts for five days, they were picked up on August 28 and returned to *Laramie*.

⁵ Several weeks before I interviewed Jock Smith in late January 2002, he saw another article about Johnnie Johnson, one that announced his retirement as vice-marshal of the Royal Air Force.

⁶ U-984 would sink four ships and damage one before being sunk by HMCS *Ottawa*, *Kootenay* and *Chaudiere* in 1944.

⁷ The press release left out the most colourful part of *Raccoon*'s history. *Raccoon* was one of twelve yachts brought to Canada as part of what's been called the "Great Yacht Plot." Devised by Rear-Admiral Leonard Murray to get around the US Neutrality Act, which was still in force in 1940, the Great Yacht Plot saw Canadian naval authorities requisitioning yachts from wealthy Canadians who then, on the advice of the navy, purchased replacement yachts in the United States. Upon receipt of the replacement yacht, the navy immediately returned the first yacht and requisitioned the new yacht, which was then converted into an anti-submarine escort ship.

⁸ Hartwig's fine military mind was recognized after he was repatriated to West Germany from Canada, where he spent four years in a POW camp after his U-boat was sunk in November 1942. In the early 1950s, he joined the *Bundesmarine*, West Germany's navy, rising to become admiral of the fleet before retiring in the early 1970s.

⁹ Degaussing neutralized a ship hull's magnetic charge—thus defeating the pistols of magnetic torpedoes.

[10] Quoted and translated by Hadley in his *U-Boats Against Canada*, 119.

[11] On October 9, 2003, the Greek ambassador placed a tombstone on Triantafyllarous's grave.

CHAPTER FOUR

[1] Heagy's Canadian-made radar lagged behind the British centimetric radar largely because, in May 1940, at the request of the British Admiralty, the Canadian government sent more than twenty of the nation's best physics graduates to man RN sets on RN ships. According to Derek Howse's history, *Radar at Sea*, "It was only the timely arrival of these Canadians that saved the [British] Navy from facing a truly disastrous position in regard to radar personnel." Prior to 1943—during the years when Canadian labs were failing to produce effective Canadian-designed asdic and radar sets, and when Canadian shipyards were unable to keep up with the modernization programs that were in effect, because they lacked the engineers who could install asdic and radar—"a very high proportion of the larger British warships were kept working at sea by Canadian radar officers." This was recognized in a letter sent by the Admiralty to the National Research Council in Ottawa.

Although Canadian asdic would continue to lag behind the RN's and the USN's until near the end of the war, by early 1943 Canadian scientists were at the forefront of the development of small centimetric radar units suitable for motor patrol boats and aircraft. After successful testing of Type 286 centimetric radar in April 1943, the Admiralty ordered 1,500 units. Type 286 radar remained in use for many years after the end of the war.

[2] According to Marc Milner, Americans serving on the North Atlantic run thought that corvettes shipped so much water, their crews deserved submarine pay.

[3] In London, the trade mission's reports must have made for depressing but familiar reading. For, as Correlli Barnett has shown in *The Audit of War: The Illusion and Reality of Britain as a Great Nation*, British yards and manufacturing firms lacked exactly the same kind of design teams the trade mission noted that Canada lacked. The UK had to turn to US sources for "fire-control gear for the main and anti-aircraft armaments of warships and anti-submarine sonar equipment." British industry was unable to provide armaments manufacturers and naval yards with the precision machine tools they needed. Nor was the UK able to supply the microvalves and other highly technical components of radar and sonar without US help.

By 1944, however, Canada had become a major supplier of such equipment. To make good a 20-million-unit shortfall in thermionic valves needed for radar, Paymaster-General Lord Cherwell recommended that an "urgent enquiry should also be made into the possibility of obtaining greatly increased imports from North America, *particularly Canada*, in 1944" (emphasis added).

[4] To save both time and money, corvettes were built to commercial, not Admiralty, standards. Accordingly, while they had many watertight bulkheads, there were only five complete transverse bulkheads that ran from the keel to the upper decking. The farthest aft divided the engine room from the aft boiler room, more than 100 feet from the after peak (propeller). By contrast, frigates, the next-largest Canadian ship, had a watertight bulkhead only 60 feet from the after peak. This difference explains the different fates of the frigate HMCS *Magog* and the corvette HMCS *Shawinigan* in October and November 1944. An acoustic torpedo destroyed 60 feet of *Magog*'s stern, but her aft bulkhead held and the ship stayed afloat. A similar explosion destroyed *Shawinigan* because, whether the aft bulkhead held or not, the flooding of some 100 feet of her 300 feet doomed it.

[5] Although I had read about this entry in Hadley's *U-boats against Canada*, I had forgotten

about it. When I came upon these last words in the logbook preserved in the National Archives, the hair on the back of my neck stood on end. It is, perhaps, the most chilling fragment I have seen from the Battle of the St. Lawrence.

6 Post-war research in BdU records indicates that there were no U-boats near ON-84. Accordingly, the Board of Inquiry's praise of Bonner's asdic operators is probably not warranted. However, given the primitive state of the asdic aboard *Charlottetown* (a school of fish could return the signature of a U-boat), the fact that the operator picked up anything at 3,000 yards is most creditable. Whether or not a U-boat was shadowing ON-84, *Charlottetown*'s reaction demonstrates that in the short time available to him, Bonner had turned his green crew into an efficient and effective fighting force.

7 On February 6, 1943, depth charges, also apparently set to safety, blew up as HMCS *Louisburg* sank after being torpedoed by Italian aircraft off Oran, Algeria. A similar tragedy befell HMCS *Weyburn* sixteen days later after she hit a mine off the Straits of Gibraltar.

8 Quoted from *The Battle of the St. Lawrence*, produced by Brian and Terence McKenna (NFB, 1995).

9 Two days later, on September 13, in the middle of the North Atlantic, U-91 sank the destroyer HMCS Ottawa, killing 113 officers and ratings, as well as 6 men of the Royal Navy and 22 merchant seamen. The six days that followed the loss of Raccoon on September 7 were the worst in the history of the Royal Canadian Navy: 160 officers and ratings died.

CHAPTER FIVE

1 St. Lawrence shipping could not be completely suspended for both national and international reasons. Many communities along the north shore of the river and up into Labrador relied on coastal shipping for their supplies and for the movement of their chief products (iron ore, timber, coal and bauxite), which were themselves vital for Canada's war industries. Additionally, the British Ministry of War Transport argued that shipping efficiency required that ships loading timber destined to shore up British coal mines be loaded at traditional timber ports on the St. Lawrence.

2 In mid-1942, Canadian escorts in the Mid-Ocean Escort Force registered four U-boat kills, more than the RN, the force's better-equipped and better-trained senior partner.

3 Only three of nine U-boats managed to penetrate the escort screen. And while U-boats did sink four ships on the night of August 24, they did so at great cost: two U-boats were heavily damaged. As Marc Milner notes in his recent *Battle of the Atlantic*, Western Approaches Command found this to be an acceptable rate of exchange.

4 One of the reasons that the RCN underperformed the RN in terms of kills was that through 1942, Canada's escort ships were equipped with 123 asdic and 286 radar and were thus a generation behind the RN's ships, equipped with 127 asdic and 271 centimetric radar.

   The decision to so equip Canadian ships was at least partially a result of the desire of the federal government to use the impetus of the war to develop Canada's own war industries. The failure of this policy can be judged not only from the repeated delays in equipping Canadian escorts with equipment as it became available in the UK, but also from the fate of HMCS *Magog* on October 14, 1944. When *Magog* was torpedoed, it was steaming with its Canadian-designed and -manufactured RX/C centimetric radar operating; it failed to pick up U-1223's periscope. In his *North Atlantic Run: The Royal Canadian Navy and the Battle for the Convoys,* historian Marc Milner writes that "in service it [RX/C] proved a disaster."

5   In *U-boats against Canada: German Submarines in Canadian Waters,* historian Michael L. Hadley summarizes Hartwig's description of the hours before the attack: "Mounting tension, fear of aircraft attack, the gnawing questions of whether one should continue with the tactic or pull out; all this pressured an already overburdened nervous system . . . . One controls one's energies cool, and runs the ever-present calculated risk."

6   Both groups safely reached shore at Cap-des-Rosiers.

7   The 4,570-ton freighter SS *Pan York* was also torpedoed but did not sink and suffered no casualties.

8   That same night, more than thirty men responded to the threat of three U-boats in the gulf by taking advantage of the full moon on a clear night and manning six Avro Ansons in what, for the time, was an extraordinary operation: an entire escort patrol at night.

9   To man the ships that were to be commissioned by the spring of 1941, in 1940 the RCN had to train fully 7,000 men and 300 officers—none of whom were even in the RCN yet.

10 The "any ship is better than none" philosophy adopted by the Admiralty in 1940 crippled Canada's ability to produced a trained cadre. At the Admiralty's request, 840 of the RCN's best-trained men were assigned to six of the four-stacker destroyers the United States had transferred to the RN. An additional 540 officers and ratings remained in Britain, manning the ten corvettes they were supposed to transfer to British crews.

CHAPTER SIX

1   The "militia myth," which in his recent *Canada's Army* Jack Granatstein has traced back to Bishop Strachan and Egerton Ryerson—the belief that citizen soldiers can rise like a Spartan band to protect the nation and its interests—is at the core of Canadian military thinking.

2   RCNVR officers were easily discernible by the gold bands on their uniforms. Instead of the solid band of the RCN, theirs was a wavy band; hence the nickname "wavy navy."

3   See Appendix B for a further discussion of anti-Semitism.

4   Mauritius-born de Marbois was the leading force behind the establishment of the WRCNS in 1942. De Marbois, who ran away to sea when he was twelve, could have stepped directly out of a John le Carré novel. According to John Bryden, whose *Best-Kept Secret* tells the story of Canada's electronic intelligence during the Second World War, by the time de Marbois was seventeen,

> he had been around the world twice in sailing vessels and had survived two shipwrecks and a bloody mutiny in which the captain and all his ship's officers died. During the First World War, he had served as a British Liaison officer aboard a Russian cruiser and had fled the Bolshevik revolution with his fiancée, a Russian countess. After the war he settled for a time in Nigeria before finally coming to Canada. He spoke French, Spanish, German and Russian fluently, and had a smattering of Arabic, Turkish and about a dozen Far Eastern languages . . . .
>
> He enthralled the boys of Upper Canada College [including Geoffrey Smith, who credits de Marbois with igniting in him the desire to join the navy] with tales of typhoons at sea, rescue by cannibals, and escape from Argentinian desperadoes. His colleagues at Naval Headquarters were skeptical. Yet the stories were true and de Marbois could tell them vividly.

5   For a discussion of how German newspapers spun the St. Lawrence sinkings see Hadley's

U-Boats Against Canada, 129f.

6 My narrative of *Caribou*'s final voyage is reconstructed from Douglas How's *The Night of the Caribou* (Lancelot Press, 1988), "The *Caribou* Disaster: William Lundrigan's story as told to *Newfoundland Woman* (*Newfoundland Woman*, vol. 3 no. 3-5, October–December 1964), "I survived the Wreck of S.S. *Caribou*: The Words of John (Jack) T. Dominie" (*Downhomer*, vol. 12 no. 1, June 2000, and "The *Caribou* Disaster: Thomas Fleming's Story" by Cassie Brown (*St. John's Woman*, October 1963).

7 Lines on the bow that tell to what point a ship can be loaded.

8 Wilkie's body was recovered. A Newfoundland Ranger found a twenty-dollar bill safety-pinned to the inside of her jacket.

CHAPTER SEVEN

1 Courchènes was nothing if not consistent. In the early 1950s, he successfully opposed National Defence's plans to turn the old EAC base at Mont Joli into a Strategic Air Command base. A new base was ultimately built at Bagotville, north of Quebec City. In 1953, Courchènes complained about the moral attitude of the Fusiliers; he was especially critical of Friday-night dances.

2 For a full discussion of the relationship between Quebec's political and religious leaders' attitudes toward Vichy, see Eric Amyot's *Le Québec entre Pétain et De Gaulle: Vichy, la France libre et les canadiens français 1940–1945*. This book is the source of Monseigneur J. Charbonneau's quote below.

3 On October 25, 1940, *L'Echo du Bas St-Laurent* also indicated its distance from the anti-Semitism of *Le Devoir* and Quebec's Catholic Church. In an editorial entitled "*La réconstruction de l'état palestinien*," *L'Echo* called for the re-creation of a Jewish state in what was then the British mandate of Palestine. Over a year before the factories of death were built at Auschwitz and Treblinka, *L'Echo* wrote that the Germans were "attacking the Jews with savage ferocity." The editorial closed with an attack on Vichy: "The men of Vichy, wanting to ape the Nazis, press themselves to also practise anti-Semitism. They are, no doubt, familiar with the writings of St. Paul [which, as the editorial stated earlier, speak of the Jewish people as 'bearing witness to the Scriptures'] and no less with the pope's decree of September 15, 1928, which condemns anti-Semitism."

4 After the war Laval was found guilty of treason; he was executed on October 15, 1945.

5 The distance between the ultranationalist view represented by *Le Devoir* or *L'Action Catholique* and the views, of the men and women who lived in the Gaspé is, perhaps, best measured from the fact that on July 9, 1942, with political emotions still rubbed raw by the conscription debate, 176 members of the Fusiliers volunteered for combat duty overseas.

6 On March 25, Roy sought to correct the impression Macdonald left—that Roy had said he, Roy, had witnessed the "battle" when, in fact, Hansard records Roy saying that Laurent Giroux claimed to have witnessed it; I've not found any newspaper that picked up Roy's correction.

7 POW Camp 30 in Bowmanville, Ontario, 65 kilometres east of Toronto, was one of twenty-six POW camps across Canada. Camps were in such unlikely places as Kingston, Ontario; Sherbrooke and St. Helen's Island (Montreal), Quebec; and in the resort at Kananaskis, Alberta. After being transferred to Canada in late 1942, Paul Hartwig spent the rest of the war in this last camp.

8 According to Michael Hadley, the Ireland code "was a system in which letters of the alpha-

bet represented dots and dashes of the Morse code; it permitted the terse communication of lean data in seemingly innocent correspondence . . . . The first letter of every word in any piece of correspondence indicated either a dot or a dash . . . . A censor would scarcely twig to the fact that a U-boat commander's lament *"Meine Kameraden und auch ich waren langen in Sorge, denn . . ."* ("My comrades as well as I were worried for a long time, for . . .") actually named the weapon that sank them. Transposed into symbols, the first letter of each word spelled "mine." In this case, nine words of seemingly innocuous plain language provided but a single word of coded communication. Clearly one could not write a lengthy military report by this procedure. But it allowed an inventive writer (or an identifiable group of writers) considerable flexibility and scope."

[9] On April 30, 1943, Admiral Murray was named commander of the Canadian North West Atlantic, making him the only Canadian to ever command a theatre of battle.

[10] Quoted and translated by Hadley in his *U-Boats Against Canada*, p. 176; Hadley, p. 183 is also my source for *"Kiebitz verpiffen"*: "Operation Magpie blown" on p. 215.

[11] Unless otherwise indicated, the following quotes from Rolf Schauenburg and Wolfgang Von Bartenwerffer come from Melanie Wiggins's *U-Boat Adventurers: Firsthand Accounts from World War II* (Naval Institute Press, 1999), 126–131.

[12] I thank Rodney Martin, author of *Silent Runner: Wolfgang Heyda, U-boat Commander*, for this information.

[13] See chapter 8 for a fuller discussion of the Gnat, an acoustic torpedo.

CHAPTER EIGHT

[1] Despite Dönitz's remonstrances, Hitler ordered the *Grossadmiral* to keep twenty U-boats in Norwegian waters to defend against an invasion that never came.

[2] Quoted and annotated by Martin Middlebrook in *Convoy* (Penguin, 1978), p. 73. At 0314 Berlin time on May 7, 1944, Dönitz signalled U-548's commander, Heinrich Zimmermann: "Daughter born 4 May. Mother and daughter well. Congratulations. Admiral Commanding U-boats." One hour and twenty minutes later, Zimmermann torpedoed the frigate HMCS *Valleyfield*, killing 125 officers and ratings. Among her 44 survivors was the same Lieutenant Ian Tate who in 1942 had been signals officer at HMCS Fort Ramsay.

[3] In July 1943, researchers at I. G. Farben informed Reich armaments minister Albert Speer that they would soon be able to supply a material that absorbed 100 per cent of radar waves. Anti-sonar panels were tested in 1941 and again in 1944 but were found wanting, first because they tended to break off, and second because they created noise that Allied hydrophones could pick up.

After eighteen months of development, on November 6, 1943, Speer ordered 287 Elektro boats. The first was launched on April 17, 1944, and commissioned June 12, six days after D-Day. Both the Russian advance from the east and Anglo-American bombing disrupted Speer's plan for the launching of sixty Elektro boats per month in 1944.

[4] Quoted and translated by Roger Sarty in his "Ultra, Air Power, and the Second Battle of the St. Lawrence, 1944" (in *To Die Gallantly: The Battle of the Atlantic*, ed. Timothy J. Runyan and Jan M. Copes, Westview Press, 1994), 189f.

[5] Quoted and translated by Hadley in his *U-Boats Against Canada*, 228.

[6] After the publication of *The Battle of the St. Lawrence*, Mr. Gilbert contacted the author to say that he was not in the cabin.

7 "Weighing off" involved docking pay and cutting off shore leave.

8 The Canadian anti–acoustic torpedo (CAT) gear was an ingenious low-tech solution to the problem raised by the acoustic torpedo. According to Marc Milner, it consisted of "one five-foot pipe (soon reduced to thirty inches) bolted to a bracket with another loosely fitted above so the two rattled, and the whole thing attached to a wire yoke. The pipes lasted for over fourteen hours and could be towed at nearly 18 knots."

9 On November 2, Kneip torpedoed the 10,000-ton Canadian steamer SS *Fort Thompson* six miles off Matane. The blast, which was originally attributed to either a mine or a boiler explosion, blew a large hole in the Vancouver-built ship's starboard bow but did not kill or injure any of its crew. Thinking that the ship was sinking, however, seventeen crew members abandoned ship. Their appearance on the shores of Quebec renewed alarm about "*l'action de l'ennemi*," as *L'Action Catholique* put it on November 3. The remaining forty-five officers and crew remained on board, and *Fort Thompson* made port under its own steam.

10 It is unclear whether Murray ordered a search for the U-boat, though given the time that had elapsed since the last sighting of *Shawinigan* and in the absence of huff-duff reports, his searchers would have little idea where to look. In fact, by the time Murray was alerted, U-1228 had transited the Cabot Strait and was some fifty miles off the coast of Nova Scotia, over two hundred miles away from where it sank *Shawinigan*.

11 *Kapitän zur See* Hermann Lessing's U-1231 entered the St. Lawrence in late November 1944. This last invader left on or about December 8 after twice firing dud torpedoes.

12 I'd like to thank Professor Mike Whitby of the Department of Defence History Directorate for drawing my attention to these two reports.

EPILOGUE: 1945

1 December 1944, which saw thirty-one U-boats launched, was, in fact, the peak of U-boat production.

2 Exactly why Macdonald chose to announce HMCS *Annan*'s role in the sinking of U-1006 on April 3, 1945, almost six months after the U-boat was destroyed, or why he overstated the facts—*Annan* shared battle honours with HMCS *Loch Achanalt* and other ships in Escort Group 6—is unclear.

3 Quoted and translated by Peter Padfield in *Donitz: The Last Fuhrer* (Cassell & Co., 1988), 419.

IN MEMORIAM

1 It is unclear whether Triantafyllarous was aboard SS *Mount Pindus* or *Mount Taygetus*. His assignment to *Mount Taygetus* is undertaken with knowledge that it might be in error.

INDEX

Naval actions are indexed under the ship name or number for the vessels involved. References in the text may be by ship name or by name of commanding officer (in parentheses).

About the author

About the book

Read on

Ideas,
interviews
& features

Nathan Greenfield:
In His Own Words

Becoming a Canadian military historian was
certainly not an obvious career path for me.
In fact, even though my father is a well-
published novelist, while growing up in
Brooklyn, New York, I gave no thought to
becoming any kind of a writer. Rather, after
getting turned on to literary theory while I
was a visiting student at McGill University in
1978–79, I intended to become an English
professor. History was, however, never far
from the surface—my M.A. thesis is entitled
"The Philosophy of History in Literary Theory:
Lukacs," and my dissertation focused on
Charles W. Chesnutt, a late 19th-century
black American novelist whose works deal
with the history of slavery and its legacy.

My first non-academic writings were published by the *Ottawa Citizen*. My first regular
gig was a five-year stint as the book reviewer
for the *Ottawa X-Press*, during which time I
was also the "Pop Culture Historian" for
CBC's *Definitely NOT the Opera*, followed by
the odd book review for the *Globe and Mail*
and the *Toronto Star*. My reviews of books on
education and history appeared regularly in
Alberta Report, a rather strange fit consider-
ing it was a conservative western based publication with a decidedly Catholic bent, and
I am a liberal central Canadian of Jewish
background.

In the winter of 1998, Algonquin College,
where I teach English, was undergoing
"restructuring"—and the layoffs were getting
awfully close to me. One depressing afternoon,

NATHAN
GREENFIELD

2

my wife, Micheline, suggested that I see if the English education newspaper I had picked up the previous weekend would be interested in an article. "Yeah, right," I said. "You want me to call the (London) *Times Educational Supplement* and tell them they need a transplanted Brooklynite to write about Canadian education?" Still, I took her advice. And as fate would have it, *TES*'s foreign editor was looking for a Canadian correspondent. Whenever I have to explain the difference between a federal and a provincial responsibility, Brendan, my editor, responds "You live in a very curious country."

My interest in the battle of the St. Lawrence was piqued during a family vacation to the Gaspé in August of 2000. I had watched *Victory at Sea* and *World at War* with my dad, so I vaguely knew something had happened "up there." When I was there, however, I realized that much more than "something" had occurred. Like most freelancers, I had been looking for an article to pitch to a magazine. I realized that the battle of the St. Lawrence would make a good *Maclean's* article. The magazine's managing editor agreed. Over the next five years, I wrote eight more military history articles for *Maclean's*.

More recently I have become a regular contributor to the *Times Literary Supplement*. I am presently working on another book for HarperCollins, tentatively titled *Ypres, 1915: Canada's Baptism by Fire.* ❧

Q & A with Nathan Greenfield

How long did it take you to write *The Battle of the St. Lawrence*?

When I tell people that the bulk of the text was written in about 12 weeks in the winter of 2002, most of them are surprised. I immediately add that unlike novelists, I didn't have to come up with a plot, counter-plot or characters. History is what it is, and once I'd organized the files into dates that corresponded to chapters, the writing was relatively straightforward.

Researching the book took about two years. Much of that time was spent doing background research, reading generally about the Second World War and specifically about the Battle of the Atlantic. I spent days in the National Archives and at the archives of the Department of National Defence, and still more days poring over the files that were sent from England. Every time I went to one of the two archives here in Ottawa or I received a package from England, I felt like a kid on Christmas morning. Researching can be tiring, but it never feels like work.

Needless to say, the interviews I conducted with the men and women who lived through the battle of the St. Lawrence were fascinating and emotional. The clarity of the memories of men and women, the youngest of whom were in their early 70s, was striking. Watching old men with stubby fingers point to their long-dead shipmates preserved in fading black-and-white photos was a moving

> ❝ Researching can be tiring, but it never feels like work. ❞

experience. More than once, voices cracked and tears welled up in the eyes that so long ago kept watch for our land.

Did you make anything up?

The short answer is "No." The more complicated answer is "No, but there were times when I took a few liberties." For example, I don't know for certain how many Sweet Caporal cigarettes were smoked on the night of September 6, 1942, while Ian Tate and his signals crew were trying to raise HMCS *Raccoon.* Nor do I know who looked at the clock and saw the minutes tick by, I do know, however, how men and women who smoked such cigarettes and who could look at the clock would behave in extremely tense moments. Likewise, I have found no document in which Admiral Murray voices the hope that now that he has a ship equipped with the most up-to-date radar— HMS *Salisbury*—in the Gulf, the Gulf Escort Force should be able to start sinking U-boats. But that is precisely how a military planner would think.

What surprised you the most while writing?

Three things. First, given the anti-military tinge of present-day Quebec politics and my knowledge of the conscription crisis of 1917 and the way Quebec voted against conscription in 1942, I was quite surprised by the support for the war and the RCN in Gaspé and especially in Rimouski. Quebec was divided; antimilitarists and pro-Vichy Quebeckers could be found in large numbers in Montreal's French elite; its mayor, Camillien Houde, ▶

> ❝ More than once, voices cracked and tears welled up in the eyes that so long ago kept watch for our land. ❞

was a supporter of Vichy. But from Quebec City to the sea, support for de Gaulle and the Allies was high. The editor of *L'Écho du Bas St-Laurent* may have been better informed than his readers in and around Rimouski, but business realities would have kept him from getting too far ahead of his subscribers. In 1940 he wrote, "We thank God that England's morale remains intact. Speaking honestly, England is at this moment alone capable of saving the world—and that includes Canada—from the darkness of barbarism and slavery."

The second most surprising fact I learned was the extent of Canada's industrial and military contribution to the Allied victory. When the war broke out, the RCN had 13 ships; when the war ended, it had more than 400, and over 90,000 officers and ratings. From a standing start, the country of a little over eight million (one million of whom were under arms) built more than 300 warships and more than 400 merchant steams (338 of which grossed 10,000 tons)—and more than 5,000 aircraft, 5,000 artillery pieces and 7,400 tanks and heavy trucks.

Third, and perhaps most important, I was surprised by the politics of the men and and women who joined the RCN to fight the Nazis. Note, I did not say Germans. The difference is important. Since the 1960s, under the influence of an all-too-justified anti-Vietnam sentiment, it has become common for historians and commentators to say that anyone who takes up arms is being duped by big business or government propaganda. Such notions permeate

> ❝ I was surprised by the politics of the men and women who joined the RCN to fight the Nazis. ❞

what history is taught in schools and even many university classes.

While it would be foolish to argue that everyone who joined the RCN or the other branches of the Canadian Armed Forces during the Second World War was a deep political thinker conversant with the way the governments of Nazi Germany and Fascist Italy offended the Rights of Man, to argue that these men and women were mindless drones is even more absurd. Yes, many joined up because the RCN represented a real job. But while recognizing this fact, not a single one of the almost 50 veterans I interviewed cited this as his or her primary motive. Each one cited the need to destroy Nazi Germany—to protect their Canadian way of life—as the main reason why they went down to the sea in ships. Those who had short wave radios and could understand German told me that in the mid-1930s they knew that, like their fathers, they'd soon be called upon to destroy German militarism.

What do you hope the book accomplishes?

I wrote the book because I feel the battle of the St. Lawrence is an important part of our history. True, it seems rather small when compared with the great battles on North Atlantic Run or Midway in the Pacific, but size is not necessarily the only criteria of importance. Between 1942 and 1944, Nazi U-boats entered Canada's waters sixteen times. One penetrated as far inland as Rimouski, Quebec; together they torpedoed 28 ships and killed more than 360 men, women and children—all just scant miles ▶

off our shores. This was the only extended campaign fought in North America. And though neither the RCN or RCAF ever got a sub, the bravery and skill of its officers pushed Hitler's vaunted fleet out of our waters. Surely, this story is worth remembering. ❧

About the book

Nathan Greenfield Talks with Survivors of the Second World War

An Interview with Lawrence Boucher

In 1942, Lawrence (Larry) Boucher, a 15-year-old sea cadet, served as a semaphore and Aldus lamp reader on SS *John Pillsbury,* a 10,000-ton laker built in Canada. Mr. Boucher called me after reading *The Battle of the St. Lawrence* to tell me that in 1942 he served in the St. Lawrence. After explaining who he was (ironically, Mr. Boucher and I once worked together—he was in his last years teaching at Algonquin College when I started there in the late 1980s), he told me "I have not seen the name of my ship in 60 years; seeing it in print was extremely emotional."

NG: How did you end up on SS John Pillsbury *in the middle of a war zone?*

LB: It was wartime and I was 15. Everyone was doing something to aid the war effort. I joined the sea cadets, my father was with the Toronto Harbour Police and before that had worked on lakers out of Ashtabula, Ohio, where I was born.

The only course open in the summer of 1942 was visual signals. The next spring, there was a meeting. At the end of it, a captain stood up and asked for a volunteer who knew signals. There were three of us who stood up and went to speak to him. When he met with us, he said that to beat the shipping ▶

9

shortage that had been caused by the U-boat attacks in the Atlantic, more and more lake boats were serving on the coast. But of course none of them had any radios. Visual signals were the only way to communicate. "Now," he said, "are any of you interested?" Before I knew it I jumped up and said "I am."

NG: It may have been wartime, but you were still only 15 years old; what did your mother and father say?

LB: My mother was dumbfounded. She didn't know what to say. My father was out with the Harbour Patrol at the time. Before he came home, about a day and a half later, I had already bought my ticket and headed for Montreal where I was to meet *Pillsbury*.

NG: How were you treated?

LB: It was common at the time for 15-year-olds to work on lakers, so having me aboard was nothing new for Captain Hawman, who, incidentally, was 5'1" tall and about 5'1" around. He was in his seventies and was a good captain who would rather have been travelling on his own than dealing with the navy brass at HMCS *Chaleur II,* the naval command station in Quebec City.

After the first sinking in May, he took me to the meetings where the captains were told what was facing them. After the sinking of SS *Nicoya* in May, the conferences became convoy conferences.

NG: Tell me about the convoys you were in that were attacked.

LB: The first attack I remember was of SS *Frederika Lensen*. She was much bigger than we were, remember. It was either 12 noon or 1 p.m. She and another big ship were off to our starboard by about one line.

Suddenly there was an explosion on *Lensen*'s port side, the side facing us. It tore a bloody great hole in their side and they started to list. The crew was able to turn her, though, and headed toward the beach, where she ended up.

I was also on the September convoy in which HMCS *Racoon* and four freighters were sunk. I remember passing the light house at Cap Chat and thinking that we were all lit up. The first ship to be hit was SS *Aeas*. Later we heard *Racoon* too had been sunk. We broke convoy during the night and put into Griffon Cove (on the north end of the Gaspé peninsula, now in Forillon Park). Sometime during the next day, I left the ship and climbed to the top of the cliffs and though I could not see any of the other ships from the convoy, I could hear the explosions of the torpedoes that sank the other ships.

NG: You were 15 years old. Weren't you scared?

LB: Only once: the first time I had to climb over the side of the ship and into the lifeboats that had been slung out on their davits after a torpedoing. My job was to put the plug [sea cock] into place at the bottom of the lifeboats.

When you're 15 you think you will live forever. I thought of it as a great adventure. It ▶

sounds strange now. After *Lensen* was hit, I thought "Well, isn't this exciting. Now, I wonder what's for lunch."

NG: When did you leave Pillsbury and what did your family and friends back in Toronto say when you told them about your wartime experiences?

LB: I was back home for my sixteenth birthday, which is in mid-September. Neither my family nor my friends believed me. You show in your book that it was in the news, but I guess there was so much happening that people missed it. When I started school my classmates didn't believe me either.

A Letter From Eric Olsen

In April of 2005, 86-year-old Eric Olsen, who served in the signals branch of the RCAF during the Second World War, sent me a letter relating his experiences in Gaspé in 1942. A Montrealer by birth, Olsen knew Lieutenant Russell McConnell, who died on September 7, 1942, when U-165 torpedoed HMCS *Raccoon*. Olsen recalls McConnell's *"McGill buddies kidding him about active service overseas and here he was practically at home and guess what . . . here also was the enemy, the dastardly Nazis, well equipped, well trained with these devastating torpedoes and coasting along with the current of the mighty St. Lawrence, and we could not fight them on equal terms with our inferior equipment."*

In 1941, Olsen was stationed at a secret RCAF H/F D/F (Huff/Duff) station on the southern side of the Gaspé peninsular called Cap-d'Espoir, not far from Percé. In his letter to me, he wrote:

The station was a couple of shacks, one for the transmitters and the other for the receivers, the largest being 12 × 12. We had a generator to make electricity. The receiver shack had places for two operators who faced the HRO (national) radios. The Air Force was there to help any lost aircraft. Dull work, as there were few lost planes. The ones we did get were usually top brass whose aircraft ran into fog coming from overseas to Halifax.

In December 1941, just after Pearl Harbour, they posted six or seven Navy wireless operators to join us. Their job was to monitor the airwaves and take the bearings when U-boats transmitted. Now that was exciting stuff. They had a list of frequencies which they monitored. . . . Lorient transmitted continuously with a BIG booming signal . . . plenty of power.

In 1942, Olsen, who had in the interim been transferred to EAC Headquarters in Halifax, recalls:

I was on duty in the WT [wireless telegraphy] room in Halifax as a morse code operator in EAC headquarters. The commanding officer came into the wireless room (which was unheard of) with the command signals officer and said: "I want a group of you fellows to go to Gaspé and get a radio station on the air immediately." (Guess he was feeling the heat from the high command in Ottawa.) "I want you on Ocean Limited this afternoon." ▶

Olsen's new base, RCAF Gaspé, was on the
main floor of the gray-clad building that also
housed HMCS *Fort Ramsay*. The main floor
was divided amongst the operations, meteor-
ological, wireless telegraphy (which included
the wireless and code & cipher room with its
secret Type X room) teletype and other
rooms.

Olsen also remembers the grizzly side of
war. He "was on the docks when they brought
back survivors of *Charlottetown*." In the fall
of 1942, he was one of half a dozen RCAF personnel who went to recover the bodies of the
men who died when a Hudson based in
Chatham, New Brunswick, crashed into a
mountainside:

*It was a terribly difficult climb for pussyfoot-
ers like us but we eventually found the terrible
wreck. Nothing left of the plane but bits and
pieces scattered throughout the dense bush.*

*The crash site was unbelievable. Two deep
holes in the ground about 5–6 feet in depth,
where the charges (the plane was carrying
depth charges) had blown up on either side of
the fuselage. A strip of earth 3–4 feet wide in
the middle of them. Sitting up in a semi-erect
position was one of the crew, his uniform
burned off him. His body was brown like over-
cooked barbecue steak, but unbelievably, not a
single abrasion, cut or bruise on his body.*

*We stood there and stared and stared . . .
horrified and unbelieving. Naturally, we had
no explanation. . . . Did he parachute into the
fire? No, one fellow surmised, the force of the
explosion blew him into the air and he fell to*

earth in the middle of the fire. . . . But where were signs of injury? Only fire damage.

We sat around the bonfire looking into the flames for a long time that night, exploring a hundred theories but none gave us any answer to his tragic death.

We then went about the gruesome task of collecting body pieces from the tree branches. We put them in our backpacks. We could find only 50–60 lbs. We wrapped the body of our mystery airman in a blanket and then tied it to a log which the lumberjacks had cut. They carried him on their shoulders.

With all the violence and tragedy he saw, Olsen also remembers, more than 60 years later, the lighter moments, such as when, thanks to the efforts Corporal Vic Cotton, CBC's national radio show *The Happy Gang* would play a song *"for the boys in the wireless station at RCAF station Gaspé."* ❧